DEMOCRACY IN CRISIS?

This volume explores the state of representative democracy on the global stage.

It does this against the backdrop of crises such as the USA Capitol attack on 6 January 2021, recent refusals to accept election results in various countries, and attempts to restrict the voting franchise, as well as longer-term trends such as the rise of populism and declining trust in political elites.

The first substantive chapter examines representative democracy in theory, history and practice today. Taking the representative model as their point of departure, the subsequent chapters explore a range of themes in relation to this model.

The contributions include timely reappraisals of democracy in countries, such as the UK and USA, with old, well-established democratic structures as well as analyses of the state of democracy in regions, such as Africa, Asia and South America, where democracy has had a more chequered history.

Across all of its chapters, the book invites readers to rethink fundamental questions about representative democracy: Why is it valuable? How should it be organised? Do steps need to be taken to strengthen representative democracy, and if so, what are those steps?

The volume's target audience – politicians, public servants and interested members of the public – will be provided with arguments and evidence to form their own views at a time when the ideals and practices of representative democracy are being challenged around the world, and new ideas and initiatives to revitalise it are being debated and implemented.

Democracy in Crisis?

The Putney Debates 2023

Edited by
Richard W Clary
Zim Nwokora
and
DJ Galligan

•HART•
OXFORD • LONDON • NEW YORK • NEW DELHI • SYDNEY

HART PUBLISHING

Bloomsbury Publishing Plc

Kemp House, Chawley Park, Cumnor Hill, Oxford, OX2 9PH, UK

1385 Broadway, New York, NY 10018, USA

Bloomsbury Publishing Ireland Limited, 29 Earlsfort Terrace, Dublin 2, D02 AY28, Ireland

HART PUBLISHING, the Hart/Stag logo, BLOOMSBURY and the Diana logo are trademarks of Bloomsbury Publishing Plc

First published in Great Britain 2025

A catalogue record for this book is available from the British Library.

A catalogue record for this book is available from the Library of Congress.

Library of Congress Control Number: 2025945685

ISBN: HB: 978-1-50998-089-5
ePDF: 978-1-50998-092-5
ePub: 978-1-50998-090-1

Typeset by Compuscript Ltd, Shannon

For product safety related questions contact productsafety@bloomsbury.com

To find out more about our authors and books visit www.hartpublishing.co.uk. Here you will find extracts, author information, details of forthcoming events and the option to sign up for our newsletters.

CONTENTS

Contributor Biographies .... *xi*

Introduction: Debating the Crisis of Representative Democracy *1*
Richard W Clary and Zim Nwokora

I. The Putney Debates 1647 1
II. The New Putney Debates 2
III. The 2023 Debates: Representative Democracy in Crisis? 2
IV. Outline of the Volume 3
V. The Volume in the Contemporary Context 5

1. *Is Representative Democracy in Crisis?* *7*
Richard W Clary

I. Introduction 7
II. Is Representative Democracy in Crisis? 7
III. What are the Structures and Basic Features of a Well-Functioning Representative Democracy? 10
A. The Primary Assumption 11
B. Basic Secondary Assumptions 13
IV. What Parts of this Model of Representative Democracy are not Bearing their Full Weight? 14
A. Attacks on the Electoral System Itself 14
B. Is Partisanship Replacing Consensus and Compromise? 20
C. Are Elected Officials No Longer the Leaders Envisioned by Madison or Burke? 22
D. Have the Checks and Balances Lost their Effectiveness? 24
E. Is the Machinery of Government Part of the Solution, or Part of the Problem? 25
V. Is there a Path Forward? 26

2. *Democracy in Crisis: A Reply* *29*
DJ Galligan

I. Representative Democracy: An Unfinished Symphony 29
II. Origins of Rule by Elected Representatives 30
A. Princely Rule 30
B. People Ruling Themselves 31
C. Rule by Representatives 32

III. Representative Democracy and the Tyranny of Form 34
  A. Tyranny of Form 34
  B. Representative Democracy as Form 35
IV. Peoples Precede Nations 36
V. Between the People and Elected Leaders 36
VI. A Competing Account 37
  A. Substance Over Form 39
  B. A Place in the Constitution 39
VII. Inside the Field 40
VIII. Sites of Government and the Place of the People 42
IX. Form Demoted, Democracy Redesigned, Crisis Reassessed 44

3. *The Challenge of Representative Democracy in Africa* *47*
Zim Nwokora
I. Introduction 47
II. Africa as a Hostile Context for Representative Democracy 49
  A. Preconditions 51
  B. Handicaps 54
  C. Institutions 56
III. Sources of Democratic Potential 57
  A. African Success Stories 57
  B. New Models of Democracy for Africa 60
IV. Mapping Contemporary Representative Democracy Performance 62
V. Conclusion 64

4. *India in Crisis: Hindu Nationalism and the Majoritarian State* *67*
Angana P Chatterji
I. Introduction 67
II. Prejudicial Citizenship in Assam | Fragment 1 68
  A. Story 68
  B. Enumeration 69
III. The Siege on Indian-administered Kashmir | Fragment 2 71
IV. Uttar Pradesh, Hindu Nationalist Heartland | Fragment 3 73
V. India in Crisis | Fragment 4 75

5. *Democratic Crisis in South America? Ten Points for Debate* *79*
Pedro Rubim Borges Fortes
I. Introduction 79
II. An Overview of the State of Democracy in South America 80
  A. The Undemocratic Exception: The Case of Venezuela 81
  B. The Partially Democratic States: Peru, Paraguay, Bolivia, Colombia, and Ecuador 82
  C. Democratic States: Argentina, Chile, Uruguay, and Brazil 87

III. Democratic Crisis in South America? Ten Points for Debate 90
IV. Conclusion 95

6. *Leadership in Democratic Systems* *97*
I. Leadership and Democracy – Ritual Performance versus Substantive Aspiration and Achievement: Some Reflections 97
Fui S Tsikata
II. Same Old or Something New? The Leadership Crisis and Political Reconciliation in Contemporary Democracies 104
Alexandra Iancu and Bogdan Iancu
A. Democratic Erosion (Decline, Backsliding, etc) 104
B. Liberal Constitutionalism vs Democracy: Shallow Pacification Through Mediation 106
C. Systemic Failures of Mediating Institutions: Politics/Policy/Polity and the Populist Turn 109
D. Conclusion: Populism as Unmediated Democracy 112

7. *Institutions of Government and their Role in Democracy* *115*
I. The Administrative State: Friend or Foe of Representative Democracy? 115
Richard W Clary
II. The Impact of the Constitution 118
Paul Craig
III. Dominance of the Executive 125
Sionaidh Douglas-Scott
A. Introduction 125
B. Executive Dominance Over Parliament 127
C. The Prerogative 129
D. Unlimited Parliamentary Sovereignty 131
E. Attacks on Judicial Review 133
F. Civil Service, Regulators and the Media 135
G. Direct Mandate? 136
H. Conclusion 137
IV. Liberal Democracy and the Dangers of Meritocratic Depoliticisation 139
Ruzha Smilova
A. Tensions in Liberal Representative Democracy 139
B. The Meritocracy Problem for Liberal Democracy 140
C. De-democratisation and the Rise of Democratic Illiberalism 141
D. 'Democracy without Choice' and Depoliticisation 142
E. Conclusion: Taming Elitist Hubris is not Enough 145

V. Policy Processes and Democracy in Crisis 146
Frank Vibert
A. Introduction 146
B. Approaches 147
C. Conclusion 150

8. *Electoral Systems and Political Parties* *153*
I. Populism, Self-Restraint and the Political Parties 153
Daniel Smilov
A. Liberal Democracy and the Importance of Constraints 154
B. Populism as the Erosion of Self-Restraint 155
C. Why the Erosion of Self-Restraint Happened Only Over the Last Two Decades? 157
D. The Populist Political Party as an Instrument for the Erosion of Self-Restraint 159
E. The Populist Party and the Evolution of Party Systems 161
F. How Far Could Populists Go? 163
G. The Twin Dangers to Liberal Democracy 164
H. Conclusion: Are Democracy and Liberalism Still Possible? 165
II. The Politics of Internet Shutdowns 167
Nicole Stremlau

9. *Democracy Threatened from Within* *173*
The Honourable Malcolm Turnbull

Conclusion: Democracy in Crisis: A Review *179*
DJ Galligan
I. Representative Democracy: Nature, Appeal, Defects 179
II. Representative Democracy under Scrutiny 180
A. Concept of Democracy 180
B. Form Over Substance or Substance Over Form? 181
C. Place of the People Reconsidered 182
D. Ideas, Principles, Values: Allies of Democracy or Rivals? 182
E. Agencies of Government, Sites of Power 183
III. Democracy Redesigned and Redefined 184
IV. Beyond Representative to Substantive Constitutional Democracy 185
V. Tensions and Instabilities 186
A. Electoral Process and Outcomes 186
B. Relations between Electors and Elected 187
C. Disaffection to Defiance 188

D. Containing the Majority: Respecting Minorities 188
E. Executive Power: Presidents, Prime Ministers, and Populists 189
F. Beyond Leaders: Recourse to Other Institutions and Processes: The Agencies of Government 190
G. Courts and the People 191
H. Social Structure 192
VI. Crisis or Not? 194

Index *195*

CONTRIBUTOR BIOGRAPHIES

Dr Angana P Chatterji is the Founding Chair, Political Conflict, Gender and People's Rights Initiative at the Centre for Race and Gender at the University of California, Berkeley. She is also a Research Fellow at the Human Rights Center at the University of California, Berkeley, and the Center for Human Rights and International Justice at Stanford University. A cultural anthropologist and interdisciplinary scholar of South Asia, her work spans issues of democracy, political violence, law, cultural survival, minoritisation, and nationalism. Publications include: *Breaking Worlds: Religion, Law, and Nationalism in Majoritarian India; Majoritarian State: How Hindu Nationalism is Changing India; Conflicted Democracies and Gendered Violence: The Right to Heal*; *Contesting Nation: Gendered Violence in South Asia*; and *Violent Gods: Hindu Nationalism in India's Present; Narratives from Orissa.*

Richard W Clary is a Fellow at the Oxford Global Society and a Lecturer on Law at Harvard Law School. He practised law for 40 years at Cravath, Swaine & Moore LLP in New York City, where he was a Partner, a Managing Partner and the Head of Litigation. He began his legal career as a law clerk for Justice Thurgood Marshall on the US Supreme Court. Mr Clary has been an active participant with the OXGS, the Centre for Socio-Legal Studies at Oxford, and the Foundation for Law, Justice and Society.

Paul Craig is Emeritus Professor of English Law, St John's College, Oxford, UK. His principal research interests and publications have been in Administrative Law, Comparative Administrative Law, Constitutional Law, EU law and more recently in Legal History.

Sionaidh Douglas-Scott is Anniversary Chair in Law at Queen Mary, London and was formerly Professor of European and Human Rights Law at Oxford University. She was Law and Public Affairs fellow at Princeton University in 2021 and her most recent book is *Brexit, Union and Disunion: The Evolution of British Constitutional Unsettlement* (Cambridge University Press, 2023).

Pedro Rubim Borges Fortes is an Adjunct Professor of Constitutional Law at the State University of Rio de Janeiro (UERJ) and a Public Prosecutor at MPRJ. He holds a DPhil from Oxford, a JSM from Stanford, a LLM from Harvard, MBE from UFRJ, a LLB from UFRJ, and a BA from PUC-Rio. He is a convenor of Exploring Legal Borderlands at SLSA, of CRN Law and Development at LSA and WG Law and Development at RCSL.

DJ Galligan is Professor Emeritus of Socio-Legal Studies at Oxford University, a position he held from 1993–2017. He was Director of the CSLS from 1993–2008. Other positions include: Jean Monnet Professor of European Public Law, Universita' degli Studi di Siena; Foundation Professor of Law, Central European University, Budapest; Visiting Professor Princeton University. Authored books: *Discretionary Powers* (Oxford University Press, 1987); *Due Process and Procedural Fairness* (Oxford University Press, 1997); *Administrative Law in Central and Eastern Europe* (with Daniel Smilov) (CEU Press, Budapest, 1999)); *Western Concepts of Administrative Law* (2002; published only in Russian); *Law in Modern Society* (Oxford University Press, 2007); *Keepers of the Common Good: The People, Opinion, and the Social Foundations of Constitutional Authority* (Oxford University Press, 2024). He is Co-Founder and Director of the Oxford Global Society.

Alexandra Iancu (PhD, Universite Libre Bruxelles) is a Professor of Comparative Politics at the University of Bucharest. She held visiting-researcher positions at EHESS Paris, Charles University, The New Bulgarian University, and the University of Leipzig. Her teaching and writing have recently focused on democratic backsliding in Romania and East-Central Europe, corruption, party politics, and political transformations in new democracies.

Bogdan Iancu is Associate Professor with the Department of Constitutional and Political History and Theory, Political Science Faculty, University of Bucharest. He held visiting researcher positions in Europe (Alexander von Humboldt Fellow in Heidelberg, Berlin, Bremen) and North America (Yale Law School, McGill, University of Toronto). Iancu teaches and writes in the fields of comparative and Romanian constitutional law and EU constitutionalism.

Zim Nwokora is an Associate Professor in Politics and Policy Studies at Deakin University, Melbourne, Australia, and a fellow of the Oxford Global Society. His research focuses on the politics of constitutions, political party systems and political finance. Recent publications include *Money, Parties and Democracy: Political Finance between Fat Cats and Big Government* (co-authored with Matteo Bonotti) (Oxford University Press, 2025) and *Constitutional Conventions: Theories, Practices and Dynamics* (co-edited with Nicholas Barry, Narelle Miragliotta and Haig Patapan) (Routledge, 2025).

Nicole Stremlau is Professor of Law and Society in a Digital World at Oxford's Centre for Socio-Legal Studies. She is a Senior Research Associate at the University of Johannesburg. Her research bridges socio-legal studies, communications/digital technologies, and international development/African Studies. She is the author or editor of several books including *Media, Conflict, and the State in Africa* (Cambridge University Press, 2018), *Speech and Society in Turbulent Times* (Cambridge University Press, 2017) and *Technology and Governance Beyond the State: The Rule of Non-Law* (Routledge, 2025).

Daniel Smilov is associate professor of political science at the University of Sofia, Bulgaria and programme director of the Centre for Liberal Strategies, Sofia. His research and publications are in the area of comparative constitutional law in political context.

Dr Ruzha Smilova teaches political philosophy and history of political ideas at the Political Science Department of Sofia University 'St Kliment Ohridski' and is a Programme Director (political analysis) at the Centre for Liberal Strategies.

Fui S Tsikata is senior partner at Reindorf Chambers, a DLA Piper Africa law firm based in Ghana. He has an LLB from the University of Ghana and a BCL from Oxford University, where he was a Rhodes Scholar at Christ Church. He taught at the Faculty of Law of the University of Ghana for 29 years. He was called to the Ghana Bar in January 1975.

Malcolm Turnbull was the 29th Prime Minister of Australia. He entered the Australian Parliament in 2004 and during that time served as Minister for the Environment and Water Resources, Minister for Communications and as Prime Minister from 2015–2018. As Prime Minister, he reformed Australia's personal income tax, education and childcare systems, oversaw the legalisation of same-sex marriage and announced the construction of Snowy Hydro 2.0 the biggest pumped hydro scheme in the southern hemisphere. Mr Turnbull embarked on the largest peacetime investment in Australian defence capabilities and set out Australia's first national cybersecurity strategy. Prior to entering politics, he enjoyed successful careers as a lawyer, investment banker and journalist. Since leaving politics, Malcolm has resumed his business career and regularly speaks at global conferences.

Frank Vibert is Associate at CARR/LSE. He has been a senior advisor at the World Bank.

Introduction: Debating the Crisis of Representative Democracy

RICHARD W CLARY AND ZIM NWOKORA

This volume, with its collection of chapters, essays and think pieces, flows from a set of lectures and panel discussions that were held in May 2023, under the umbrella title of *The Putney Debates 2023: Democracy in Crisis?* Organised by the Oxford Global Society (of which the co-authors of this Introduction are Fellows), The Putney Debates 2023 followed on from prior debates in 2017, 2018, 2019, and 2021, which in turn derived their inspirations from the original Putney Debates of 1647. To put in context the goals of this volume, it is useful to briefly describe its historical roots and its more recent predecessors.

I. The Putney Debates 1647

The original Putney Debates began on 25 October 1647, at St Mary's Church, Putney, England. Presided over by Oliver Cromwell, the debates covered 'matters of high concernment' related to the crisis then facing England: the civil war was over, won by Cromwell's New Model Army; the king was a prisoner, taking the monarch (temporarily) out of the constitutional order; and the Parliament could be characterised as 'in disarray'. As our co-editor, Professor Denis J Galligan, aptly summarised it, 'The balanced [English] constitution, balanced among king, peers and commoners, had been destroyed.'[1] The debates that followed concerned competing visions of a new constitutional order and the role of the people and their representatives (particularly the House of Commons). The debates publicly aired various theories of constitutions, of government, and of the relationship between the people and the government, and those theories continue to be debated today.

[1] DJ Galligan, 'Introduction' in DJ Galligan (ed), *Constitution in Crisis: The New Putney Debates* (London, IB Tauris, 2017) 1. The description 'matters of high concernment' comes from *The Moderate Intelligencer*, published on 25 October 1647.

Professor Galligan has called the original Putney Debates 'a constitutional convention of a kind and importance not seen since'.[2]

II. The New Putney Debates

The New Putney Debates were created in 2017, and organised by the Foundation for Law, Justice and Society, as a vehicle to address yet again the relationship between the people and the government. Entitled 'Constitution in Crisis', the idea was sparked by the results of the United Kingdom's referendum in 2016 on leaving the European Union, but the debates ranged far and wide on parliamentary sovereignty, the role of the people and the balance between the people, Parliament, the executive and the courts.[3] The following year, The Putney Debates 2018 focused on issues of federalism, in part arising from the ongoing debates after the defeat of the 2014 referendum on independence for Scotland. And in 2019, The Putney Debates addressed the question of 'The Courts and the People: Friend or Foe', which flowed in part from political reactions to Brexit litigation in the United Kingdom.[4] After a temporary break due to the Covid pandemic, The Putney Debates returned in 2021, with the Oxford Global Society taking over the mantle from the Foundation for Law, Justice and Society. The topic in 2021 was 'The Unity of a Nation', looking at lessons to be learned from the constitutional structures of a variety of nations.

III. The 2023 Debates: Representative Democracy in Crisis?

As described more fully in Chapter 1, the topic in May 2023 – 'Representative Democracy in Crisis?' – derived from what various studies called an erosion of democracy, or a backsliding of democracy. Two events in particular led to the selection of this topic: (1) in the US the refusal of the loser of the 2020 presidential election to accept the results of a free and fair election, leading to the unprecedented 6 January 2021 insurrection at the US Capitol building; and (2) the rapid turnover of prime ministers in the UK, three prime ministers in the span of six months in 2022, with no intervening election at all. Since many would point to the UK and the US as established beacons of representative democracy, these

[2] Galligan (n 1) 2. It should be noted that some have argued the US constitutional convention of 1787 rises to the same level: see RW Clary, 'Thoughts from Across the Pond: The U.S. Constitution (1787, 2017)' in Galligan (ed) (n 1).

[3] A volume of the 2017 Debates was published: see Galligan (ed) (n 1).

[4] Again a volume of essays was created, entitled *The Courts and the People: Friend or Foe? The Putney Debates 2019* (Oxford, Hart Publishing, 2021).

events – and similar events in countries around the globe – suggested a need to revisit the fundamental assumptions and identify the stress points and hopefully possible solutions. Numerous countries and topics were explored, as reflected in the chapters and essays that follow.

It must be acknowledged that much has happened between May 2023 and the publication of this volume, in the US, the UK, and in various countries around the globe. Has the 'crisis' dissipated? Sadly, no, and we respectfully submit that this volume remains highly relevant today. The individual authors, with limited exceptions, have not tried to update their essays to the present, and readers should keep that in mind. But clearly representative democracy is still in choppy waters, as described later in this Introduction.

IV. Outline of the Volume

This round of The Putney Debates explores representative democracy. Its first chapter sets the scene, asking 'Is Representative Democracy in Crisis?' After explaining the basic theoretical and institutional pillars of representative democracy, Richard W Clary suggests some reasons why these pillars may be under threat. There have been challenges to legitimate elections, the bedrock of (representative) democracy, compounded by increasing polarisation and parochialism and a loss of civility in elite politics. These arguments are developed with a focus on the US and UK, but they resonate beyond these countries. Taking Clary's depiction of representative democracy as its starting point, Chapter 2 by Denis Galligan draws 'the people' into the account of representative democracy. Galligan argues that, far from being passive recipients and objects in the representative relationship, the people in a democracy need to present a complex of behaviours, ranging from self-restraint, support and engagement to vigilance and censure.

Chapter 3 by Zim Nwokora considers representative democracy in Africa, assessing the challenges to it in this region. While the region has not historically been a conducive one for representative institutions, Nwokora contends that there is more diversity today (and likely even more in the future) in terms of the region's capacity to support such institutions. Continuing the exploration of different geographies, Chapter 4 by Angana Chatterji examines developments in India, identifying the rise of 'political majoritarianism' as a result of the extended rule by the BJP. Its dominance, argues Chatterji, has led to the marginalisation of and violence against minority groups. In Chapter 5, Pedro Fortes presents an overview of representative democracy in South America, beginning with the case of Venezuela which has degenerated from being a 'beacon of democracy' to an authoritarian regime. Fortes also teases out broader lessons, as 'ten points for debate'.

The subsequent chapters focus squarely on issues, rather than countries and regions. Chapter 6 delves into leadership, which is fundamental to representative democracy but also implicated in the accounts of its crisis. Its first section, by Fui

Tsikata, reflects on the risk of leaders deploying democratic language as cover for more sinister efforts to concentrate power, enrich themselves, dominate minorities and otherwise undermine the spirit of democracy. Alexandra and Bogdan Iancu give attention to the role of mediating institutions (eg political parties, interest groups, tertiary education institutions) in the crisis of democratic leadership. These institutions used to conciliate between elitism and democracy but in the Iancus' analysis are now failing, opening the door to dangerous populist leadership.

Chapter 7's contributions look at the institutions of representative democracy. Richard W Clary debates the proper role of the administrative state and the judiciary. He asks: are they essential to the functioning of a representative democracy, or part of the current problem? Paul Craig analyses how constitutions impact on democracy. This discussion extends to consider constitutional design, constitutional conventions, and challenges to judicial independence. Sionaidh Douglas-Scott turns the spotlight on the UK executive, which she sees as the source of accountability deficits. These, she argues, might be remedied by the legal entrenchment of domains that traditionally have been left to 'good chaps' to run. Ruzha Smilova points to the dangers of 'meritocratic depoliticisation' by which key decisions are insulated from democratic pressures and instead made by well-credentialed experts. It can lead to elite hubris and mass resentment, and thus fertile ground for populism. The contribution by Frank Vibert also gives a prominent place to expertise, this time as essential to effective policymaking. Vibert draws attention to the expertise housed in agencies that lie beyond the central government, seeking to define their role in relation to traditional democratic mechanisms.

The contributions in Chapter 8 turn the focus to electoral systems and political parties. Daniel Smilov analyses the features of contemporary populism which, he explains, share a common basis in the erosion of self-constraint among politicians and the people at large. He situates the rise of populism in a broader history, suggesting that it is driven by the growing self-confidence of the people stoked by populist political entrepreneurs. Nicole Stremlau examines the politics of internet shutdowns, revealing the tensions linked with the partial or complete closing of the internet during election time. This action goes against liberal democratic rights to expression and access to information. But this point must be weighed against the unbridled power of Western internet companies operating in contexts such as Africa where colonial entanglements continue to shape the state and society.

The volume's final chapter, by Malcolm Turnbull, proposes that democracy is severely challenged 'from within', and especially by polarisation of the media. This has eroded the common ground needed for democratic debate in the United States, and intensified polarisation in the public at large. Australia, he points out, has been somewhat protected from this extreme polarisation by institutions like compulsory voting and its preferential voting system.

V. The Volume in the Contemporary Context

This edition of The Putney Debates occurred in May 2023, a moment in time defined by certain actors and events. In the US, President Joe Biden attempted to manage conflicting pressures as the US offered military and financial support to Ukraine following Russia's full-scale invasion of the country in the previous year. The Ukraine war also exacerbated domestic challenges, notably high inflation. The presidential election was still more than a year away, but speculation was building about who would be the Republican nominee and whether Donald Trump would return to the political stage. In the UK, Prime Minister Rishi Sunak was also focused on the Ukraine war, though another significant domestic event was the coronation of King Charles III following the death of Queen Elizabeth II in late 2022.

The US and UK were among many countries still reeling from the disruptions of the Covid pandemic, which peaked a couple of years earlier. Other prominent elections that provided the backdrop for the debates included the presidential election in Nigeria, Africa's most populous country, which took place in February 2023 and saw a controversial victory for Bola Tinubu amid allegations of electoral maladministration; and the 2022 general election in Brazil, South America's most populous country, which saw defeat for the populist firebrand Jair Bolsonaro and a return to power for Lula da Silva for a third, non-consecutive term.

While some authors have chosen to add a few updates to their chapters, the contributors to this volume were on the whole taking stock of how things looked in May 2023, around the world, and across the various aspects of representative democracy. This Introduction is being written two years later, and in the time that has elapsed global developments have either addressed or underscored some of the big questions posed by the volume's contributors while also raising new issues.

While the US two years ago seemed to be in a challenging place, the situation today is arguably much graver from the standpoint of the priorities endorsed by the volume's contributors – goals such as constitutional constraints, protection of rights, and effective representation. The legitimacy of the 2020 presidential election continued to dominate the discussions leading to the 2024 election, and attempts continue in 2025 in some states to disenfranchise voters through gerrymandering, changing voter identification rules, and litigation asking for absentee ballots to be discarded to change the announced results in local elections. Polarisation is more entrenched than ever, in both the House and the Senate, and civility continues to decline. One can argue that 'enlightened conscience' and 'mature judgement' are being openly replaced with raw political power achieved by the slimmest of margins.[5] It is still early days in the second administration of Donald Trump, but

[5] Donald Trump claimed a 'mandate' for sweeping governmental change with less than 50% of the popular votes cast, and the Republican party similarly claimed a 'mandate' for sweeping change from an election that produced a historically small split between Republicans and Democrats in the House of Representatives (a margin of three).

what we have seen so far shows that the subject of this latest round of The Putney Debates remains highly relevant as we write. The populism of President Trump continues to pose real challenges to the ideals of representative democracy and especially its liberal aspects.

It is not only in the US that we see a strengthening of populist sentiment. The BJP continues its dominance of Indian politics following its election victory in 2024. In France, the National Rally (RN), led by Marine Le Pen, made significant electoral gains in the 2024 National Assembly elections, securing 29 per cent of first-round votes (and was prevented from forming government only by the coalition strategies used by the other parties). Likewise, the 2025 German election saw a historically strong performance by the country's main populist party, the AfD as it surged to 21 per cent of the overall vote share, placing it second behind the CDU/CSU (29 per cent) but well ahead of the main social-democratic party, the SPD (16 per cent). The UK general election was won by the Labour Party in what some interpreted as a return to normality. But even here there were signs of populism, especially in the continued rightward shift of the Conservative Party as it strives to fend off the challenge further along on the ideological spectrum.

In these and other countries, recent developments show that representative democracy is in a fragile condition. They are a powerful testament to the need for scholars of politics and law, practitioners in these fields, and the public to be engaged in asking questions about their democracies and how to make them work better.

1

Is Representative Democracy in Crisis?

RICHARD W CLARY

I. Introduction[1]

There are several goals for this first chapter of a volume of essays evolved from the Oxford Global Society's 2023 New Putney Debates. First, I will explain briefly why the Oxford Global Society chose 'democracy in crisis' as the topic. One can debate whether the title should be a question or a statement. There are enough examples around the globe to suggest that representative democracy is in fact in a state of crisis, or at least under serious stress, in several nations previously considered exemplars of well-running representative democracies. This chapter will focus primarily on the US and the UK. The intervening two years since the conference have presented us with several more examples from both countries related to the topic, some suggesting optimism and others suggesting further concerns.

My second goal is to suggest at least some of the causes of this stress. To address that topic, it is necessary to start with the basic pillars of what we call representative democracy today, look at the basic assumptions underlying a well-functioning representative democracy, and then decide which pillars and assumptions appear to need reinforcement. I will also identify some proposals currently under discussion as alterations to the existing pillars. Finally, I will end with my own thoughts on where we should start the reinforcing process.

II. Is Representative Democracy in Crisis?

According to the Economist Intelligence Unit (the EIU) in its report, 'Democracy Index 2023, Age of Conflict', more than half the world's population was eligible to go to the polls in 2024 in 76 countries. But the EIU defines only 43 of those 76 countries as meeting the criteria of 'fully free and fair' elections. Moreover, out

[1] This chapter is derived from the keynote lecture I delivered on 9 May 2023 to open *The Putney Debates 2023: Democracy in Crisis?*, sponsored by the Oxford Global Society. The full set of lectures and panel discussions is available online through the OXGS YouTube channel.

of 167 countries studied, the EIU identifies only 24 countries as being 'full democracies'. The UK is in the full democracy category, but sadly the US is in the 'flawed democracy' category (and has been since 2016).

The International Institute for Democracy and Electoral Assistance (the International IDEA) at the end of 2022 issued a report suggesting that half of the world's democratic countries are experiencing an erosion of democracy. The US, Brazil, Hungary, India and Poland were all included in the report's list of 'backsliding' democratic countries.

The generalised assertion that democracy is being challenged has been used to cover a multitude of different situations, but most can be placed into two basic categories: a refusal to accept election results; and a repeated, rapid change in executive leadership with no election at all. The US is a startling recent example of the first category; the UK was an example of the second category, now 'corrected' by the recent 2024 general election.

In the US, there is an ongoing refusal by some on the losing side to accept the outcome of the 2020 presidential election, which led to the unprecedented 6 January 2021 insurrection at the Capitol building. Refusal to accept the outcome of the 2020 election – notwithstanding the total absence of proof of election fraud after numerous recounts and investigations – continued to be an issue in the 2022 mid-term elections and remained a critical issue in the run-up to the 2024 presidential election. Numerous prominent Republicans – especially Mr Trump and those who hoped to be his vice-presidential running mate – refused to say whether they would accept the 2024 election results should Mr Trump lose again. While the US is the most startling example of this phenomenon, it is by no means the only one.[2]

For the second category – repeated, rapid change in executive leadership – examples can be found in the UK and some of its constituent parts. The UK saw three prime ministers in a six-month span in 2022, with accusations of 'coups' and 'coronations'. Thus Boris Johnson, becoming Prime Minister in 2019 as a result of a duly held general election, resigned under pressure effective September 2022. His replacement, Liz Truss, lasted only 49 days, announcing her resignation in October 2022. Her replacement, Rishi Sunak, was the subject of numerous rumours of coup attempts, although none, in fact, occurred before a snap general election was finally called for July 2024. Of course, in a parliamentary system such as the UK, the majority party in Parliament has the right to change the Prime Minister without going to the national polls. It is not the change per se that raised eyebrows, but the frequency and rapidity with which it occurred. 'Coups' and 'coronations' are not the normal terminology of an elected representative democracy. No less

[2] In Brazil, supporters of the losing Presidential candidate (Mr Bolsonaro) urged the military to nullify that country's 2022 election. In 2022 in Peru, the then President (Mr Castillo) attempted to dissolve the duly elected legislature in anticipation of being impeached. Following his impeachment, riots in the streets pitted Mr Castillo's supporters against those of the new President (Ms Boluarte). Both sides rejected the legitimacy of the other's 'President'.

an 'authority' on democracy than Vladimir Putin felt comfortable saying that the multiple changes in Prime Minister had been 'far from democratic'.[3]

Similar rapid leadership changes occurred in Scotland in 2023–2024. Nicola Sturgeon was the duly elected First Minister of Scotland for over nine years (2014–2023) but abruptly resigned in March 2023. Her replacement, selected by the Scottish National Party and then by the Scottish Parliament (Holyrood), Humza Yousaf, only served for 13 months before he resigned to avoid losing a no-confidence vote. His replacement, John Swinney, has been serving since May 2024, achieving the First Minister post unopposed. Thus, as with the UK more generally, Scotland has seen three First Ministers in relatively short order. In Wales, the new First Minister (Vaughan Gething) was only in office for 78 days before he lost a no-confidence motion in the Senedd. Because the vote was non-binding, the First Minister said he would carry on, but ultimately he resigned after only four months in office when four of his own Ministers resigned in protest. His replacement, Eluned Morgan, was the only candidate seeking to replace Mr Gething as head of the Welsh Labour Party, and she was confirmed as First Minister by the Senedd. Thus, Wales, like Scotland and the UK, saw a change in executive leadership in a short period of time. As noted previously, the parliamentary system allows for such changes without the need to return to the national electorate, or even the party electorate, but the rapidity, frequency and circumstances of the changes at least raise questions as to whether government is functioning as the voters anticipated when last they went to the polls.

One more example, more difficult to categorise, comes from Northern Ireland. In May 2022, elections were held for the Stormont Assembly, resulting in Sinn Fein securing the largest number of seats for the first time. This should have resulted in Sinn Fein having its first First Minister. However, the Democratic Unionist Party (DUP), having lost its plurality and thus its leading position in the Stormont Assembly, refused to allow the Assembly to elect a speaker and resume the business of governance. The refusal was characterised as a protest against the Windsor Framework between the European Union and the UK, which adjusted the operation of the prior Northern Ireland Protocol. That stalemate remained in place for two years, until February 2024, when Michelle O'Neill became First Minister, finally achieving the outcome of the 2022 election.

Thus, both the US and the UK, albeit for very different reasons, have been cited as examples of representative democracy under stress, surprising additions to a growing list.

In fairness, it must be pointed out that some of these examples were eventually resolved in a manner consistent with their respective electoral systems. In the US, President Biden was sworn in on schedule after the 2020 election. Many of the people participating in the January 2021 insurrection were duly convicted and sent to prison (but have now all been pardoned). Numerous investigations – including

[3] *The Guardian*, 7 September 2022.

investigations launched by highly partisan Trump supporters – concluded there was no evidence of election fraud. Polls suggested that most voters preferred to move off that issue in the 2024 election, and the 2024 election itself was relatively peaceful. In the UK power sharing has been restored in Northern Ireland, and the general election in July 2024 reset the elected order in the UK (although the representativeness of the election results can be debated, as discussed below). Taken together, though, these examples – and there are more around the globe – can justify a concern that representative democracy is under stress.

III. What are the Structures and Basic Features of a Well-Functioning Representative Democracy?

What are the causes of these challenges to representative democracy? What lessons can be learned from these examples, and what can be done to reinvigorate the democratic ethos?

One way to approach the question is to look at the pillars generally understood as supporting the structure of representative democracy, at least from an Anglo-American perspective. Four basic pillars have been identified:

1. The *constitution*: the basic framework for governance (written or not), establishing the basic relationship between rulers and ruled, between government and the people, and the terms under which the many consent – actually, or at least theoretically – to governance by the few.
2. The *institutions* of government: the formal mechanisms by which the national leaders are selected and rule, subject to constitutional limitations. These include both the electoral systems and the underlying machinery of government, such as the civil service, independent agencies, regulatory authorities, and the courts.
3. The *political actors:* the people who step forward to provide leadership, legitimately selected through the electoral system, and hopefully acting in a manner consistent with constitutional norms and in cooperation with the underlying machinery of government.
4. *Acceptance*: the acceptance of the people of a system of authority by which the few govern the many, even when (or especially when) the many would have made a different choice from the few.

Based on recent examples, which of these four pillars are under stress, or at least have been weakened and need reinforcement? To address that question, it is best to start with a more fundamental question: what are the basic features of a representative democracy that is *functioning well* and consistent with the four pillars?

I will focus on the models of the UK and the US, which have rich histories of representative democracy, notwithstanding some recent events. The model in the UK, derived from an unwritten constitution, is based fundamentally on parliamentary sovereignty. The model in the US, derived from a written constitution, is based on a complicated set of interwoven checks and balances, with political power shared by the President and the legislature, subject to judicial review. Thus, the models are quite different in structure and operation. Nonetheless, these two models share certain basic assumptions, which I will divide into what I call the primary assumption and a series of related secondary assumptions upon which the primary assumption relies.

A. The Primary Assumption

What I call the primary assumption is easily summarised: the country's government should be selected through fair and open elections in which: (i) all citizens may participate equally; and (ii) all citizens will abide by the results. Such elections are considered to reflect the basic elements of *participation in*, and *consent to*, governance by the people.

It must be acknowledged that the concept of universal suffrage entered the stage rather late in both the US and the UK, but it is now part of the primary assumption. In the US, the right to vote was originally limited to white males, and they only voted for the members of the House of Representatives (the lower house of the national legislature) for their individual district.[4] The members of the Senate (the upper house of the national legislature) were originally elected by the legislature of each respective State.[5] The President was elected by 'Electors' (colloquially referred to today as the 'Electoral College') selected by the legislature of each State.[6] It was not until the passage of the Thirteenth, Fourteenth, and Fifteenth Amendments in the 1860s, following the American Civil War, that suffrage was extended to all male citizens 21 years old or older, without regard to race, colour, or previous condition of servitude. Direct election of Senators did not occur until the passage of the Seventeenth Amendment in 1913, and women were not given the right to vote until the Nineteenth Amendment in 1920. The voting age was lowered to 18 by the Twenty-Sixth Amendment in 1971. The Electoral College remains alive and well, and due to its odd structure produced the anomaly that the winners of both the 2000 and 2016 presidential elections lost the popular vote.[7]

[4] US Constitution, Art I, s 2.

[5] ibid Art I, s 3.

[6] ibid Art II, s 1.

[7] The Electoral College was one of numerous compromises included in the Constitution to obtain its passage. Rather than having a direct national popular vote for President, each State was assigned a number of electors equal to the total of its Congressional delegation: its number of representatives in the House based on comparative population (measured through a national census every ten years), plus two for its Senators. Each State, regardless of size, was given equal representation in the Senate, to protect smaller States. The electors were originally envisioned as wise, independent men selected by each State's legislature for the particular purpose of voting for President. As it works today, the candidate who wins the plurality of the popular votes cast in a particular State gets the votes of all the electors for that State. (In Nebraska and Maine, that State's Electoral College votes are distributed to whichever

The right to vote started out similarly limited in the UK. According to the National Archives blog, in 1831 only approximately 4,500 men could vote in parliamentary elections, out of a population of more than 2.6 million people. Even after the Great Reform Act 1832, the franchise was restricted through property qualifications. It was not until the Representation of the People Act 1918 that male universal suffrage was passed, along with suffrage for women over the age of 30 who satisfied a property qualification. The Equal Franchise Act 1928 finally extended voting rights to women over the age of 21. The voting age for Parliamentary elections was lowered to 18 in the Representation of the People Act 1969. Thus, in fits and starts in both countries, universal suffrage was achieved and its results accepted, satisfying the primary assumption.

Of course, having the ability to vote once every few years is a fairly thin reed on which to base either 'participation' or 'consent'. Many citizens, especially those who are not active participants in a political party, have no meaningful ability to influence who the candidates are and thus their electoral choices are limited by others. A substantial number of citizens choose not to exercise their right to vote at all. The 2020 presidential election in the US had the highest rate of eligible voter participation in 120 years, and still only 66 per cent voted. The 2024 general election in the UK had 60 per cent participation, the lowest percentage turnout since 2001. Nonetheless, the *potential* to effectuate change through voting can be considered the base minimum required to satisfy the theoretical necessities of participation and consent.

Obviously that primary assumption, standing alone, is insufficient. Many nations have 'elections', but one would not characterise Russia, for example, as a representative democracy. What other essential attributes are required?

President Abraham Lincoln, in his famous Gettysburg Address delivered in the midst of the American Civil War, encapsulated a basic view of democracy as 'government of the people, by the people, for the people'. As inspiring political rhetoric, the Gettysburg Address is a masterpiece. Of course, it is not – and was not intended to be – a full-blown description of how that government in fact works. Rather, Lincoln used this phraseology – often quoted by Americans – as shorthand for the far more complicated system of government embodied in the Constitution: *representative* democracy, in which voting for representatives constitutes 'of the people' and actions by those elected officials constitute – or at least substitute for – actions 'by the people', hopefully 'for the people'. In England in the 1770s, the idea of 'by the people' was captured by the theory of 'the people in parliament', envisioning the House of Commons as the embodiment of the people as a whole. The US skipped over this theoretical construct, going straight to representatives. Today, in both countries, 'by the people' really means by the elected representatives of the people. This leads me to the related secondary assumptions.

candidate won each of the Congressional districts in the State, with the remaining two electoral votes assigned to the overall winner of the State as a whole.) The overweighting of the smaller States in the Electoral College is what permits an outcome whereby one candidate wins the national popular vote, but the other candidate wins the Electoral College vote and hence the presidency.

B. Basic Secondary Assumptions

I will summarise three basic secondary assumptions for representative democracy as follows:

1. The representatives so elected should work together for the common good of the nation as a whole, rather than simply focusing on narrow, partisan or parochial preferences.
2. The representatives so elected should, through knowledgeable debate and deliberation, arrive at solutions that most likely reflect consensus through compromise.
3. The representatives should be chosen for the purpose, expected to exercise independent judgement that may well be different from the views of the subset of the voters that elected them.

James Madison in his Federalist Papers Number 10, arguing in 1788 for ratification of the proposed Constitution, described the benefit of representative democracy as the ability:

> to refine and enlarge the public views, by passing them through the medium of a chosen body of citizens, whose wisdom may best discern the true interest of their country, and whose patriotism and love of justice will be least likely to sacrifice it to temporary or partial considerations. Under such a regulation, it may well happen that the public voice, pronounced by the representatives of the people, will be more consonant to the public good than if pronounced by the people themselves, convened for the purpose.

Edmund Burke used different but related concepts when he described the role of the representative in a democracy in his famous 1774 Speech to the Electors at Bristol:

> [H]is unbiased opinion, his mature judgment, his enlightened conscience, he ought not to sacrifice to you [the electorate], to any man, or to any set of men living … Your representative owes you, not his industry only, but his judgment; and he betrays, instead of serving you, if he sacrifices it to your opinion.
>
> [P]arliament is a *deliberative* assembly of *one* nation, with *one* interest, that of the whole; where, not local purposes, not local prejudices, ought to guide, but the general good, resulting from the general reason of the whole. You choose a member indeed; but when you have chosen him, he is not a member of Bristol, but he is a member of *Parliament*.

Both sets of quotes – one American, one English – eloquently capture what I have referred to as three basic secondary assumptions about the nature and role of representatives in a democracy. Madison and Burke may have had very different assumptions about the qualities of a representative vis-à-vis the electorate more broadly, but they described similar *roles* once elected.

There is also a fourth assumption, at least in the US model: A system of checks and balances within the constitutional order should keep the government from overstepping its bounds, whether that be due to fear of factions (particularly factions within the so-called 'lower' class likely to sway the lower house of the legislature, as Madison and others emphasised) or fear of executive overreach leaning towards 'princely rule'. Put simply, there should be a *balanced* constitution to keep the elected representatives within their assigned duties.

IV. What Parts of this Model of Representative Democracy are not Bearing their Full Weight?

Of the four pillars identified above – the constitution, the institutions of government, the political actors, and acceptance by the people – in most recent examples, the constitution (written or unwritten) seems to be largely surviving the test of time. But the institutions of government – both the electoral systems and the underlying machinery of government – are being sorely tested, and political actors are playing a major role in that testing. Distrust of government – the institutions and the relevant actors – naturally leads to the undermining of acceptance by the people. I will address each element in turn.

A. Attacks on the Electoral System Itself

We are witnessing attacks on the electoral system itself in numerous countries, both in the refusal to accept election results by candidates and voters, and in attempts by government officials to skew electoral systems towards their own desired outcomes. I will use recent events in the US as examples of both.

i. Refusing to Accept Electoral Results

As noted previously, in the US we saw the shocking refusal of the loser to accept the results of the 2020 presidential election. That refusal continues to reverberate in American politics today. For example, a majority of Republican candidates in the 2022 elections for the House of Representatives, the Senate, and key statewide offices (such as governor) denied or questioned the outcome of the 2020 presidential election.[8] Some candidates used their rejection of the outcome of the 2020 election as their defining platform, as if the refusal to accept the outcome of an election is itself a qualification for elected office. The Republican candidate for the 2024 presidential election and politicians seeking his endorsement refused to commit to accepting the results of the 2024 election if he lost again. An investigation by CBS News revealed that in the 2024 election cycle there were over 80 candidates for positions as election officials – State officials responsible for *running* the presidential election and certifying the results – who still denied that President Biden

[8] *Washington Post*, 6 October 2022.

won the 2020 election and were campaigning to 'stop the steal' in 2024.[9] A steady drumbeat began that any loss by Mr Trump in 2024 could only be explained by fraud, which is the same pattern the country saw starting in the summer of 2020.

ii. Trying to Manipulate Future Elections

There has been an increased effort by some political actors to alter future election results by making it more difficult to vote, or by redrawing districts to control the outcome. For example, in both the US and the UK, there has been the recent enactment of voter identification laws. At least in the US there is a strong suspicion that the intent behind those laws was not protection against voter fraud, as publicly stated – a problem frequently discussed in theory but rarely identified in practice – but rather the expected disparate impact on the poor who simply do not have basic government-issued picture ID cards such as drivers' licences or passports.

The intent is far less clear in the UK, but questions have been raised. Some analysts have suggested that the categories of approved voter IDs in the UK were skewed to favour older voters, and a senior Conservative politician seemed to concede that the intent behind the voter ID law had been to suppress young voters (presumably liberal voters) who might lack the necessary IDs, although he suggested that the law instead had unintentionally suppressed older (Conservative) voters. Sir Jacob Rees-Mogg was quoted after the 2023 local elections: '[p]arties that try and gerrymander end up finding their clever scheme comes back to bite them, as, dare I say, we [the Conservatives] found by insisting on voter ID for elections'.[10] In the 2023 local elections in the UK it is estimated that more than one per cent of voters were turned away because they lacked an approved ID[11] – admittedly not enough to have likely influenced the outcomes, but that does not address the question of how many otherwise eligible voters did not even try to vote because they realised too late that they lacked (or could not readily find) the necessary ID. Prior to the May 2024 election for the Mayor of London, there was speculation in the media that voter ID requirements might suppress the youth vote to the detriment of Labour. (There is no concrete evidence that this, in fact, occurred.) Whether the new voter ID requirements, in fact, impacted the vote in the July 2024 general election remains to be analysed, but the mere fact that the possibility was widely discussed in the media could undermine faith in the electoral system.

In the US, the issue is more pronounced. Some State legislatures have recently sought to pass new laws cutting back on methods of voting. In the 2020 presidential election, largely as a result of the Covid-19 pandemic, the methods by which votes could be cast were expanded. (Each State sets its own standards for permissible voting methods.) The expanded methods included allowing a broader time

[9] *CBS News*, 14 May 2024.
[10] Quoted in *The Observer*, 20 May 2023.
[11] ibid.

frame for early voting, the use of drop boxes for early voting, and the broader use of ballots returned by mail, including ballots post-marked by election day but received thereafter. Of the votes cast in that election, 69 per cent were cast non-traditionally, rather than at the ballot box on election day: 43 per cent by mail and 26 per cent by early voting. (By comparison, only 21 per cent of voters mailed in their ballots in 2016.) In a country accustomed to having the winner of the presidential election declared on the night of the election, the delay in counting due to voluminous mail-in ballots provided ample room for conspiracy theories about election fraud and opened the window for misleading premature declarations of 'victory' before all votes were counted.

In response, some State legislatures are seeking to require in-person voting, eliminating absentee and mail-in ballots, and prohibiting so-called 'ballot harvesting' (allowing an individual to collect the ballots of voters in a family or community and drop them off in a collection box in early voting, rather than making each voter make the trip to the polling station on election day). Mr Trump has gone so far as to suggest that only paper ballots should be allowed (no voting machines[12]) and that all votes should be received and counted on a single day (no early voting). The combined effect of these proposed restrictions would be to expedite the counting by dramatically suppressing voting itself. Such changes would have a disparate impact on poorer communities lacking adequate transportation to distant polling stations. Given the long lines on election day, such changes can force individuals to choose between getting paid for a day of work or voting. If enacted in full, such measures could potentially disenfranchise military personnel serving overseas.

The US has also seen instances of State legislatures redrawing Congressional districts in order to water down the voting power of certain identifiable groups, for instance by splitting natural communities across multiple electoral districts where those communities will be in the minority and therefore cannot win an election going forward. Another version of the same tactic is to redraw districts to make sure an entire community is consolidated in a single district with one representative, if that community was previously large enough to form a majority or plurality in two districts and elect two representatives. Either approach to gerrymandering is designed to skew future elections.

iii. The Sense of Disenfranchisement

There is also evidence of an increased sense of disenfranchisement for portions of the electorate. Here I will draw from recent examples from the UK. For example, there is the curious case of the 2022 'election' of Liz Truss as Prime Minister by the votes of 81,326 members of the Conservative Party (to Rishi Sunak's 60,399 votes),

[12] Dominion Voting Systems was falsely accused of rigging its voting machines in the 2020 election; it recovered $787.5 million from Fox News to settle Dominion's defamation case. No evidence of problems with the voting machines has ever been discovered.

in a nation with a population of over 66 million total and over 46 million registered voters for parliamentary elections. Shortly into the job there were already questions whether she in fact had a mandate from the people to govern, as she claimed, and she announced her resignation six weeks after taking office. Ms Truss's successor, Rishi Sunak, became Prime Minister by the vote of a majority of the Conservative Party MPs. With no declared competing candidate crossing the heightened threshold to run, not even Conservative Party members – much less the electorate as a whole – had any say in the matter of who would next lead the government. While that is fully consistent with the UK parliamentary system, at least viewed from the outside it has the appearance of a shrinkage of the franchise (from national poll to party poll to Conservative MP poll) on a matter of national importance.

As previously noted, in Northern Ireland the results of the May 2022 election for the Stormont Assembly were rendered a nullity through the simple mechanism of the Democratic Unionist Party refusing to participate. Presumably having no working government at all was not what *any* of the voters had in mind in casting their ballots, and thus *all* of them were effectively disenfranchised.

The argument over whether Scotland may hold another independence referendum has been cast by the Scottish National Party (the SNP) in terms of democracy: that blocking another referendum disenfranchises the people of Scotland. Having lost a legal challenge in the UK Supreme Court, the then leader of the SNP (Nicola Sturgeon) announced she would view her party's performance in the next national election in Scotland (assuming it won the majority of the available Parliamentary seats) as a de facto independence referendum, even though individual voters could have something else entirely on their minds on election day, such as which candidate will be the best representative for delivering basic government services. This plan was repeated in the SNP's 2024 party manifesto, although the SNP's poor performance in the general election rendered it moot. The fact remains that choosing in advance to select a single-issue message out of a complicated, multi-issue, multi-candidate election is itself a form of disenfranchisement for all the voters who are not so single-minded.

iv. The Effect of Party Control Over Candidate Selection

There is a growing sense that the electoral process is being skewed by an unrepresentative subset of the electorate. The candidate selection process is controlled by a very small, highly active partisan group within an already small and partisan political party. That, of course, is not a new phenomenon. But the 2024 general election in the UK produced vocal complaints against both major parties that the party apparatus was 'parachuting' some unwanted candidates and 'deselecting' other, wanted candidates without consultation with the relevant local constituencies.

Events in the 2024 presidential election in the US presented an extreme example of party control over candidate selection. The incumbent, Joe Biden, had already won all of the Democratic Party primaries across the country and was clearly going to be the official Democratic nominee. But following a televised debate that did not go well for Mr Biden, a concerted effort was launched by party leaders and influential donors to force him to drop out of the race. After a drumbeat of negative speeches and articles, Mr Biden in fact withdrew, to be replaced by his Vice-President, Kamala Harris. The rank-and-file party members who voted overwhelmingly for Mr Biden in the primaries were not consulted in the slightest, either about forcing his withdrawal or substituting Ms Harris. While a majority of Biden delegates quickly followed his lead in endorsing Ms Harris to be the new nominee, it was a startling display of the power of a small party elite to force even an incumbent President to acquiesce in their demands. In the US this was essentially unprecedented, although some politicians in the UK expressed parallels to the unseating of Boris Johnson and then Liz Truss as Prime Minister without consultation with the rank-and-file members of the Conservative Party.

Party control over candidate selection is then coupled with the increasing expense of elections themselves, which discourages independent candidates. This is particularly true in the US, where spending on elections – by candidates and parties, and by outside sources – has reached extraordinary levels, not just in national elections but also in State and even local elections. This combination leaves large portions of the electorate with very little participation in democracy except to vote on election day, choosing among candidates selected by others. This too can be seen as a form of disenfranchisement, especially for those who do not want to be forced to formally join a political party. At least in the UK there are multiple parties to choose from;[13] in the US there are really only two, and in 2023 roughly 43 per cent of the American electorate – the largest bloc – self identified as independent.

v. Unrepresentative Results

There is evidence of a growing feeling that current electoral systems are not in fact producing a representative government, in two different senses: (1) the individual elected only received a plurality of the votes cast and in theory could be the last choice of a majority of voters in the constituency; and (2) in a legislature, a series of extremely narrow victories per constituency could produce a majority in the legislature that seriously overstates at a national level the mandate of the winning party. These two senses can work together in countries with multiple parties, producing a legislature heavily dominated by plurality-only members, to the detriment of many other parties.

The recent 2024 general election in the UK is a clear demonstration of these electoral dynamics at work when the first-past-the-post system is combined with a substantial expansion of the political parties fielding candidates. The Labour Party won 411 seats in Parliament – 63.2 per cent – with only 33.7 per cent of the votes

[13] There are 13 political parties represented in Parliament after the 2024 general election, as well as six independents.

cast. The Conservative Party won 121 seats – 18.6 per cent – with 23.7 per cent of the votes cast. The Liberal Democrats won 72 seats – 11.1 per cent – with 12.2 per cent of the votes, making them the third largest party in Parliament with only the fourth largest number of votes. New party Reform UK had the third largest number of votes (14.3 per cent) but only won 5 seats in Parliament – fewer than the SNP and Sinn Fein, both of which received substantially fewer votes. Of the 650 seats at issue, 113 were won by so-called 'thin majorities', which really were thin pluralities, with less than 5 per cent of votes separating the winner from second place; in some instances, only 20 votes separated the winner from second place. Thus, the overall result, characterised as a landslide win for the Labour Party, masks the fact that two-thirds of the participating electorate voted for someone other than Labour. Put another way, with 13 political parties and six successful independents splitting the votes, the first-past-the-post system essentially doubled Labour's representation in Parliament with only a tiny percentage increase in its vote share compared to the 2019 general election.[14]

As a reaction to these types of skewed results, various efforts are underway to redesign electoral systems, either to ensure majority support for the winner or to ensure that smaller political parties are included in the legislature. For example, in the UK, the Labour Party voted at its September 2022 annual conference to replace first-past-the-post voting with 'proportional representation', although that idea did not make it into the party's 2024 manifesto. The leader of Reform UK, looking at the 2024 results, has already suggested revisiting first-past-the-post, and the Liberal Democrats called for proportional representation in their manifesto. The Scottish Parliament is selected by giving each voter two votes: a constituent vote for an individual candidate, with the winner being the first past the post, and a regional vote for a political party; regional MSPs are allocated so that the number of seats a party gets in total across a region is about the same as the percentage of votes that party received. This additional member system helps to correct the potential danger of smaller parties being excluded.[15]

Some States in the US are experimenting with ranked choice voting (as in Alaska and Maine) or with requiring a run-off vote between the top two candidates if the candidate first past the post fails to get an outright majority (as in Georgia, Mississippi and Louisiana). Either approach ultimately produces a winner who has the support of a majority of the votes cast, but both delay the ability to declare a winner and thus leave room for rumour and speculation trying to undermine in advance the validity of the ultimate outcome.

[14] In the 2019 general election in the UK, the Conservative Party won approximately 44 per cent of the popular vote but over 56 per cent of the seats in the House of Commons; Labour had 32 per cent of the popular vote (only 1.7 per cent less than in 2024) but only captured 202 seats in Parliament that year.

[15] New Zealand is another example of a mixed-member proportional system with two votes per voter, one for an individual candidate and one for a political party: 72 seats are filled through direct vote, and 48 seats are allocated proportionately among parties.

It should be noted that one recent election in the UK featured a return to the first-past-the-post system of voting. The Mayor of London had previously been selected using a supplementary vote system (somewhat similar to a ranked choice system), in which voters selected both a first and second choice. This was a form of automatic runoff to produce a majority winner: if no candidate received over 50 per cent of the ballots cast, all but the top two candidates were eliminated and their voters' second choice votes were reassigned to one of the remaining two if applicable, and the candidate with the most total votes (first and second choice combined) was the winner. The Elections Act 2022, passed by the Conservative government, changed that supplementary vote system to first-past-the-post, applicable in the May 2024 mayoral election. There was substantial speculation in the media that this change could diminish – and was intended to diminish – the re-election chances of Mayor Sadiq Khan from Labour. The speculation was that the candidates for Labour, the Liberal Democrats, the Greens, and numerous independent candidates would split the left-leaning votes, whereas the Conservative candidate would only split votes with the Reform UK candidate. Whether or not that was in fact the plan behind the change in systems, Khan won the May 2024 election with a plurality of 44 per cent of the votes. In any event, it is a notable example of a retreat back to first-past-the-post at a time when there seems to be a broadening push for something more representative, and it generated media speculation about election manipulation.

Whether alternatives to first-past-the-post plurality winners are improvements can and should be debated. The case for such alternatives is probably at its strongest in countries with multiple, robust political parties, such as the UK. But at the very least, proposals to get majority winners or proportional winners, rather than merely plurality winners, reflect a frustration with the electoral process. To some extent, so does so-called 'tactical voting', a self-help work around by individual voters to which both Labour and the Liberal Democrats attribute some of their 2024 success.[16] Loss of faith in the election process's ability to produce the voters' intended results undermines acceptance. Without a nation's full embrace of the primary assumption, representative democracy is on shaky ground.

B. Is Partisanship Replacing Consensus and Compromise?

It can be argued that successful representative democracies require a common set of basic cultural norms that are at least largely embraced by the electorate. 'We the people', as the US Constitution famously begins, assumes that commonality

[16] The 7 July 2024 runoff election in France was a powerful demonstration of tactical voting conducted at the political party level. The National Rally party had anticipated having an outright majority in the French National Assembly but ended up in third place behind the New Popular Front and the Ensemble alliance after those two blocs agreed to withdraw their respective third place finishers before the runoff occurred. The leader of the National Rally decried the agreement as a 'dishonest alliance', but the result was that each successful candidate won with a majority of the votes cast, which seems entirely consistent with representative democracy.

of basic interests, values and beliefs. That assumption may have seemed reasonable at the time the US was founded because 'We the people' really only referred to a specific subset: white males. With today's far more expansive definition of the people, commonality is harder to achieve.

But in recent years achieving commonality does not seem to even be the goal: 'We the people' seems to have been replaced by 'us versus them', a growing sense that there is a 'culture war' underway that only one side can win. For example, the US has seen the rise of the so-called 'replacement' theory – a fear that the 'them' are taking the rights, jobs and opportunities rightfully belonging to the 'us'. There have even been public calls by some elected officials for the 'return' of the country to being a 'white Christian nation', leaving aside that from its very founding the country was neither wholly white nor wholly Christian (although much of the original leadership was both). Moreover, the Constitution now guarantees freedom of religion and equal rights for all members of what is a substantially diverse, multicultural society.

In parts of Europe, far right political parties have had success emphasising nationalism combined with anti-immigration: the need to exclude the 'others', the 'them', combined with demands that 'they' change their cultural ways to become more like 'us'. Anti-immigration has become a major political talking point in both the US and the UK.

Part of the growing 'us versus them' mentality appears to be a reaction to the dramatic increase in multiculturalism, particularly as groups have increasingly embraced the unique aspects of their own cultures rather than prioritising assimilation. The 'great melting pot' theory of national culture that was once popular (at least in the US) has been replaced with something more resembling a collage. Certain groups – particularly those who dominated or at least thrived in the old social order – are feeling threatened by this redefinition of national identity, describing it as a rejection of national values rather than as a new, expanded definition of national values.

The rise of increasingly partisan media groups, embracing not only their own opinions but their own facts, only accentuates the divide by spreading disinformation that now travels at the speed of the internet. As Theresa May put it in her farewell speech in Parliament, social media 'amplifies extreme views which then become accepted views unless we are very careful'.[17]

The 'us versus them' mentality can also be traced to some extent to the expanding inequality in wealth in both the UK and the US. Such inequality has, of course, existed for a very long time, and certainly was evident at the first Putney Debates and at America's founding. Madison's fear of factions in Federalist Papers Number 10 bears testimony to the concern that the 'have nots' would use representative democracy to challenge the property rights of the 'haves'. Suspicion of the Levellers at the original Putney Debates shared similar concerns. The recent uproar

[17] Quoted in *The Independent*, 27 May 2024.

in the UK over a Conservative government proposal – subsequently withdrawn – to cut the highest tax bracket for the highest earners while failing to increase benefits to keep up with inflation for those at the bottom of the economic ladder dramatically demonstrated the financial aspect of 'us versus them'. Perceptions that some groups are gaining at the cost of others, and that the government is actively favouring one group over another, undermines acceptance by those feeling disfavoured.

If one's outlook is that the nation is engaged in a culture war of values and economics in an 'us versus them' tug-of-war that only one side can win, it is not surprising that consensus and compromise are seen as weaknesses rather than strengths in government. Thus, a basic tenet of representative democracy – the achievement of good national policy through educated debate among open-minded elected officials seeking to find consensus for the greater good – becomes a negative, to be replaced by raw political power that gets recalculated at every election. To again quote Theresa May from her final speech to Parliament, '[c]ompromise is not a poisonous word … Polarisation is bad for politics.'[18] Sadly, that view is not consistent with the current views of many elected representatives, in the UK or the US.

The shift in the vision of a representative's proper role in governance is starkly demonstrated in the US by the recent attempt by Representative Marjorie Taylor Greene to remove Speaker of the House Mike Johnson, a fellow Republican. Johnson's transgression, in Greene's view, was allowing the bipartisan passage of legislation in the House of Representatives. The good news is that her motion was itself defeated through a bipartisan vote. Such was not the result for the recent attempt to pass a new immigration law, even though both Republicans and Democrats have been calling for such legislation. A small group of Senators – one Democrat, one Republican, and one independent – negotiated a bill that reflected give-and-take and compromise to achieve a proposal that all three could accept: an example of Madisonian representatives at work. Sadly, the bill was defeated by hard-line Republicans, acting at the urging of candidate Trump, to avoid the appearance of handing President Biden a 'win' on immigration before the 2024 election. Openly embracing chaos at the border for use as an election issue, rather than actually doing something about the chaos, should be viewed as a failure of the representatives' role in government, not a goal to be achieved.

C. Are Elected Officials No Longer the Leaders Envisioned by Madison or Burke?

It must be admitted that historically there has been suspicion about, if not outright disrespect for, an *active* role of the people in representative democracies. Madison in Federalist Papers Number 10 envisioned instead a 'better sort' of elected

[18] ibid.

officials – wiser, more open-minded, and better able to see the greater good than those who elected them. Those better, wiser elected officials would be able to decide what was best for the country as a whole, freed from the dictates of their less informed and more parochial constituents. Burke envisioned the members of the House of Commons as free to follow their 'mature judgment' and 'enlightened conscience', freed from 'local prejudices' of their electorate, although he did not share Madison's vision of a 'better sort' of elected official, just officials willing to aim for the collective good.

Such notions of the elected official – whether it be Madison's or Burke's – have been replaced by something far more partisan. In the US, members of the House of Representatives, subject to the pressure of election every two years, are more and more simply reflections of the majority views of their own districts or even the plurality's views if the plurality can deliver electoral victory, with seemingly little or no consideration of the greater good of the nation as a whole. This was perhaps most starkly demonstrated by the decision of a majority of Republicans in the House of Representatives to oppose certification of the 2020 Presidential election results, notwithstanding the total lack of evidence of voting fraud, apparently because they thought that tracked the views of their voters, uninformed as those views might be.

Moreover, representatives acting in that more parochial way are not even representing the consensus view of their constituencies. They are instead representing the views of those who have voted or hopefully will vote for them in enough numbers to win the next election. Political party allegiance has become a dominant feature of government in the US and in the UK. Neither Madison nor Burke seems to have anticipated the oversized role that political parties would come to assume, although President George Washington predicted the danger in his famous Farewell Address in 1796 when he described political parties as 'potent engines, by which cunning, ambitious, and unprincipled men will be enabled to subvert the power of the people'.

Partisanship, instead of the deliberative leadership described by Madison or Burke, is also demonstrated by a notable decline in civility in government. Politics has often – perhaps always – been a nasty business, but it seems to have sunk to a new low. It is hard to imagine that an elected official would interrupt the President's State of the Union national address with catcalls and jeers, yet members of Congress have done so and are proud of it. Attention-grabbing posturing, catchphrases such as 'Fake News' and 'The Big Lie', name-calling, and the substitution of hastily written tweets for thoughtful political discussion are hardly conducive to representative democracy. A willingness to lie outright about an opponent's positions and actions is becoming more and more commonplace. All of this has the effect of lowering the people's faith in elected government as a whole.

The decline in the art of compromise and the rise of increased partisanship helps explain another relatively recent development: the failure of coalitions. In Scotland, the coalition of the SNP and the Green Party fell apart over a culture war issue, and the resignation of the First Minister in the face of a no-confidence vote followed shortly thereafter. In Wales, it was the coalition of Labour and Plaid Cymru that collapsed, followed shortly thereafter by a non-binding no-confidence vote that the First Minister lost but said he would ignore until his own Ministers forced his resignation. If electoral systems are to be changed to create greater proportional representation, then those representatives will have to be able to form coalitions, broadly or at least on an issue-by-issue basis, in order to accomplish the role of government.[19]

D. Have the Checks and Balances Lost their Effectiveness?

In the UK historically there was in effect a tripartite government: the Crown; the Lords; and the Commons. Of course, in the modern world, the Crown's political role is essentially non-existent, and the Lords' role is substantially diminished, denounced as 'undemocratic' whenever the Lords' actions are inconsistent with a majority vote in the House of Commons. Thus, the House of Commons has become the decision-maker, consistent with parliamentary sovereignty. More accurately, the members of Parliament who are in the majority party are the decision-makers, assuming the majority is sufficiently large not to require propping up by one or more smaller parties. And even more accurately, given the energetic whip system of the parties, the actual decision-makers are the Prime Minister and his/her selected Cabinet – the executive – who in recent times seem to have been given fairly free range, subject to the disciplining fears of national electoral loss or an intraparty coup, with the coup being more prominent of late. If the Prime Minister fills the Cabinet with like-minded people chosen for their personal loyalty to the Prime Minister, the decrease in meaningful debate becomes acute, and lends itself to fears of the return to princely rule, albeit with an elected prince subject to periodic recall. Such a description, when coupled with partisan representatives in place of Burkean statesmen, hardly lends itself to any effective checks and balances. This in turn puts a substantially increased burden on the judiciary as the remaining bulwark against an increasingly powerful executive – a bulwark that is then attacked as undemocratic whenever it stands in the way of the executive's desires.

The US has its own far more structured three-part system of checks and balances, enshrined in the Constitution: an executive, a two-chamber legislature (the Senate and the House of Representatives), and a federal judiciary (overseen by the Supreme Court). The political branches, with separate electorates on separate election cycles, have intertwining duties and powers that were purposefully designed to encourage consensus and compromise. The problem in the US is not that checks and balances have stopped existing but that the 'checks' work too well,

[19] The results of the recent French National Assembly election, producing essentially a three-way split of the left, the centre, and the right, should make for an interesting case study on coalition building.

to the exclusion of the balances. In the current highly partisan world, for example, a majority in the Senate from one party can stymie a President from the other party, even one who won their own national election by a substantial margin. By way of a recent example, the Republican Senators refused to even hold a hearing on President Obama's nomination of Chief Judge Merrick Garland to the Supreme Court, simply leaving the seat vacant for a year in the hope that a Republican would be elected President in the next election. Those same Republican Senators then rushed to fill a new vacancy on the Court basically a month before the next presidential election, an election they correctly feared their party would lose. Nothing in the Constitution anticipated such blatant and inconsistent political steps or anticipated that the majority in the Senate would exercise its duties to advise and consent by refusing to even participate in the constitutionally-mandated process. Political manipulation of the membership of the Supreme Court in turn has undermined faith in its legitimacy, leading to attacks that it has become an unelected, undemocratic and largely unchecked political force of its own: another political arena for culture wars, rather than a check and balance as envisioned by the American founders.

A different but equally concerning issue has arisen following the 2024 elections: a decision by the Republican Senators to rubber-stamp presidential nominations for the Cabinet, notwithstanding those Senators' own public announcements of concerns about the nominees, because of a fear of offending the President from the same political party. That too abandons the constitutional duty of advise and consent. And checks and balances work far less well when one political party controls the presidency and both parts of the Legislature, albeit by the smallest of margins, especially if some legislators fear retribution from the President if they fail to comply with his wishes.

E. Is the Machinery of Government Part of the Solution, or Part of the Problem?

It is important also to consider two other well-established institutions of government: the civil services and independent regulatory agencies. Elected officials alone cannot actually run the vast machinery of modern government. But in both the US and the UK, there has been growing controversy over the role of the supposedly non-partisan civil service and the supposedly non-partisan or bi-partisan agencies: are they 'undemocratic', and has their power grown at the expense of duly elected representatives?

When Prime Minister Liz Truss began her short-lived tenure, she promptly fired two top civil servants at the Treasury. The dismissals were attacked by the opposition parties as partisan politics at the expense of government expertise, but they were defended as necessary to put duly elected officials back in charge. When allegations by civil servants of bullying led to the resignation of Deputy

Prime Minister Dominic Raab, the response by some legislators was to challenge the result as undemocratic. The airways and internet are filled with complaints by politicians that 'the blob' – the civil service – is standing in the way of the politicians' ideas, even though those civil servants are specifically charged with checking the legality and fiscal sustainability of elected officials' plans. Does a representative democracy need its civil servants and regulators to be impartial, acting on experience and expertise, or must the machinery of government automatically follow the lead of the elected officials? That is a legitimate debate to be had (I am admittedly in the former camp), but it is hardly advanced by simply using derogatory terms such as 'the Mandarins' and the 'deep state' whenever a particular politician feels thwarted, which is the situation today.

V. Is there a Path Forward?

Albeit in different forms, representative democracy has long been enshrined in both the UK and the US and has been held up as a beacon for the world. How can that beacon be polished and restored? That is what the following chapters of this book will be addressing.

I would suggest a variation of a Madisonian starting point: we need a better sort of politician, one who recognises that the goal of governance is to advance the common good of the nation as a whole, not just to stay in office as long as possible. In a multicultural society, this includes recognising the values of all those cultures and the need to find common ground among them: a willingness to live and let live coupled with the need and even desire to live together. It means that elected representatives have to rise above parochial and party interests and actually exercise independent wisdom and judgement for something bigger than themselves, bigger than the plurality or majority in their constituency, and bigger than their party. They must actually represent 'we the people,' not just 'my people.'

Necessarily, such representatives must be willing to live with the results of elections, and they must be willing to reject efforts to manipulate elections through voter suppression and gerrymandering, even though such steps in the short run might help their party seize or maintain control of government. Such elected representatives could then help restore checks and balances by behaving the way they were intended to behave.

I say a variation of Madison because Federalist Papers Number 10 described the better sort of elected official in terms of class: wealthier, better educated. That aspect of Madison's vision of a good representative needs to be left behind, but his vision of how a good representative should *act* remains useful.

There is an expression in the museum world that can be helpful here: 'No stories about us without us.' Similarly, one could say, 'no governance of us without us.' With expanding multiculturalism, representative government needs to reflect those varied cultures and include their values and ideals by including their voices as voters, as candidates, as party leaders, and as elected officials. The concept of better-elected representatives, in my view, should include more inclusive selection processes for candidates as well as changes to the electoral system to better represent the totality of the people in participation and results.

Is it naïve to ask for better-elected representatives? Yes, absolutely. Political party leadership and party donors exercise extensive control over who the choices are in an election, and most people do not become involved until far too late in the process. In my opinion, that, too, needs to change. Effective representative democracy requires more vigorous participation by the citizens in the initial selection of candidates at every level, both local and national, not just a vote on election day. Positives coming out of the 2020 and 2022 elections in the US include increased participation in voting and a better appreciation of the need to participate in the selection of candidates. But there is work still to be done, as reflected in the decline in turnout for the 2024 general election in the UK notwithstanding the obvious importance of that vote for the next five years. And greater participation by citizens is needed in between elections as well; representatives need to know that they are being watched by those who voted for them and those who did not.

Notwithstanding the somewhat gloomy picture I have been painting, today, both the UK and the US have examples of Madisonian or Burkean representatives in the best sense of those visions. By rising above party, by reaching across the aisle, and by demonstrating that compromise and consensus can produce good government that benefits the entire country, those representatives can help restore the people's faith in representative democracy. It is that faith on the part of the people that allows the few to govern the many in a way that advances the common good.

2

Democracy in Crisis: A Reply

DJ GALLIGAN

I. Representative Democracy: An Unfinished Symphony

The opening chapter begins by citing Abraham Lincoln's definition of democracy as 'government of the people, by the people, for the people'. Rhetoric and reality, plainly, are not natural companions. The oddness and obscurity of that definition need not detain us. Richard Clary proceeds with a different and distinct model of democracy. Representative democracy, as a form of constitutional authority, is defined as rule by an elected few for a fixed term. The people choose the few from among candidates, whose authority they accept. The elected few are deemed to be representatives who 'work for the common good', which means adopting policies that, according to Richard, 'reflect consensus through compromise'. Just what the concept of *representation* means or adds is left unsaid. Critical to this form of rule is the claim that the elected few do not act under the direction or instruction of voters; instead, they exercise 'independent judgement' in deciding the common good. Their judgements might differ from those of 'the voters who elected them'. This model of compromise, consensus, and the common good is under attack for the reasons set out in the opening chapter: the peoples' losing confidence in their elected leaders; distortion of the electoral process by minorities; domination of certain interests; and above all the poor quality of leaders.

My aims are twofold. The first is to trace representative democracy to its origins in two different and competing sources, then to lay bare the social foundations of each. The second aim is to propose and construct a fuller account of the people's relations with elected leaders and other officials. Election, on this approach, is a framework within and around which to build a more complete account of the social relationship between the people, elected leaders, and officers of government, whether executive, administrative, or judicial. Two matters prompt scrutiny: one, relations between the people and elected leaders; and the other relations between the people and officials. As to the first, the election of leaders, while a critical feature, is not enough to express the fullness of the relationship; as to the second, officials exercising power at the many sites of government are absent from accounts of representative democracy. If allowed a place at all, it is on the margins and being outside the representative relationship is of scant interest. Yet, officers of state, other than the elected few, are essential to constitutional authority and to governing well. Elected leaders command the ship of state and set the direction of sail; the voyage depends on the sailors, the many officials from the high to the low, from executive officers, to administrators and regulators, to prosecutors and judges, and many others. The point of view here is that of the people: how they encounter and what they expect from the constitutional order; how they perceive and experience relations between themselves and officials; how officials elected or appointed fit within the relationship.

II. Origins of Rule by Elected Representatives

Representative democracy or, to be more precise, rule by representatives elected by the people, is the ungainly offspring of ill-matched parents, one princely rule, the other the people ruling themselves. Rule by representatives has its origins in two different sets of ideas and experiences, sentiments and dispositions, the one descending from princely rule, the other ascending from the people's self-rule. The legacy is a concept of rule showing the awkwardness of adolescence: uncertain in meaning and insecure as to purpose, yet holding potential promise and the prospect of maturing into a form of authority attractive to the people, while securely founded and effective in serving the common good, the well-being of the people. The blemishes are made plain and the potential pencilled by tracing, briskly, the provenance of each parent.

A. Princely Rule

James Stuart, king of England, in an address to Parliament in the early seventeenth century, captured the essence of princely rule in declaring his having being 'ordained for the procuring of the Wealth and Prosperitie of his People'. The 'Weal of the Publick', the common good and the good of each subject, is safe in his hands.[1] Twin virtues stand out: the king knows the common good and has the power to achieve it. The king consults counsellors, listens to the voice of Parliament, and receives petitions and addresses from the towns and shires. The decision as to the common good and the power to rule are his. His son and successor, Charles I, in a last bid to avoid civil war, conceded that the House of Commons, the elected chamber and hence the democratic element, had a role as protector of liberty, but not to govern, for that was the right and responsibility of the king. The concession proved, as we shall see, to be prescient in signalling an alternative approach to relations between the ruler and the people, an approach reflecting the opinion of

[1] James I: *Works* (London, 1616).

the people embedded in history, but ignored and ridiculed by the superior sectors of society.

The appeal of princely rule is strong rule, the firm and decisive rule needed to protect a nation from external threats, while maintaining order internally and delivering to the people essential aspects of well-being. Princely rule is based on the claim that strong rule is best provided by power being entrusted to one person, whose relationship with the people is simply stated: the prince rules and the people obey. The case for power being so concentrated is strengthened and the risks softened by a constitutional discourse, on the one hand praising the virtue of the prince, on the other hand draping the relationship between prince and people in abstractions, fictions, and pleasing metaphors. The discourse on virtue, the qualities needed to rule well and how to cultivate them in the prince, drew endless debate and filled treatises over the centuries. Another discourse imagines a *body politic*, parallel to the body natural, where each sector of society has its place, the prince the wise head at the top, at the bottom the people, the feet to bear the weight of the body. According to a third discourse, the prince embodies the realm and represents all its members, who in turn become an abstract notion of the *people*, which consents to princely rule. The relationship transcends social reality to become an abstraction based on two symbols, one of the people, the other the prince.

B. People Ruling Themselves

The people ruling themselves, by contrast, is 'founded on the authority of the people only'.[2] Abstractions and fictions have no place. Each citizen is entitled to have a say in governing, in deciding how to protect and advance well-being. Liberty is the guide; the liberty of each person to engage in and to influence the process of governing; to watch over, criticise, and censure. Among attempts by the people to rule themselves, from Anglo-Saxon society to the present, the *Constitution of Pennsylvania* 1776 stands out. The approach was inspired by the constitutional order of the freemen of Anglo-Saxon England, as depicted by Obiadiah Hulme, whose ideas were much admired by the freemen of the former colonies. The Constitution of 1776 declared the people to have 'the sole, exclusive and inherent right of governing'.[3] For practical reasons, some powers have to be delegated to officials, some elected, others appointed. All officers of government, elected or appointed, are 'trustees and servants and accountable to the people'. The English Levellers had earlier accepted the need for delegation of power to a few, loosely referred to as *representatives*, because too many people engaging in deciding major policy and making law would be 'confusing and lead to desolation'.

[2] *Constitution of Pennsylvania* 1776, Art III.

[3] O Hulme, *An Historical Essay on the English Constitution* (London, Edward and Charles Dilly, 1771; reprinted in Gale Print Editions).

Nevertheless, all institutions and processes are designed to ensure the people stay in charge. They know their own interests and how to advance well-being; they accept the need for a system of authority and the utility, but insist on being involved in the processes of governing and keeping officials, including elected representatives, under supervision. Self-rule ensures that laws enacted 'be more maturely considered' by the people. Among the measures taken to sustain the place of the people as the foundation of authority, several stand out. The doors of the legislature are to be kept open; the matters decided by vote are to be printed each week and accessible to the people; elected members may add their reasons for voting; bills are printed in advance for the people to ensure against 'hasty determination'; 'motives and reasons' for each bill are printed in the Preamble. An independent Council of Censors had wide powers to keep watch over the legislature and, if thought necessary, to impose censure. The measures open to it included asking for reasons and calling for papers, ordering impeachment, recommending repeal of a law; even summoning a constitutional convention if needed 'for preservation of the rights and happiness of the people'.[4] The constitutional order of 1776 was a serious attempt by the freemen to be self-ruling. It lasted just two years before collapsing, the self-ruling workers, shopkeepers, and hill-billies, mocked and scorned as 'upstarts drunk with liberty'.[5]

C. Rule by Representatives

Out of the tensions within rule by the prince and the people ruling themselves, and the vulnerabilities of both, arose the modern form of rule by representatives. The form of princely rule, championed by James I and confirmed by Charles I, could not cope with changing economic conditions and social relations, the rising expectations of the people and their clamour for a place in governing. As their demands rose and the franchise widened, the risk of the people dominating the constitutional order became real. The power of rule was shifting, slowly, from king to Commons, the chamber whose members were elected by a fraction of the people, the qualification based on property. As the franchise under pressure widened, the demands of the people to have their interests protected and advanced had to be addressed. The House of Commons of the late eighteenth century found in the submerged subjunctive an ingenious solution. When the House assembles, it is *as if* the people, through their representatives, assemble. Actions of the representatives become the actions of the people, while the real people are defined out of the constitution, their voices at best in the background beyond the constitutional field.[6] The sovereignty

[4] For a fuller account see DJ Galligan, *Keepers of the Common Good: The People, Opinion, and the Social Foundations of Constitutional Authority* (Oxford, Oxford University Press, 2024) XII:8.

[5] Discussed in *Keepers of the Common Good*, Ch XII.

[6] Discussed in P Ihalainen, *Agents of the People: Democracy and Popular Sovereignty British and Swedish Parliamentary Debates, 1734–1800* (Leiden, Brill, 2010).

of the people in parliament was born. Reference to the people was soon dropped to leave the sovereignty of parliament the foundation of the constitution.

Behind the fictions, abstractions, and submerged subjunctive, were grave matters to confront: the call for a wider franchise; the agitation of sectors of the people for a say in government; that government be more active in advancing the well-being of the people. Constitutional authority was moving from the prince to the elected chamber, but the basic premise of rule, the relationship between the people and rulers, stayed the same. The few replaced the prince, but they, like the prince, knew the common good, knew what was best for all. The voices of the people in the background could be heard, while the House of Commons, its members drawn from the superior sectors of society, became the centre of government, as the powers of monarch and peers waned.

The shift from the prince to the few was familiar elsewhere in Europe, not least in the Italian city-states. Describing the constitutional order of Venice in the early seventeenth century, Gasparo Contarini wrote of the balance of forms of government: princely sovereignty, governance by the nobility, and rule by citizens.[7] Form masks reality. Behind the form, 'the delicate artifice of constitutional engineering', the reality is starkly different. Authority is vested in 'men who were distinguished by their nobility, virtues and merits for the good of the republic'.[8] Words that echoed over in the New World, where James Madison, in designing the federal constitution, had need for neither the people as an abstraction nor the pretence of representatives becoming them. The case is purely practical. Property rights arise from 'diversity in the faculties of men', the preservation of which is 'the first object of government'.[9] Popular government, or rule by the people themselves, puts at risk both 'the public good and private rights'. And yet it was too late to deny the people the vote. To secure property, and at the same time 'to preserve the spirit and form of popular government', is 'the great object' to which his 'enquiries are directed'. Pure democracy, or the people ruling themselves, is suitable only for a society of a few. In larger societies, the alternative is a republic, which means 'a scheme of representation' takes place, according to which government is delegated 'to a small number of citizens elected by the rest'. The justification is plain: 'the chosen body of citizens – may best discern the true interest of their country', while blessed with 'patriotism' and 'love of justice'. Notice the reversal. According to the freemen of Pennsylvania, the people display 'mature judgment' in measuring laws against the common good. Madison claimed the opposite: representatives are the best judges, their 'views being more consonant with the public good than if pronounced by the people themselves'.[10]

[7] G Contarini, *De republica Venetorum libri quinque* (Leiden, Lugd Batavorum, 1626).

[8] Quoted in V Conti, 'The Mechanisation of Virtue: Republican Rituals in Italian Political Thought in the Sixteenth and Seventeenth Centuries' in M v Gelderen and Q Skinner (eds), *Republicanism: A Shared European Heritage*, Vol II: *The Values of Republicanism in Early Modern Europe* (Cambridge, Cambridge University Press, 2002) 76.

[9] J Madison, *The Federalist*, No 10 in A Hamilton et al, *The Federalist or The New Constitution* (London, Everyman's Library, 1970) 42.

[10] ibid 45–46.

Whether Madison had read Contarini we do not know. The sentiments are similar, the means for calming the voices of the people the same: they cannot be denied the vote; but once elected, the representatives, being a better class of persons, know and rule for the common good, which means at base the protection of property. Nor do we know if Madison was following the debates in the House of Commons. The outcomes are similar: the people have the power to elect representatives, who once elected become the effective chamber of government. Madison goes one step farther: representative democracy is to be distinguished from pure democracy, the latter suitable only in a society 'consisting of a small number of citizens'. In a large and diverse society, the risk of pure democracy is that the majority of the people becomes a faction, which 'is incompatible with the personal security or the rights of property'. The representatives, the men of property and owners of slaves, not only rule; they know 'the true interests of their country' and 'are least likely to sacrifice it to temporary or partial considerations'. The freemen elect the representatives; beyond that they have no constitutional role.

III. Representative Democracy and the Tyranny of Form

A. Tyranny of Form

Writing during the troubled 1640s as the nation sank into civil war, John Warr warned of the 'tyranny of form', of the unstoppable slide in human affairs from substance (or 'principle' in his words) to form.[11] He wrote of the 'divine principle' as 'the clear light, equity, reason, and understanding of things themselves, abstracted from all human constituted form'. Until substance is restored, 'civil darkness' prevails; 'an ignorance of principle, an idolising of form', all a 'badge of our inward darkness'. Whatever the form, it is a yoke that 'keeps us in subjection to others' and inures the people to bondage. Form at first serves substance; but soon emerges from 'the covert and shadow of equity', to become the weapon of the strong by which to sustain their power. 'True reason' is the remedy.

The constitutional order designed according to the 'divine principle' will 'free rulers from the bondage of form and guide the use of power' of a few over the many. The danger is that constitutions and laws made under them serve not reason but 'lust, greed, and ambition'. Form is necessary in structuring and guiding human affairs, and may advance the first principles of equity and reason. Form has a place, not as a 'standing rule' but as 'a temporary help in advancing the people's interests'.

[11] S Sedley and L Kaplan (eds), *A Spark in the Ashes: The Pamphlets of John Warr* (London, Verso, 1992).

Quite what that place is, and how form and substance can work together, Warr left unsaid. The message, however, remains powerful: between form and substance a balance has to be found, rough and ready and ever under revision, so that neither loses contact with the other.

B. Representative Democracy as Form

Representative democracy takes for granted that form serves substance: if the form is right, the wanted outcome follows. If the right persons be elected, they can be relied on to govern for the common good. Madison thought property to be the essence of the common good, and so it follows that the owners of substantial property can be relied on to govern for the protection of property.[12] There are several reasons for doubting the worth of this approach.

First, the common good, even in eighteenth-century America, included but went beyond protection of property. The common good is wider, more complex, and rather than being settled in advance emerges, not only from deliberation and discussion, but from the tug-and-scramble, the discord-and-dispute among competing interests.

Second, the electoral process is not designed to find persons who show the qualities needed to work out the common good and who have the resolve to govern for its protection and advancement. Candidates for election emerge from the dark recesses and haphazard ways of the party system, where being selected to stand for election depends on factors quite apart from having the quality to govern. If the outcome sought be the selection of 'proper guardians of the public weal', in Madison's words, the processes of selection fall far short, on two grounds: the qualities needed to be 'a proper guardian' are unknown, and anyhow the selection process is not geared to the identification of proper guardians.

Third, even if the candidates standing for election have the right qualities or display the required virtues, good government does not necessarily follow. Qualities and virtues may be a condition of governing well, but they are not enough. Not only does the common good mean more than protecting property, it is not handed down as if from on high, but has to be worked out. Account has to be taken of the interests at stake, how they rank in importance, and, crucially, how they are viewed and valued by persons, groups, and sectors.

The defects are inherent in the very concept of rule by representatives. As soon as the people are inserted, additional issues arise and problems appear. Two in particular call for attention: one is the need to reconsider the relationship between

[12] Madison might have known of The Putney Debates more than a century earlier, where Henry Ireton persuaded the assembly that those without an 'estate', a certain amount of property, 'have not a permanent interest' and should be denied the vote: discussed in Galligan (n 4).

the people and elected leaders; the other concerns the many sites of power and the nature of relations between the people and officials of several kinds. That means approaching the constitutional order from the perspective of the people.

IV. Peoples Precede Nations

The people approach the constitutional order as a means to protect and advance their well-being, which means the aggregate of interests they value, whether material or abstract, self-serving or altruistic. Variations occur across communities, but the core is constant, the concern for civility and humanity, needs and utilities, common to all. Social relations form and function, rules and conventions are made or emerge, action is designed and directed, all to protect and advance well-being. Two features are noteworthy. First, each community no matter how seemingly simple or backward has a sense of well-being; which, second, forms a foundation from which to view the constitutional order. An idea perfectly and precisely expressed in three words: *peoples precede nations*, the words of Susan Reynolds, which might be rephrased for present purposes as *peoples precede constitutions.*[13] Far from their being 'a stop for fortune's fingers to sound which stop she pleases',[14] from that hinterland of interests and understandings, the people confront, criticise, and contest the constitutional order, whatever form it takes. In assessing rule by representatives, two features draw the people's attention: one is the relationship with elected leaders; the other is the many sites of authority at which officials, who are not elected, have authority and exercise power over them.

V. Between the People and Elected Leaders

Constitutional authority depends on two relationships, one between the people and the leaders, the other relations among the people themselves. The former is defined by the constitution; the latter is prior to and more fundamental. It is rooted in the social understandings of the people, drawing on their ideas of community, their sense of well-being, and the place of institutions, including those of the constitutional order. The constitutional relationship of rule by representatives is plain and simply stated. The people elect the leaders, who have the power to rule for a term, during which they rule as they judge best, and at the end of which they submit to the people's vote. During the term of office the leaders decide the common good and how best to achieve it. They are inclined to take account of opinions of the people, whether individual persons or certain sectors, regions and communities,

[13] S Reynolds, *Kingdoms and Communities in Western Europe 900–1300* (Oxford, Clarendon Press, 1997).

[14] W Shakespeare, *The Tragedy of Prince Hamlet* Act 3: 2: 2.

or special interests. Whether they do and, if they do, how much notice they take is at their discretion. They may be influenced by but are not subject to the opinions of the people. The relationship in practice is more complex. At one level it includes the many encounters between people and leaders, some of which are aimed at influencing how rule is conducted, others guided by other aims and purposes, all rather haphazard, undisciplined, and unstructured. That is the view from above; the view from below is very different.

The people view the constitutional order as a means to well-being, a set of institutions capable of protecting and advancing their interests. The power of election is the starting point. That the leaders serve a fixed and fairly short term before having to seek re-election is for the people a source of influence between elections. The image of election as framing relations between the people and leaders, as a starting point, proves useful, but leaves the relationship otherwise empty of content. Between elections the people have no constitutional place or status. Why would they accept such a situation? Why entrust power to a few leaders, whose qualities for office and abilities to rule are questionable; whose understanding of the common good is variable, open to dispute, and often unpredictable, their commitment often doubtful. Form starts to exert its tyranny. The acceptance of rule by a few, regardless of how well they rule, how seriously the people's interests count and how well they are served, seems perilously close, in John Warr's words, to 'idolising form'. Form is well-protected by fictions and abstractions and the power of the submerged subjunctive, the *as if* style of argument: as if by having voted the people consent to whatever action follows; as if the leaders represent them, even become the people; as if they are sovereign, the power of which the leaders exercise in their name. The people know that unless they are able to give content to the framework, structure the relationship, their well-being is at risk whether from incompetence, the influence of special interests, or the wolf of appetite itself.

How to give content and structure to the relationship between people and leaders, in the period between elections, is the issue. Let us imagine the constitutional order as a field, a distinct area of activity fenced off from other areas; a field defined by the constitution. On the conventional account of rule by representatives, the people from time to time enter the field to cast a vote; then leave, have no further place in the field, and stay behind the fence, constitutionally in the wilderness. Their voices might be heard in the background, just as the House of Commons in the eighteenth century heard and could not ignore the voices of the people. Prudence might induce the leaders to listen, even take action, but that is for them to decide, bearing in mind the people will soon return to the field to cast their vote.

VI. A Competing Account

There is a competing account, another way of imagining the field. Rather than being outsiders, strangers to the field except when casting a vote, the people are occupants, engaged in cultivation, their relationship to elected leaders permanent rather than occasional. Far from being outsiders looking in, behind the fence voicing their views and hoping to be heard, the people have a place at the centre of constitutional authority. History viewed from the perspective of the people, plainly and movingly portrays how in conditions of poverty and oppression, starkly shown in episodes of resistance and rebellion, their sentiments and dispositions towards the constitutional order are manifest.[15] The people view the field as a means to well-being, offering protection of settled interests and opening avenues to advance other interests. The problem for the people, and the persistent complaint, is their exclusion from the field, their being held behind the fence, their well-being wholly in the hands of the prince or the few. The power to elect leaders is a major advance, an opening of the gate to admit the people to the field and to allow them a direct role in cultivation. The trouble is the vote in isolation is of limited value; a beginning rather than an end; a first step in giving content to the frame of relations between people and representatives. How to build on that base by adding more content is the question.

Keeping the people out of the field has been a prominent theme of constitutional history, in England, other European nations, and elsewhere. A theme rule by representatives illustrates well. The founding purpose was not to welcome the people as full members of a thriving constitutional order; rather the opposite. Faced with the people's rising demands, allowing the vote was a concession, a necessary measure to calm them, while preserving the economic, social, and political order. And yet there are signs that rule by representatives is incomplete, that it does not follow and apply rigorously its own logic. Tucked into the undergrowth, hidden from sight, largely ignored, is another way of reading constitutional history. The signs are subtle, the shift seemingly minor, but once noticed prove to be of major potential constitutionally. Early signs could be seen in the medieval Italian city-states, hints dropped in the writings of observers and commentators. Niccolò Machiavelli, a controversial figure of the sixteenth century, his writings open to wildly different readings, some of dread, some of admiration, is clear and to the point. The people do not rule themselves but have a *share* in ruling. Although rather cryptic and much left unexplained, the idea at core is plain: the people do not rule, do not constitute government, but they have a place, a justified role in the processes of governing.

Another sign appears a century later in Charles I's conceding that while he governs, the elected chamber has a place in protecting *liberty.* Liberty at the time was broadly construed and regarded as a valued aspect of well-being. The king's words are brief and cryptic, the concession hard to evaluate. Nevertheless, for the prince to grant the elected chamber, acting in the name of and on behalf of the people, a place in the constitutional order of princely rule, strikingly at odds with his father's account, is noteworthy.

[15] C Levi, *Christo si e' fermato a Eboli* (*Christ Stopped at Eboli*) (Florence, 1943; London, Penguin, 2000).

A. Substance Over Form

The concession relates to substance not form. Princely rule as displayed by James I is based on form, that whatever the prince decides is by definition for the common good. Form now gives way to substance, to the idea that the meaning of the common good is not whatever the prince says, but has to be considered and constructed. That suggests a process open to opinion, taking account of the interests at issue, and reaching a resolution. Persons, groups, and sectors with interests, some in common, others diverse and competing, have a claim to be included in the process.

B. A Place in the Constitution

The concession may be read as a first step towards accepting the people as members of the constitutional order, granting them a place in deciding the common good. A place at first filled by the elected leaders, who claim they are not just acting on behalf of the people, but embodying them. The fiction deflated, the people could distance themselves from elected leaders and apply to them the logic Charles I applied to rule by the prince. Whoever rules, whether the prince or the elected few, in deciding the common good, needs the people – persons, group, and sectors – to be engaged in the process, for two reasons. On the one hand, the common good is not a concept settled and awaiting discovery; it has to be constructed, given content by reasoning from practical experience, taking into account and making sense of the many elements. Included among and indeed central to which are the interests and aspirations of the people in all their diversity and variety. Madison later pronounced the 'regulation of diverse interests' to be 'the principal task of modern legislation'. On the other hand, the people know elected leaders are as fallible as the prince and subject to the same appetites, weaknesses, and poor judgement. They understand the furtive power of form and the lure of idolatry. The people insist that just as the king of England needed the elected chamber to be engaged and vigilant and capable of censure, the elected leaders need the people.

The concept of rule by representatives presented by the architects of the eighteenth century is, at first sight, clear and plausible, even convincing. According to Madison, the leading architect, the people enter the field to vote then, having no further part to play, leave. The common good is best entrusted to the elected few who 'discern the true interests of the country'; whose 'patriotism and love of justice' means their decisions 'will be more consonant to the public good than if pronounced by the people themselves'.[16] And yet, 'the principal task of government' is 'the regulation of diverse interests', the virtue of rule by a few being their ability 'to refine and enlarge the public view', not to disregard it. But how do the

[16] Madison (n 9) 45–46.

few know of the interests, 'the diverse interests' at issue if after voting the people leave the field?

Madison's argument is incomplete, not followed through to its logical conclusion. The logic and, we should add, common sense if applied with rigour, is plain and compelling. The few know 'the public view' *only* by engaging the people at the many sites of government, including and especially at the top. That means hearing and taking account of the range and diversity of their opinions, their preference, and their aspirations. That is done most effectively by keeping them in the field, accepting their place in the constitutional order, and adopting processes of government to match. The elected few govern, make the major decisions, design the administrative system, and engage the people. The architects of rule by the elected few are guided by an image of society inherited from the past but now obsolete. An image of the needs, utilities, and aspirations of the people, of relations between the people and the leaders, of the nature of power and the risks and the purpose of the constitution. Exposed to the course of history, the image has faded. Knowledge and understanding of constitutional authority have matured, from rule by an elected few, the callow youth of awkward parents, to a form of constitutional authority, attuned to and capable of serving the common good as projected by the people, for which their presence, their sharing in the processes of government, is a vital part.

VII. Inside the Field

Once admitted to the constitutional field, what is the role of the people? How, between elections, do they contribute to cultivation; how do they give content to their relationship with elected leaders? It is enough to note in outline the avenues open, the kinds of actions open to the people. First a note of caution. The people's constitutional role, their relationship with leaders between elections, goes beyond form to embrace substance and principle, addressing content and outcome rather than mere process. This not to abandon form, for form as process is a necessary companion to substance, not to replace it, but a means to substance. Processes serve substance and are critical to doing justice, but raise two risks. First, processes are imperfect in achieving outcomes; second, processes not only tend to detach themselves from substantive outcomes but become their substitute. With that caution in mind, the people approach the constitutional field, guided by two main ideas: one that effective government depends on their self-restraint and their support; the other that they can influence the course of governing by three kinds of action: engagement, vigilance, and censure.

The people know that for government, whatever the form, to be effective depends on their restraining their own actions. Hobbes wrote at length and with eloquence of need for 'the introduction of that restraint upon themselves'.[17] The

[17] T Hobbes, *Leviathan* (ed N Malcolm) (Oxford, Oxford University Press, 2012) Ch 17, 234.

need for support is equally obvious and compelling, and takes many forms, some open and declared, others subtle and concealed. The Reverend Meriton, preaching in Norwich Cathedral in 1696, reminded the congregation that without the people's support government will 'totter and shake'.[18] Restraint and support are needed for stable rule; but the people want more. Stable rule is a foundation but not enough. The people want to influence the course of government and seek ways of being *engaged* in the processes, being *vigilant* in keeping leaders under scrutiny, and holding in reserve the power of *censure*.

Each kind of action signifies a broad and open category into which many different processes can be inserted. Engagement with leaders takes many forms, from expressing an opinion to deciding the course to be taken. Some modes of engagement are provided for in the constitution, such as the referendum and the people's initiatives, abrogation and consultation.[19] Most are devised and designed in the course of governing, in responding to issues as they occur, sometimes at the initiative of leaders, often prompted by persons, sectors, or interests. The range is wide and the process variable, from the formal to the informal. Some processes become permanent, others after serving the purpose fade away. Whatever the form, however formal or informal, the people's aim is to structure their relationship with elected leaders in a way that enables them to guide and influence decisions and actions. Vigilance speaks for itself: keeping watch, keeping leaders under their gaze, knowing their reasons and scrutinising their actions. Vigilance opens the way for censure, the many ways and means, formal and informal, from expressing disapproval to having the decision over-turned, the action reversed.

The upstarts of Pennsylvania in designing the Constitution of 1776, despite the deadly opprobrium, understood how the people could be engaged, vigilant, and censorious of officials, elected or appointed. If the language of self-rule, the claim to be ruling themselves, be put aside, the 'upstarts' retained a sense of realism. They knew the need for elected leaders and appointed officials in governing for the well-being of all, while aware of the dangers. The guiding principle that every freeman has an equal interest in ensuring well-being and so has an interest in the conduct of government, from which follows the need to find ways of ensuring that well-being, genuinely, is served by government. A few examples from the constitutional order are worth noting. Delegation of power is a practical matter; elected leaders are simply agents of the people. The legislative process is highly and carefully structured. The doors of the assembly are open to all. Bills are printed in advance and available to the public to prevent 'hasty determination'. Each week, details of voting are printed, while each member can give his 'motives and reasons', which are then included in the Preamble to a new law. The Council of Censors, a separate institution independent from elected leaders, has wide powers: to impose

[18] H Meriton, 'A Sermon Preacht at the Cathedral Church in Norwich' (1696) in M Knights, *Representation and Misrepresentation in Later Stuart Britain* (Oxford, Oxford University Press, 2005) 156.

[19] Explained more fully in *Keepers of the Common Good* (n 4) Ch VI.

censure, including impeachment of members; to recommend repeal of a law; even to call for a convention on the constitution. The processes of governing are 'open and accessible to the people'; free speech is guaranteed; the printing presses are free to any person who wants to comment on proceedings in the legislative house.

The list of measures could continue but the point is made. The freemen of Pennsylvania grasped both the need for power being given to officials, and the need for the people to be engaged, vigilant, and capable of censure. If in retrospect the order of government seems quaint, the measures crude, the rhetoric inflated, despite all the upstarts had a sound grasp of the principles. First: the purpose of a constitutional order from the people's point of view is to serve their well-being. Second: well-being, rather than parcelled and packaged and awaiting discovery, has to be constructed. Third: in settling the common good, the people have opinions, a place, and a vital role to play. Fourth: that means having a place in the constitutional order, starting with the election of leaders and then building the relationship through restraint and support, combined forms of engagement, vigilance, and censure, the precise nature and extent of each to be worked out according to the context, the interests at issue, and the need for effective government. The principle holds firm regardless of who holds the power to govern, whether prince, people, or elected few.

VIII. Sites of Government and the Place of the People

Elected leaders sit at the centre of the constitutional field, deciding matters of high policy, while most governing takes place in other agencies, executive, administrative, and judicial. In the discourse around rule by representatives, the agencies are largely absent, as if they were irrelevant to constitutional discourse. The superior courts are the exception, just how they fit a matter of contention, the reasons for which help to explain why scant attention is paid to administrative agencies. Put starkly and over-simply, the superior courts have their own constitutional status and are beyond the power of the elected leaders.[20] Administrative agencies by contrast, in general, are created by laws made by the elected leaders. A few agencies are likely to have a base in the constitution itself, although most owe their existence and their authority to elected leaders. The assumption is then made, but rarely stated, that the agencies serve the common good by discharging the functions defined by legislation, under the watch of elected leaders and answerable to them, and of no interest constitutionally.

An alternative approach is to regard the administrative agencies as the very core of the constitutional order, the many sites at which matters of well-being are decided, where constitutional ideas and principles guide and structure the

[20] The place of courts in the constitutional order is examined in DJ Galligan (ed), *Courts and the People: Friend or Foe?* (Oxford, Hart Publishing, 2022).

process. In other words, start with the agencies, study the processes, observe and chart the reasoning, from which will emerge the constitutional principles. Each agency occupies a site of power, the purposes of which are defined partly by legislation and partly left to the agency's discretion. Discretion has two sources, one the empowering legislation, the other the space inherent in the exercise of power for purpose, the *discretionary space* at each site of power. Each agency acquires a certain autonomy and independence from the legislative base and, notably, from the elected leaders, the shift both inevitable and necessary if an agency is to do its job. Rather than being a corruption of the constitution, the usurping of power, the shift is both necessary and commendable in enabling the agency to decide the common good within the borders of each site of power, and then to take action for its protection and advancement. Several features follow.

First: the statutory concept of purpose is likely to be broadly stated, leaving the content and the boundaries to be settled by the agency. That means reaching down to the deeper recesses of the discretionary space, to the foundation of substance, in other words deciding the common good at that site and how it is best served.

Second: the task at each site is to settle the nature and scope of the power, the actions to be taken, and the processes to be followed. Guidance from the legislation is likely to be variable, sometimes precise, at other times left to the agency. Actions are of three main kinds: deciding matters of general policy; setting rules and standards and guidelines; applying them to decide specific cases. The borders between the three are neither fixed nor exact: policies are rendered partly into rules and standards; rules are surrounded by contextual contingencies; standards and guidelines are relatively open as to meaning and scope.

Third: the next task is to decide which persons, groups, and sectors are to engage at each site in the process of giving content to purpose, to settling the meaning to the common good. The people encounter officials and work together to settle the common good. The credentials to engage are based on interests, on which interests are serious enough and affected enough to justify taking part in the process of settling the common good. Rules, by nature, identify who has an interest, who is directly affected. As rules edge into more open standards, room for interpretation widens, the range of interests at issue expands to include other persons and sectors. Decisions of general policy and setting standards by nature affect a range of persons, sectors and interests. Who has the right to engage is at times defined by the legislation, but often the onus falls on the agency to decide who has a good ground for being engaged and whose interests fall outside the site of power.

Persons, groups, and sectors bring to bear their interests, their sense of well-being; how they are likely to be affected, and how at each site they are best protected. Engagement takes many forms, from being right at the centre, closely involved in the decision-process, to being on the margins, with many points in between. Those with an interest are vigilant, keep close watch over the agency; they scrutinise the reasons for the action proposed and the reasons for the action taken. The dissatisfied have available forms of censure, from criticism to appeal, from appeal to judicial review. The task at each site of power, each area of agency authority, is to determine the common good, taking account of competing interests, conflicting claims of the parties, the tug-and-scramble for attention, an agency has to determine how at that site the common good is served. There are two components, one the resolution among interests, the other a sense of the common good more generally according to the constitutional order, and how the two go together.

The constitutional order depicted is different from the conventional accounts, according to which the elected leaders define the common good and then authorise agencies each to implement a portion. On this authorisation approach, implementation is considered to be a routine matter, an almost bureaucratic process, simply putting into practice the common good decided by leaders and defined in legislation. The study of administrative agencies, and the legal framework around them, suggests an alternative account, functional or purposive by nature. Although agencies are authorised from above, in order to perform their functions they look to purpose, to the substantive ends and goals at each site of authority. Within the bounds of guidance from above, each agency has to determine: first, how at that site the well-being of persons, sectors, and communities is best served, the substantive issue; second, the process suited to the site; third, keeping in mind, an eye on, and the discretionary power to protect and advance the common good of society more generally.

IX. Form Demoted, Democracy Redesigned, Crisis Reassessed

Whether democracy is in crisis depends on two elements: settling the concept, then testing practice against the concept. The first is a theoretical enquiry, the second empirical, the gathering of evidence to determine whether, within one constitutional system or another, the practice falls short of the concept. Only then can a judgement be made that democracy is in crisis, at a turning point, in danger of disappearing. The concept of democracy under scrutiny is representative democracy, or rule by elected representatives. The assumption is that representatives know and have the power to realise the common good, the well-being of the people. As the evidence tends to show, the representatives seem to be failing in their task of governing well, and putting democracy at risk.

An alternative approach, as outlined in this chapter, is to demote form, look behind democracy as rule by representative to expose substance and content, and then propose a modified concept of democracy. Rule by representatives is the base, the youth with potential, yet to mature into a convincing concept of democracy. The conventional approach is to present democracy as a *form* tied to the people ruling themselves: *demos* + *cracy* = the *people* + *rule*. How form came to overshadow, indeed replace substance, is yet to be explained. For now it is enough to suggest an alternative, another way of construing the concept of democracy, implicit in the account above. A conception more realistic, more likely to serve better the well-being of the people, more closely tied to the common good of the nation. It starts with the people, the *demos*, who want to advance well-being and know the utility, indeed the need, for the power of the state. The issue is how to structure the state and allocate power. The temptation to keep rule in their own hands is strong, but common sense suggests otherwise and points out the merits of delegating authority to a selection of officials, some elected, some appointed.

The case is persuasive and the concept of constitution starts to take shape: the guiding purpose, the substantive end, is the well-being of the people, delegation of power the means. That is just the first stage, the process far from complete. The next stage involves the people, the Keepers of the Common Good, who find ways of keeping the power of officials to purpose, exerting influence, keeping it on course in protecting and advancing their well-being. That is best achieved by encouragement and influence, the first by exercising restraint and giving support, the second by processes of engagement, vigilance, and censure. Election of leaders is the founding process around which others gather, at all levels of government from the high executive to the lowest administrative agency. Some processes are designed, others emerge from practice; some are formal, others informal, the range practically unlimited. All share the common purpose of trying to make sure that at every site in the constitutional field the interests of the people, in all their diversity, are taken into account, where the common good, the well-being of all is the guiding principle. Once the structure of the constitutional order is understood and the many sites of power mapped, the evidence gathered, then and only then may success or failure be judged, whether there is a crisis or not.

3

The Challenge of Representative Democracy in Africa

ZIM NWOKORA

I. Introduction

Theoretically, democracy can take a variety of forms. But, in practice, the representative model stands out as by far the most commonly implemented model. As imagined by theorists such as Edmund Burke and James Madison, it is an intricate and balanced set of formal and informal institutions working in tandem to enable good governance. 'The representative', typically a lawmaker in a parliament, congress or assembly, plays an indispensable role in this system, and the collective of representatives should be concerned with 'acting for' – that is, on behalf of and in the interests of – the public. As Hanna F Pitkin explains, '[t]he representative system must look after the public interest and be responsive to public opinion, except insofar as non-responsiveness can be justified in terms of the public interest'.[1]

Elections are the central process of representative democracy (RD), since they are the means through which representatives are chosen. Elections, therefore, also serve as a mechanism to validate the performance of the rulers by those they govern and to remove and replace unresponsive rulers. This mechanism is not available to citizens who live under an autocratic government. Conversely, citizens are not expected (or desired) to be continually active in politics and governance under RD, unlike in a direct democracy. Limited participation protects against an unconstrained and crude majoritarianism that tramples on minority rights. This is a risk of direct democracy. Further rights protection is achieved through constitutional checks and balances, and conventions and norms, which are also institutional features of RD. However, RD should not be reduced to 'electoral democracy plus constitutional guardrails'. What is key to the system, at least when it is operating well, is how its structures meld to create space for deliberation, judgement and

[1] HF Pitkin, *The Concept of Representation* (Berkeley, University of California Press, 1967) 224.

collaboration.[2] As Nadia Urbinati puts it, '[t]he crucial factor of representation is the relationship between the inside of state institutions and the outside *created by elections*' (emphasis added).[3]

Despite these features and their supposed qualities, the practical workings of real-world representative democracies have always posed a challenge to the devotees of this model. For example, elections can sometimes (even often) be a blunt tool for fostering responsiveness. Political parties that are meant to capture, integrate, and moderate citizens' demands may become 'irresponsible' and do none of these things. Checks and balances may turn out to be too weak (as in the UK at times) or too strong (as in the US at times). Yet, even with such deficiencies, defenders of RD could, for a long time, credibly point out that other models of government seemed to be less sustainable and effective. What's more, RD proved itself to be a fairly flexible arrangement, as shown, for example, by the important differences between the American and British versions (and also the evolution of these countries' arrangements over time).

In more recent times, however, as Chapter 1 of this volume explains, the critique of RD has gone deeper, with many describing the state of affairs as one of 'crisis.' Richard Clary points to developments in the media environment, rising economic inequality, various forms of disenfranchisement, and the diversification of societies as new and significant pressures on RD. As a result, RD needs to be 'polished and restored'.[4] Versions of this deep critique of RD now resonate powerfully across established democracies, and they have prompted calls for measures to improve RD institutions (eg by reforming political parties), or for the introduction of institutions and practices such as citizens' assemblies that could circumvent RD or at least supplement its processes with new forms of citizen engagement.

The debate about the condition of RD and potential solutions to its 'crisis' has focused on the core of the West (and Global North), especially the US, UK and European Union countries. Thus, an important question to consider, at this juncture in the history of RD, is how the model is faring in the less-discussed regions beyond the West. These Global South contexts bring to the debate distinctive features, including, among other things, a history of colonialism and its ongoing legacies, as well as acute economic and development challenges in areas such as health, education and public services provision. There is, of course, huge variety in the Global South. Its many countries and populations each bring their own distinctive histories of collective action, community and division, which shape governance opportunities and choices. In this chapter, I examine the RD model in Africa. The scope of the analysis is regional, seeking to draw out experiences that

[2] N Urbinati, *Representative Democracy: Principles and Genealogy* (Chicago, University of Chicago Press, 2006); see also A Kavanagh, *The Collaborative Constitution* (Cambridge, Cambridge University Press, 2023).

[3] Urbinati, ibid, 8.

[4] See Ch 1, above, at 26.

are fairly common across the continent while pointing to some of the key contrasts across countries.

My discussion of RD in Africa proceeds in three stages. First, since an influential view among observers has been that Africa is a challenging, and perhaps even hostile, context for institutionalised democracy of any form (including RD), my first task is to flesh out some reasons underlying this view. Yet, RD has taken root in some African countries. This fact, along with other considerations, has led to qualifications of the view that RD is incompatible with African society. In the second part of this chapter, I discuss the reasons for this (partial) reappraisal of the region's democratic potential. Having detailed these sources of pessimism and optimism about Africa's democratic prospects, I then map, very roughly, the present conditions for RD across the region, taking account of three specific criteria: constitutional endurance; democratic performance; and political violence. These criteria do not provide a complete framework for assessing RD, but they do help to identify some empirical patterns that show the diversity of situations confronting African countries today.

II. Africa as a Hostile Context for Representative Democracy

The received wisdom has been that Africa is not hospitable to democracy, including RD, and perhaps even that African societies may be, to some extent, incompatible with democracy.[5] A recent account likens democracy in Africa to 'a flashlight without batteries'.[6] As I explain later, I think the relationship between democracy and Africa is complex. But before exploring the nuances, we should first consider the general proposition head-on. On this point, I believe it is fair to say that the conventional wisdom contains more than a grain of truth.

To see why this is the case, let us begin by asking the descriptive question: has Africa been a hostile place for democracy? The short answer is 'clearly yes'. In the decades since the region gained independence, only two countries, Botswana

[5] See eg M Bratton and N van de Walle, *Democratic Experiments in Africa: Regime Transitions in Comparative Perspective* (Cambridge, Cambridge University Press, 1997); N Cheeseman, *Democracy in Africa: Successes, Failures, and the Struggle for Political Reform* (New York, Cambridge University Press, 2015); N Cheeseman, 'Introduction: Understanding African Politics: Bringing the State Back in' in N Cheeseman (ed), *Institutions and Democracy in Africa: How the Rules of the Game Shape Political Developments* (Cambridge, Cambridge University Press, 2018) 1; N Cheeseman, 'How Could we Design Democracy to Make it Work in the African Context?' in CM Fombad and N Steytler (eds), *Democracy, Elections, and Constitutionalism in Africa* (Oxford, Oxford University Press, 2021); G Sartori *Parties and Party Systems: A Framework for Analysis* (Colchester, ECPR Press, 2005).

[6] MG Wentling, 'Democracy in Africa is Like a Flashlight without Batteries' *American Diplomacy* (May 2022), available at americandiplomacy.web.unc.edu/2022/05/democracy-in-africa-is-like-a-flashlight-without-batteries, accessed 28 May 2025.

and Mauritius, have been able to sustain democracy continuously.[7] If, rather than looking back through history, we instead focus on just contemporary African countries, how many of these countries qualify as 'democracies'? As is well known, the concept of 'democracy' is contested, and there are several ways to measure it. One influential metric is the democracy index produced by the Economist Intelligence Unit (EIU).[8] It is based on indicators in five categories: electoral process and pluralism; functioning of government; political participation; political culture; and civil liberties. Using scores in these categories, a country can be classified as a 'full democracy', 'flawed democracy', 'hybrid regime' or 'authoritarian regime'. The first two categories (ie full or flawed democracies) describe countries with free and fair elections and basic civil rights protections, and in full democracies, 'a political culture conducive to the flourishing of democracy'.[9] In hybrid and authoritarian regimes, by contrast, the opportunities for political participation, and especially for the development of organised opposition, are either suppressed or explicitly forbidden.

According to the EIU criteria, the Sub-Saharan Africa (SSA) region presently (in 2023) hosts seven countries that satisfy the basic requirements for democracy. They are Botswana and Mauritius, of course, but also five other countries: Ghana, Namibia, South Africa, Cape Verde, and Lesotho. The EIU list for SSA does not consider the Seychelles, but we should probably add it to the list, making the total eight. This is out of 44 countries in the region. Following the EIU's taxonomy, most African countries are classified as 'authoritarian' or 'hybrid regimes' that mix elements of democracy and autocracy. Many African countries occupy the lower reaches of the global democracy index ranking, and the Middle East and North Africa is the only region with countries that are, on average, less democratic than those of Africa.

Evidence such as this suggests quite clearly that the African experience with democracy has been an uncomfortable one, almost a mismatch. With only a few exceptions, the region has struggled to implement and consolidate the institutions of RD and its accompanying values. So, naturally, we might ask: why has this been the case? Any account of the reasons why democracy has struggled across the region will be partial and incomplete because the relevant set of factors, and the weight given to each, will differ between countries. However, as an organisational frame to make progress with this problem, I think it is useful to consider three groups of factors. The first group of factors, which we can call the preconditions for RD, are the circumstances which, experience and research suggest, are conducive to RD seemingly everywhere (ie in general). The presence of these factors makes

[7] See eg Cheeseman (2015) (n 5) 2.

[8] This index is easy to access and apply and regularly updated. This makes it highly relevant and useful for policy debates, but its methodology is less sophisticated and transparent than that underlying other metrics, such as those produced by V-Dem.

[9] *Democracy Index 2023: Age of Conflict*, Economist Intelligence Unit, available at www.eiu.com/n/campaigns/democracy-index-2023/, accessed 17 June 2025.

RD more likely, effective, and sustainable. The second group, which we can call handicaps on RD, are the various factors distinctive to Africa that have weighed negatively on its democratic prospects. The third group of factors are the constitutional/institutional designs of RD used in Africa. These are the specific models that have been used to convert the idea of RD into institutional forms.

A. Preconditions

Let us first consider the background conditions that set the stage for RD. In this category, I consider factors that have a general scope, which are relevant for understanding the fortunes of RD in Africa but also in other regions. Arguably, the most important factor from this standpoint is state capacity, and more particularly, the presence or absence of a strong state, which in turn is intimately linked with another condition: the ability to control corruption.

The state, in political science theory, is presented as the locus of organised political power. As Weber famously said, the state holds a monopoly on violence. But going beyond this baseline, the state is 'encoded' in the broader notion of sovereignty. It is therefore assumed that, because the state is sovereign:

> It owes to no other power its control over the population in question; that it responds to no other organisation for the modalities and the outcomes of that control. It exercises that control on its own account, activating its own resources, unconditionally.[10]

Ideally, the state should use its sovereignty to look after its citizens. It should supply law and order, health, education, and social welfare, secure taxation revenue, and organise modes of citizen engagement and participation. It should deliver these public goods across the breadth of its territory – that is, as Jeffrey Herbst[11] puts it, project power over space. These are the hallmarks of a strong, capable state. Viewed against this benchmark, the African region suffers from chronic state weaknesses, with the capital standing out as an exception in many countries. The Fragile States Index, produced by The Fund for Peace, draws on various quantitative and qualitative sources to measure state capacity. It takes account of factors such as the degree of national integration, whether the state holds a monopoly on the deployment of force, and state finances. According to this index, four out of the world's top five most fragile states in 2024 are in Africa (Somalia, Sudan, South Sudan, and the Democratic Republic of Congo), and the region contributes 14 of the top 20 most fragile states globally.[12] In practical terms, in many of these countries, the state often lacks the legitimacy (ie social licence) to carry out its functions. Personalised

[10] G Poggi, *The State: Its Nature, Development and Prospects* (Oxford, Polity Press, 1990) 21.

[11] J Herbst, *States and Power in Africa: Comparative Lessons in Authority and Control* (Princeton, Princeton University Press, 2014).

[12] Fragile States Index, 'Global Data' *The Fund for Peace*, available at fragilestatesindex.org/global-data/, accessed 28 May 2025.

networks of power and influence often trump official state laws and directives in terms of social significance.[13] In this sense, the state may not be respected, trusted, or even recognised across much of the territory that it purports to govern.

From the standpoint of RD, many African countries are locked in a 'vicious cycle' in which the state lacks the capacity to deliver basic public goods, leading to disillusionment and the withdrawal of support for initiatives (eg taxation) that could strengthen state capacity.[14] The cycle is reinforced by elite corruption. Its manifestations are varied and include bloated cabinets and senior public administration positions that result from the need for rulers to dispense largesse to remain in power.[15] This corruption drains states of their material resources but also, and no less importantly, of their potential for democratic legitimacy. RD is difficult to achieve and sustain in these conditions because this model of governance depends on representative 'linkage' between citizens and their state. On the one hand, citizens, through their representatives, direct the state's actions; and, on the other hand, the state is able to meaningfully respond to citizens' demands. The weakness of African states creates a massive gap in the mechanics of this process, which severely limits the chances of there being any effective linkage between citizens and the state.

The reasons for state weakness in the region are deeply rooted, so it makes sense to briefly consider the history out of which contemporary state weakness has emerged. To begin with, it should be noted that countries in regions such as Western Europe, with capable, legitimate states today, and which are often cited as examples of 'state capacity', did not always have this quality. If we go back in time to, say, around the 1600s, the patchy evidence that we have suggests that there were parallels between the varied and unstable forms of governance in Europe and those in Africa at the time. In Africa, a variety of governance arrangements could be found at the start of the early modern period.[16] There were absolutist empires (such as the Kuba Kingdom in modern-day Congo and the Oyo Empire in West Africa). Alongside these grander arrangements, many small petty chiefdoms existed, as did grand chiefdoms and societies that were ruled by tribal councils. These varied arrangements were probably not so different from the variety of governance forms that existed in Europe at the start of the early modern period.

However, what happened during that critical period of history set the two regions on vastly different trajectories. On the one hand, Europe underwent a period of massive technological, social, and political change. These processes of change included the Enlightenment and the Age of Revolutions, which created a new appreciation of rationality that would become an important principle in the

[13] Bratton and van de Walle (n 5).

[14] M Bratton, 'State Building and Democratization in Sub-Saharan Africa: Forwards, Backward, or Together' (2004) 43 *Afrobarometer Working Paper*.

[15] AC LeVan and A Assenov, 'Parties or Portfolio? The Economic Consequences of Africa's Big Cabinets' (2016) 51(4) *Government and Opposition* 661.

[16] See eg Herbst (n 11); GP Murdock, 'Ethnographic Atlas: A Summary' (1967) 6(2) *Ethnology* 109.

development of bureaucracy, as well as ideas about democracy and the organisation of public power. Perhaps most important were the many wars fought between (and within) countries. As Charles Tilly explains, war-making was decisive in the emergence of organisations (eg bureaucracy) and activities (eg taxation) that were essential to state-building. As Tilly puts it, '[w]ar wove the European network of national states, and preparation for war created the internal structures of the states within it'.[17]

In Africa, state strengthening did not happen at this critical time. Glaringly absent in the African context were the endless series of interstate wars that were common in Europe,[18] while modern ideas and ideals stemming from the Enlightenment spread more slowly within this region, largely because the process was 'pre-empted' by the adventures in Africa of the European powers who had earlier acquired strong states.[19] Of course, here we are referring to the effects of the slave trade and colonialism, which I highlight below as handicaps in this account of why Africa has been a challenging context for RD. The result has been that much of the region has never developed the capacity to deliver security, law and order, and basic public services. These states draw low levels of income from their societies, as reflected in taxation rates that are typically below 15 per cent of GDP, and they rely on revenue sources that can be volatile and economically inefficient, such as customs duties, natural resources, and foreign aid.

Another significant facilitating condition for democracy, suggested by comparative research, is national income/wealth (preferably equitably distributed). There are intimate connections between state capacity and national income. These include the fact that the state is often a driver of economic growth, whether the state actively takes up this role in the mould of a so-called 'developmental state' or merely through its support of a national environment, including, for instance, a legal system that can enforce contracts, that is conducive to sustained economic growth. However, these two factors are worth considering independently of each other, not least because they affect the groundwork underlying RD in different ways. As noted earlier, RD is imperilled by weak state capacity because, in this scenario, the state is unable to deliver on citizens' demands, which is key to effective representation.

The story for national income is somewhat different. The belief here is that democracy is more valued, and better practised, whenever a country's citizens can take for granted the satisfaction of their material needs. For instance, in SM Lipset's view, it is 'only in a wealthy society in which relatively few citizens live in real poverty [that] a situation [can] exist in which the mass of the population could intelligently participate in politics and could develop the self-restraint necessary to

[17] C Tilly, *Coercion, Capital, and the European States, AD 990–1990* (Oxford, Basil Blackwell, 1990) 2.

[18] Herbst (n 11).

[19] O Taiwo, *How Colonialism Preempted Modernity in Africa* (Bloomington, Indiana University Press, 2010).

avoid succumbing to the appeals of irresponsible demagogues'.[20] Adam Przeworski provides support for this point with empirical data, showing (in the late 1990s) that no democracy with a per capita income higher than $6,055, that of Argentina in 1975, had ever collapsed.[21] If we adjust that figure to today's value, Przeworski's benchmark is around $10,000. Only one African country exceeds that mark (Seychelles, $14,600), and there are five countries that approach it if we consider that to be a per capita income exceeding $6,000 per annum: Botswana, Equatorial Guinea, Gabon, Mauritius, and South Africa. Thus, Africa remains a very poor continent, and that makes it a tough place for democracy in any form. The story with education – another facilitator of democracy, which is highly correlated with national income – is similar. Here, again, Africa is impoverished in comparison to other regions. Twenty per cent of primary-aged children do not go to school; by the age of 15, that figure rises to 60 per cent.[22] It is the lowest education completion rate of all developing regions.

B. Handicaps

The second category of factors to consider are handicaps, the presence of which has impeded RD in Africa. Unlike the preconditions identified earlier, these are context-specific factors that have shaped the African experience in decisive and distinctive ways. The factors that stand out here, as noted earlier, are slavery and colonialism and their ongoing legacies.

The trans-Atlantic slave trade involved the mass movement of Africans into slavery in North and South America from the sixteenth to the nineteenth centuries. This factor is distinctive to Africa not because of the fact of slavery itself – which has intermittently occurred in other regions – but because of its unprecedented scale. It involved the transportation of 12 million Africans. Estimates suggest that Africa's population in 1850 was approximately half what it would have been had the slave trades not occurred.[23] Often, the trade involved communities turning on their own (eg to settle scores), causing a massive deterioration in social trust, which matters for democracy in several ways.

For example, elite trust was key to the pact that the Tories and Whigs formed to constrain the British monarchy.[24] Political trust is needed for a stable dynamic of alternation in power, where incumbent losers accept defeat (knowing that they

[20] SM Lipset, 'Some Social Requisites of Democracy: Economic Development and Political Legitimacy' (1959) 53(1) *American Political Science Review* 69, 75.

[21] A Przeworski, 'Democracy and Economic Development' in ED Mansfield and R Sisson (eds), *Political Science and the Public Interest* (Columbus: Cohio State University Press, 2006).

[22] 'The High Price of Education in Sub-Saharan Africa' *World Bank Blogs*, 23 March 2023, avaiable at blogs.worldbank.org/en/developmenttalk/high-price-education-sub-saharan-africa, accessed 28 May 2025.

[23] G Bertocchi, 'The Legacies of Slavery In and Out of Africa' (2016) 5 *IZA Journal of Migration* 24.

[24] BR Weingast, 'The Political Foundations of Democracy and the Rule of Law' (1997) 91(2) *American Political Science Review* 245.

will not face retribution). Low-trust settings are also more violent, more prone to corruption, and more susceptible to other vices that undermine effective governance of any kind, perhaps especially the more intricate kinds such as RD. As such, the diminution of trust in African societies as a result of the slave trade has had a hugely detrimental impact on the region's democratic prospects. These effects endure. For example, research by Nathan Nunn and Leonard Wantchekon shows that the geographical regions in Africa where the slave trade was most active continue to have lower levels of trust and cooperation than the regions that were less affected by the slave trade.[25]

The prospects for RD in Africa were subsequently undermined by colonialism, beginning in the late nineteenth century – during the so-called 'Scramble for Africa' – until the late 1960s. The different colonial masters (especially Britain and France, but also Belgium, Germany, Italy, and Spain) bequeathed somewhat different institutional legacies. For example, some scholars have argued that the French were more interventionist than the British, choosing to replace local structures with their own, while the British ruled more indirectly, through local intermediaries and strategies of co-optation.[26] However, the overall imprint of colonialism bore common themes, which greatly complicated the possibilities for RD. One was its authoritarian ('might is right') logic, which established a dysfunctional norm: the disenfranchisement and disengagement of the mass of citizens. Another effect was the poorly constructed national boundaries. In several cases, a new nation was put together with little attention to the structure of the society on the ground. The result was countries that amalgamated rivalrous tribes, and other countries without a viable means of economic development beyond subsistence.

It should be noted that the problems here were thorny. With the huge ethnic and linguistic diversity in the region, constructing classic-style nation-states with a correspondence between national and ethnic boundaries may not have been a practical idea in the African context. Though, as Herbst points out, '[f]ew ask if it would be better to try to redesign at least some African states …'.[27] Therefore, the problem must be seen in a more nuanced way: it is not only that various ethnic groups have been forced to co-exist within a nation-state, but also that the mechanisms of intergroup accommodation and cooperation have been weak. Some of this can probably be traced to slavery, as I have noted. However, other drivers can be linked more directly to colonialism. For example, sometimes the colonial master set up a game of 'divide and rule' among local tribes, and in other cases they favoured one or some tribes, entrenching imbalances and resentment. Indirect rule often created handpicked delegates whose authority scrambled preexisting authority structures and created a new axis of conflict. For these reasons

[25] N Nunn and L Wantchekon, 'The Slave Trade and the Origins of Mistrust in Africa' (2011) 101(7) *The American Economic Review* 3221.

[26] See eg C Müller-Crepon, 'Continuity or Change? (In)direct Rule in British and French Colonial Africa' (2020) 74(4) *International Organization* 707.

[27] Herbst (n 11) 58.

and more, intergroup relations – often termed ethnic politics – in Africa have been an enduring problem. Of course, devising a way for different ethnic, linguistic, and religious groups to get along is not a uniquely African conundrum, but the challenge has proved to be a defining one for the region, as shown by the difficulties of national integration experienced by countries such as Nigeria, Kenya, Ethiopia, and Rwanda.

C. Institutions

I have argued so far that in Africa the preconditions for RD were weak. Metaphorically, we might say that the soil was poor. It is always tough for democracy to take root under conditions of extreme state weakness and widespread poverty. Colonialism, slavery, and ethnic politics might be considered large weeds that further undermined the quality of the soil. Nonetheless, the institutions of RD were implanted into this context. Consideration of these institutions is the third limb of our explanation of the circumstances for RD in Africa.

In the immediate aftermath of independence, most African countries experimented with the trappings of RD, such as written constitutions and multiparty elections. But, of course, these experiments were short-lived in most cases. One reason was the poor soil, in which even the 'right' designs would struggle. RD institutions that depended on intricate background structures often failed to take root. For example, the parliamentary regime of Nigeria's First Republic was cited as 'weak' when it was overthrown in 1966,[28] but it is important to recognise that it operated without strong supporting institutions. Political parties, which are so crucial to parliamentary governance, were poorly developed and lacked a national orientation and structures. The bureaucracy, legislature, military, and electoral commission also underperformed in their core functions, often becoming embroiled in the political fray. All of this set the scene for the military coups and countercoups that followed, which used the weakness of parliamentary politics as a pretext for ruling by decree and introducing a highly centralised form of presidentialism.

This kind of pattern – promising designs but weak institutions being overturned in a rapid descent to highly centralised military or strongman rule – occurred throughout the region. Furthermore, as Nic Cheeseman has observed, the range of models considered by the newly independent African countries was limited and unimaginative.[29] In most cases, they copied the constitutional forms operated by their previous colonisers. Just how restricted the range of design options

[28] YT Baba, 'Executive Dominance and Hyper-Presidentialism in Nigeria' in AC LeVan and P Ukata (eds), *The Oxford Handbook of Nigerian Politics* (Oxford, Oxford University Press, 2018) 259.

[29] N Cheeseman, 'Introduction: Understanding African Politics: Bringing the State Back in' in N Cheeseman (ed), *Institutions and Democracy in Africa: How the Rules of the Game Shape Political Developments* (Cambridge, Cambridge University Press, 2018) 5.

considered by constitution-makers at the time was becomes apparent when one sees the innovations that have characterised the post-1990 African constitutions (and other constitutions globally). For example, efforts to integrate indigenous governance into governance arrangements have been a feature of this modern wave of constitution-making, including in Africa.[30] With the benefit of hindsight, then, it seems likely that a more expansive approach to design possibilities, with greater attention given to local constraints and resources, might have served Africa well at independence in the sense of providing a more pragmatic and context-sensitive basis for governance through RD.

What has followed the immediate post-colonial decades has been much debated. Crawford Young is among those who stress the need to go beyond thinking of the 'post-colonial' African state. He claims the post-colonial moment ended with the Cold War.[31] For our purposes, what has followed this period, as I explain below, bears some promising signs as far as the prospects of RD are concerned. However, since we are at present detailing the negative side of the ledger, it should also be noted that the practices of the post-post-colonial period also contain some bad news for the advocates of RD. For one thing, several of the promising openings have been snuffed out as regimes have struggled to escape the logic of patrimonialism. As another problem, the post-1990s period has seen a surge in domestic political violence across the region, which has exacerbated the basic challenges of governance.

III. Sources of Democratic Potential

Having reviewed various kinds of obstacles to RD in Africa, I would now like to approach the question of Africa's democratic prospects with a more positive lens, in particular by identifying markers of significant democratic potential across the region. In some cases, the potential identified is consistent with the requirements for RD. However, in other cases, the potential speaks to the possibility of a different form, kind, or style of democracy – not RD.

A. African Success Stories

The first important piece of evidence is the proof of concept. There are a handful of countries in the region which, under most reasonable definitions of functioning RD, would qualify. As mentioned earlier, these are Botswana, Mauritius, Ghana, Namibia, South Africa, Cape Verde, Lesotho, and Seychelles.

[30] See eg Cheeseman (2015) (n 5).

[31] C Young, 'The End of the Post-Colonial State in Africa? Reflections on Changing African Political Dynamics' (2004) 103(410) *African Affairs* 23.

Botswana has received significant attention as an African 'success story'. In terms of the three-tiered account fleshed out in the previous section, the country's success with RD can be traced, to a large extent, to a promising set of preconditions. To be more precise, Botswana had pre-colonial, tribal institutions that encouraged cooperation and distributed and constrained power. In the 1840s and 1850s, the many Tswana tribes, whose relations until then had been turbulent, came together to oppose the growing threat from the Boers, who sought to expand their lands into the territory that is today Botswana. Their cooperation to resist proved to be formative and has been cited as a decisive moment in the country's nation-building.[32]

The existence of multiple centres of power – a kind of ethnic separation of powers – provided accountability. But cooperation across tribes was also achieved and sustained. Furthermore, Botswana had an unusual relationship with its eventual colonial power, Britain. The Tswana leaders were keen to have British support to help them ward off the Boer threat. The British, not immediately but eventually, agreed, so Botswana was incorporated into the Empire. The British had their own reasons, of course. They wished to check the expansionism of other colonial powers and saw the territory as strategically located and endowed with resources. Nonetheless, and partly as a result of the way Botswana bargained its entry into the Empire, the British adopted an especially light-touch form of administration there.

Since independence, Botswana has been governed by one political party, the Botswana Democratic Party. However, all accounts suggest that its election victories have been legitimate, not rigged. Its majorities have sometimes been slim, and there is plenty of evidence that the party has governed responsibly and responsively. To use the terminology of Giovanni Sartori's party systems framework,[33] this is a case of a predominant party in a democratic system, not a hegemonic party in an autocratic system. Botswana's economic development, which, as we have seen, is conducive to democratic development, was enabled by its vast diamond resources. Many other African countries have vast natural resources but have struggled to use these to support public goods provision. Indeed, the resources of countries such as Nigeria have probably contributed to the problems of democratic consolidation, for example by generating conditions conducive to corruption.[34] In Botswana, by contrast, the fact that the resources have been exploited within an accountability framework has been key to their use for public benefit.

Promising signs can also be found beyond Botswana. For example, South Africa's constitutional project has largely been a success, despite many frustrations and unfulfilled expectations. The country has established a framework for airing and resolving disputes, which seems to be widely accepted as legitimate. Given

[32] D Acemoglu et al, 'An African Success Story: Botswana' in D Rodrik (ed), *In Search of Prosperity: Analytic Narratives on Economic Growth* (Princeton, Princeton University Press, 2003) 80.

[33] Sartori (n 5).

[34] M Basedau, 'Context Matters – Rethinking the Resource Curse in Sub-Saharan Africa' (2005) 1 *German Overseas Institute (DUI) Working Paper*.

the country's history and potential for division and violence, that alone is a fairly remarkable achievement. The South African Constitution is frequently lauded as an example of a new 'transformative constitutionalism'.[35] While liberal models of constitutionalism have tended to preserve the status quo and prioritise stability and order, the South African Constitution is designed to compel socio-political change towards a more egalitarian society. For example, it includes positive, potentially justiciable rights to food, healthcare, education, housing, and social welfare. The model also gives courts a highly prominent role in the constitutional order, which is unusual in the African context.

Likewise, in Ghana, which has also been included in the class of African success stories in more recent times, one of the interesting developments has been the emergence of a powerful informal mechanism: the inter-party advisory committee (IPAC), through which representatives of different parties meet to discuss electoral processes and reforms. IPAC emerged after the disputed 1992 presidential elections led to boycotts of the subsequent parliamentary elections, and it has been praised for trust-building and fostering more collegial inter-party relations. Among its contributions has been the implementation of a code of conduct for political parties, including a complaints investigation procedure. This code, according to one group of observers, 'has been an effective means of checking abuse of process by political parties',[36] thus easing a key pressure point that had led to violence in the past.

Even if we go beyond the group of 'success stories' to countries whose democratic status is lower and more tenuous, we see some reasons for optimism. Take Nigeria as a prime example in this group. It remains a deeply flawed democracy, coded as a 'hybrid' regime by the EIU. Yet the norm of civilian control of the military seems to have taken hold. Term limits for the executive are now well-observed. The 1999 Constitution has proven to be enduring, despite the country's deep governance problems. This is a country, after all, that cycled through six post-independence constitutions prior to its current one. The 2023 election revealed a potentially decisive role for new electoral technologies – in this case, a new voter accreditation system (BVAS) that reduced the scope for electoral manipulation. That scope was not eliminated – and the available evidence suggests strong suspicion of manipulation[37] – but technology may ultimately be a key part of the strengthening of electoral practices in Nigeria and elsewhere on the continent.

Numerous other developments, on the positive side of the ledger in terms of Africa's democratic prospects, could also be cited. Consider, for instance, Kenya's 2010 Constitution, which was a response to ethnic conflict in the

[35] KE Klare, 'Legal Culture and Transformative Constitutionalism' (1998) 14(1) *South African Journal on Human Rights* 146.

[36] 'The Electoral Political Process' (*Devex*, 30 November 2012), available at www.devex.com/news/the-electoral-political-process-79863, accessed 17 June 2025.

[37] R Maclean and E Peltier, 'Opposition Parties in Nigeria Call for Election Rerun, Citing Vote Rigging', *New York Times* (28 February 2023).

early 2000s. It bears similarities with South Africa's because it also enshrines a thick notion of socio-economic rights available to all citizens. This constitution, too, has emerged as a critical device of democratic strengthening and an important marker in the 'gradual sedimentation' of constitutionalism across the region.[38]

Along different lines, but also encouraging, has been the enhanced role in democracy promotion taken up by the African Union (AU) in recent decades, particularly following the adoption in 2007 of the African Charter on Democracy, Elections and Governance. The AU and its predecessor, the Organisation of African Unity, had followed a strategy of non-interference in the domestic affairs of union members. But since 2007, the Union has supported constitutional changes of government, opposed extra-constitutional changes, and become more active in election observation throughout the region. There are calls for the AU to do more – for example, Adem Abebe and Charles Fombad[39] argue that it should establish a full set of benchmarks of democratic quality and create a panel of experts to monitor constitutional developments, much like the Venice Commission does for Europe. That said, the AU has become a generally positive influence on the democratic development of the continent.

B. New Models of Democracy for Africa

Another important consideration is the development of new constitutional models for Africa. This reflects the realisation that the representative model of democracy, at least as it has traditionally been understood and implemented, may not be an ideal fit for the region given its pressing problems of poverty, disenchantment, and insecurity, but also given its history of governance and social characteristics. Decolonial researchers such as Mahmood Mamdani[40] make this case most forcefully, demanding a profound reimagining of the political community in Africa, which goes beyond the Westphalian model of the nation-state and even the idea that Africa's ethnicities are real. These identities, Mamdani argues, are largely constructed, and therefore nations and states should not be built around them.

Less radical innovations have also been proposed as part of this broader effort to devise more context-specific institutions for Africa. For example, some innovations involve proposals to synthesise traditional/indigenous and liberal elements of constitutionalism. While this kind of integration has sometimes been described as 'legal pluralism', Berihun Gebeye goes one step further in identifying

[38] AK Abebe et al, 'Introduction to Comparative Constitutional Law in Africa' in R Dixon et al (eds), *Comparative Constitutional Law in Africa* (Cheltenham, Edward Elgar, 2022) 1, 3.

[39] AK Abebe and CM Fombad, 'The African Union and the Advancement of Democracy: The Problem of Unconstitutional Retention of Governmental Power' in CM Fombad and N Steytler (eds), *Democracy, Elections, and Constitutionalism in Africa* (Oxford, Oxford University Press, 2021) 61.

[40] M Mamdani, 'Beyond Settler and Native as Political Identities: Overcoming the Political Legacy of Colonialism' (2001) 43(4) *Comparative Studies in Society and History* 651.

a distinctively African kind of merging, which he describes as 'legal syncretism'.[41] This model contends that the resources for constitutional development in the region need to come from multiple sources, including colonial history, traditional structures, and liberal models.

In other work, I have made the case for a more 'dynamic' approach to constitutional design.[42] This approach is similar in some ways to transformative constitutionalism, in the sense that the constitution is future-oriented, but this principle is applied beyond the domain of rights to the institutions of constitutional governance. These structures can be designed to include adaptive mechanisms that pre-empt future problems and the likelihood, and not merely the possibility, of fundamental change. This temporal perspective is highly relevant to Africa because one of the standout features of the region's politics and society is its exposure to significant change, whereas the standard approaches to constitutional design are premised on the assumption of fundamental continuities in a society and its politics.

Kwasi Wiredu[43] and Emmanuel Ani[44] reveal the deeply deliberative, consensus-based decision-making that was, and in many cases continues to be, standard practice in African traditional societies. From this standpoint, majoritarianism – in which political decisions, lawmakers, and citizens alike, are determined by 50 per cent plus 1 of the population (or often by a smaller plurality) and which is central to RD – stands at odds with deep-rooted African traditions. This unearthing of integrative models of politics in African societies coincides with two trends that may foreshadow a greater role for such principles in the future. The first is the realisation that majoritarianism is implicated in the high-stakes, sometimes conflictual struggles over political office in the region. Thus, as Cheeseman has argued, there is a strong case for future constitutional reform (and informal developments) in the region to proceed along a more accommodationist path in the hope that this will reduce conflict.[45]

The second development is growing global interest in deliberative democracy, a movement which prioritises reason-giving, listening, and reflection in decision-making. Deliberative democrats are critical of decision-making based on preference aggregation and majoritarian rules,[46] arguing that it produces crude and impulsive decisions that often ignore minority values and interests. There are parallels between the consensualism of traditional African communities, identified by Wiredu and

[41] BA Gebeye, *A Theory of African Constitutionalism* (Oxford, Oxford University Press, 2021).

[42] Z Nwokora, 'Constitutional Design for Dynamic Democracies: A Framework for Analysis' (2022) 20(2) *International Journal of Constitutional Law* 580.

[43] K Wiredu, 'Democracy and Consensus in African Traditional Politics: A Plea for a Non-Party Polity' (2000) 39(1) *The Centennial Review* 53.

[44] EI Ani, 'Africa and the Prospects of Deliberative Democracy' (2014) 32(3) *South African Journal of Philosophy* 207.

[45] Cheeseman (2021) (n 5).

[46] A Bächtiger et al, 'Deliberative Democracy: An Introduction' in A Bächtiger et al (eds), *The Oxford Handbook of Deliberative Democracy* (Oxford, Oxford University Press, 2018).

Ani, and the ideals of deliberative democrats. Indeed, some deliberative scholars include African tribes such as the Tswana (of Botswana) in their accounts of deliberative democracy in practice.[47] The frustration with RD is not limited to Africa, and the search for refinements and alternatives is a truly global effort.

IV. Mapping Contemporary Representative Democracy Performance

So far, I have presented two lists of factors, which represent both sides of the ledger in the debate about Africa's democratic prospects. In this section, I try to bring greater focus to the discussion by homing in on trends that capture the region's contemporary performance in terms of RD. This is a reflection both of the democratic challenges that African countries face, as well as their capacity to overcome them. I should note that while it is important to keep in mind the recent efforts to conceive models of government that challenge RD, the criteria I discuss do not have a direct bearing on the emergence of new governance models. These innovations may arise under various conditions, including in contexts where RD is performing effectively and in countries where RD has struggled to take root.

As a first indicator, I consider the constitutions of African countries, in particular their duration or longevity. Constitutional stability has long been seen as a facilitating condition for representative processes. The importance of this factor has been highlighted by Zachary Elkins, Tom Ginsburg, and James Melton in *The Endurance of National Constitutions*.[48] They explain that a stable constitution provides an organising framework for the development of the institutions and practices of RD, including institutionalised political parties, constitutional norms, and a developed body of jurisprudence.

Their book shows that the average constitution globally lasts for approximately 19 years. This resonates with other research by political scientist Milan Svolik,[49] which shows that 20 years is a critical threshold or cut-off in the process of democratisation. Before that point, the odds of constitutional collapse are quite high, but they recede substantially after that point. So, if we consider 20 years as a critical threshold along this dimension of constitutional endurance, how many African countries qualify? The answer is about two-thirds – around 33 countries in the region. I calculate the average age of an African constitution to be about 26 years – still young, but not extremely so.[50]

[47] J Sass, 'Deliberative Ideals Across Diverse Cultures' in Bächtiger et al, ibid.

[48] Z Elkins et al, *The Endurance of National Constitutions* (New York, Cambridge University Press, 2012).

[49] M Svolik, 'Authoritarian Reversals and Democratic Consolidation' (2008) 102(2) *American Political Science Review* 153.

[50] Data accessed from the Comparative Constitutions Project. See Comparative Constitutions Project, 'Informing Constitutional Design', available at comparativeconstitutionsproject.org/, accessed 28 May 2025.

As that suggests, the region is maturing in terms of the age of its written constitutions. While that is correlated with constitutional performance, and indeed may be a requirement for an effective constitution, it is certainly not sufficient. We also want to consider, more directly, how a constitution and the democracy it creates work in practice. Are elections fair and characterised by party pluralism? Is democratic participation vibrant and enabled? Are civil liberties respected and executives constrained? Are government policies implemented? These questions are at the core of the measures of democratic performance such as those compiled by the EIU, Polity, and V-Dem. These indicators are also quite highly correlated, as you might expect. As I mentioned above, the EIU measure identifies a handful (7) of functional democracies in the African context. Looking more closely at this measure, we see 14 hybrid regimes and 24 authoritarian regimes.

The final indicator I would like to consider is political violence and political stability. The argument here is again quite intuitive: to have a functioning RD, you need not only a working constitution but also reasonably peaceful and stable background conditions. In their absence, constitutional collapse is likely or at least quite possible. Furthermore, low political violence is a sign of a legitimate constitutional order, an indication that those who are governed by the constitution broadly accept the outcomes that it delivers. High political violence or instability can often be a sign that this is not the case. The World Bank computes a series that captures this intuition: the Political Stability index, a series in its Worldwide Governance Indicators, measures the perceptions of the likelihood of political instability and politically motivated violence, including terrorism.[51] If we take the global average of this series, we see that about 10 African countries have scores that are above that mean. We can describe this set of countries as having a 'high score'. Twenty-four countries have scores that are a little below this mean (within one standard deviation), a group with a 'middling score'; and about 16 countries are well below the mean and can be described as having a 'low score'.

Taking these three indicators together, we can distinguish several distinctive country profiles. To begin with, there is a set of (fairly) mature responsible democracies. The countries in this group have a low risk of political violence (in other words, high political stability), they have stable and enduring constitutions, and a high level of democracy. These countries are the high performers in RD terms, a group that includes Botswana, Cape Verde, Ghana, Mauritius, and Namibia. As a second group, we can identify countries such as South Africa, Madagascar, Lesotho, The Gambia, and Rwanda that are excellent prospects in RD terms. There are two ways to be classified into this group. First of all, some of its members (eg Madagascar) are countries with a new constitutional order that is stable and already moderately or highly democratic. Alternatively, another kind of excellent prospect is a country with an established constitutional regime but a mixed performance

[51] 'Worldwide Governance Indicators', World Bank, available at www.worldbank.org/en/publication/worldwide-governance-indicators, accessed 28 May 2025.

with respect to the other two criteria. In other words, these countries have strength in democracy (South Africa) or in political stability (The Gambia), but not in both.

A third group of countries might be described as promising but at risk. They are characterised by medium political stability, an established constitutional order, and medium democracy. This group includes Benin, Kenya, Senegal, and Tanzania. A fourth group is at high risk or teetering on the brink of collapse. Here we have countries with a low political stability score, a new or old constitutional order, and a medium or low democracy score. In this category are countries such as Angola, Gabon, Guinea, Nigeria, and Togo. A fifth group of countries are what might be described as distant prospects – they are far from the requisite conditions for RD. There is a high risk of violence (ie low stability), new or old constitutions, and low democracy. Examples include Burkina Faso, Burundi, Cameroon, Ethiopia, and Sudan.

As this mapping suggests, the region hosts significant variety in terms of RD performance. This reflects the fact that some countries have been able to overcome, to varying degrees, a challenging set of preconditions (and perhaps in some cases, the preconditions were not so harsh). The mapping, of course, represents no more than a rough snapshot, but I hope it is a useful one in terms of identifying where African countries are located at the moment in relation to some key benchmarks of RD.

V. Conclusion

This chapter has explored representative democracy in Africa, seeking to understand how an essentially liberal and Western idea has fared in a region characterised by a long history of non-Western governance forms, a lengthy period of Western intervention through slavery and colonialism, and ongoing and pressing developmental challenges. Against this backdrop, it has become clear that African countries have diversified over time in terms of their RD status and characteristics. It was easier in the past to generalise about the situation of African countries: there were a couple of star performers (Botswana and Mauritius) and a vast bulk of democratic laggards. The situation now is more variegated and complicated. There is a greater range of performance situations, which my taxonomy attempts to capture. Several African countries have been able to break out of a challenging context and history to become reasonably established RDs. The various performance categories that I identify are not evenly balanced in terms of numbers – the lower performance groups have more members – but there are substantial numbers in each category.

These observations raise an important question: how can a country move up the scale from group 5 (distant prospect) to group 4 (at high risk), or from group 2 (excellent prospect) to group 1 (fairly mature responsible democracy), etc? At a superficial level, this involves remedying weaknesses in stability, constitutional endurance, or democratic performance, all of which are complex tasks. Some upward movements may involve institutional strengthening in RD terms, but, crucially, it is also possible that gains could be made by implementing new design innovations that go beyond the traditional RD framework. This would especially be the case if the new forms of governance are viewed as being more legitimate in the communities they serve. In that scenario, we would expect, for example, less political violence. Indeed, Namhla Thando Matshanda stresses this point in a recent analysis, arguing that the instability seen in the Horn of Africa is precisely because these countries are 'actively searching for new and alternative forms of political organisation'.[52] Of course, we should not assume that the trends will be one-way – it is possible that a country may move down the scale. Considering these possibilities together, there is now evidently a wide range of alternative pathways for the future of democratic development and decay across the region.

[52] NT Matshanda, 'The Crisis of the Postcolonial Nation-State and the Emergence of Alternative Forms of Statehood in the Horn of Africa' (2022) 20(10) *History Compass* e12750, 2.

4

India in Crisis: Hindu Nationalism and the Majoritarian State

ANGANA P CHATTERJI

I. Introduction

I was honoured to present this lecture at the 2023 New Putney Debates, the topic for which examines 'Democracy is in Crisis'. My talk speaks to 'India in Crisis: Hindu Nationalism and the Majoritarian State', addressing issues in four fragments.

The Narendra Modi and Bharatiya Janata Party (BJP)-led[1] government was elected to power in 2014. The notion of 'consent' in Indian democracy raises crucial questions of how assent is manufactured, translates to electoral victories and what energised the world's largest electorate to vote right-wing nationalists into power twice, in 2014 and 2019 (and, since then, again in 2024).

The Modi-led government's reach to configure a Hindu nationalist state in India since the national elections of 2019 has enforced states of emergency across the country. The ascent of political majoritarianism[2] has manifested an extra-legal and authoritarian-to-dictatorial apparatus. Experiments to enforce the latter are amplified via nationalist, populist, authoritarian and majoritarian strategies in governance. The BJP's local cadre number in the tens of millions at the grassroots. Hindu Right political leaders and militias have proliferated the spatial habitus, institutional structures and practices, and local and symbolic imaginaries to incite the Hindu majority to unparalleled dominance.[3]

Disillusion and breakage among marginalised Hindus and, among the elite, the greed to consolidate privilege and fear of losing privilege, together with silence and indifference, have been manipulated to swell the BJP's vote-bank. India, the world's most populous country of 1.4 billion, has a burgeoning middle-class

[1] Parliamentary wing of Hindu nationalism.

[2] AP Chatterji et al (eds), *Majoritarian State: How Hindu Nationalism Is Changing India* (London, Oxford University Press, 2019).

[3] See Chatterji et al (n 2).

of 31 per cent,[4] more than the entire population of the US. Approximately 22 per cent of upper caste Hindus control 41 per cent of India's wealth[5] and command disproportionate power. India remained the world's largest arms importer in 2022, even as it ranked 107 out of 121 countries on the Global Hunger Index.[6]

The BJP's furtherance of forms of coloniality in Kashmir (through forcing citizenship on people in dissent to Indian rule),[7] while removing citizenship from Bangla Muslims and other vulnerable communities in Assam in Northeast India through prejudicial laws,[8] seeks to actualise long-standing promises to 'unify' India. Old and new forms of violence have been activated through decrees, speech-acts, aggression, and assault whose signs, symbols and performative agency intersect and intertwine. Majoritarian depictions of Hindus as the national race and Muslims as enemy-infiltrators aid the Hinduisation of national culture and cultural citizenship. 'Bulldozer justice', 'love jihad', arbitrary detention, social and economic boycotts, prejudicial citizenship, juridical breakdowns, the 2019 siege on Kashmir, and the regularisation in India of long-standing techniques in militarised governance habitual to Kashmir's administration, are elements of an epistemic enterprise constructed by Hindu nationalists and sanctioned by those who are dominant.

II. Prejudicial Citizenship in Assam | Fragment 1

A. Story[9]

29 January 2020: a Muslim man committed suicide by hanging himself in the building of a primary school in Assam where his two children studied. He had been missing for two days. Originally from another district in Assam, at the time of his death he had been resident in his current village on the char (river islands) for several years. His spouse was the recipient of a house through a government

[4] S Gupta, 'Nearly 1 in 3 Indians Middle Class, to Double in 25 Years: Report' *Times of India*, 2 November 2022, available at timesofindia.indiatimes.com/business/india-business/middleclass-nearly-1/3rd-of-indias-population-to-be-2/3rds-by-2047-report/articleshow/95239621.cms, accessed 28 May 2025.

[5] 'Five States Own 50% Wealth in India, Upper Caste Hindus Richest with 41% of Total Assets: Study' *Financial Express*, 14 February 2019, available at www.financialexpress.com/india-news/five-states-own-50-wealth-in-india-upper-caste-hindus-richest-with-41-of-total-assets-study/1487084/,accessed 28 May 2025.

[6] 'India Falls to 107 among 121 Countries in Global Hunger Index' *The Telegraph*,15 October 2022, available at www.telegraphindia.com/india/india-ranks-107-out-of-121-countries-in-global-hunger-index-2022/cid/1892205, accessed 28 May 2025.

[7] AP Chatterji, 'Kashmir: A Place without Rights' *Just Security*, 5 August 2020, available at www.justsecurity.org/71840/kashmir-a-place-without-rights/, accessed 28 May 2025.

[8] The Citizenship (Amendment) Act, 2003, Act 6 of 2004, available at www.refworld.org/legal/legislation/natlegbod/2004/en/14043, accessed 28 May 2025.

[9] This narrative is based on conversations and interviews with civil society leaders, lawyers, and community members undertaken by the author, taken from AP Chatterji et al, 'Breaking Worlds: Religion, Law and Citizenship in Majoritarian India; The Story of Assam' (Berkeley, Center for Race & Gender, 2021) 1, available at escholarship.org/uc/item/6w56781n, accessed 28 May 2025.

scheme. Previously, he had also worked in construction in Guwahati, the largest city in Assam. On settling down in the char he commuted to Guwahati to work as a daily wage labourer while his wife earned a living as an agricultural labourer in their village. Notwithstanding the hardships, in the words of his family, they felt truly blessed to have each other and their home.

The protracted process of the National Register of Citizens (NRC) to verify their family's citizenship status was daunting and painful. As a non-formally literate person and someone without means, it had been extraordinarily difficult and incapacitating for him to navigate the bureaucratic obstacles, misinformation, and procedural requirements and to locate and procure the requisite documents to establish their family's legacy as apposite residents of Assam. Despite repeated verifications, his name, and the name of one of his very young children, were absent from the NRC list published on 31 August 2019. The father of his spouse was also identified as a 'D voter' ['doubtful voter'] and omitted from the NRC.

He could not fathom why he and his family and community were being estranged from their homeland. His family was apprehensive that their being Muslims and the multiple local migrations necessitated by poverty had cast them as people 'without roots', and therefore as 'foreigners'. He began to experience mental health issues, which escalated with loss of income, debt, anxiety, increasing depression, and severe stress. He lived with foreboding about his future and that of his family. He started to consume alcohol in excess and was easily angered. At one time, he had attempted to break their home down with an axe. He had consumed pesticide to kill himself, and at another time, tried to hang himself. His wife used to watch over him all the time. Just before his death, he had rowed with her.

His family lived through a vortex of threat, sadness, humiliation, and deprivation. They were uneasy about the trials of the Foreigners Tribunal process in which they felt increasingly pre-judged. Exhausted, they withdrew from various aspects of collective social life. They feared for his well-being and the impact his deterioration was having on his children. Then, one day, he took his life. With his death, fragments of hope and history were irreparably broken for his family.

B. Enumeration

The Modi-led BJP government has sought to reconstitute the basis of Indian citizenship, citing national security, through exclusionary changes to the law. Prejudicial citizenship laws in India, akin to the Nuremberg Laws instituted in September 1935 in Nazi Germany, fortify legal discrimination based on religion and privilege Hindus in defining citizenship, placing the rights and protections of religious minorities at risk, particularly Muslims.[10] The government of

[10] AP Chatterji, 'Citizenship Laws and the Nazification of India' Berkley Center for Religion, Peace & World Affairs, 9 March 2020, available at berkleycenter.georgetown.edu/responses/citizenship-laws-and-the-nazification-of-india, accessed 28 May 2025.

India: (1) passed the Citizenship (Amendment) Act (2019); and (2) determined to commence an all-India register (the NRC), also in 2019.[11] The BJP's pilot implementation focused on the state of Assam in the northeast, with injurious, gendered impact on its sizeable Muslim population, also affecting Adivasis, Dalits and other caste-oppressed groups, and communities identified as the 'tea [plantation indentured labour] tribes' and those orphaned, deserted and destitute.[12]

Three parallel and intersecting changes to citizenship laws have been enacted through the years: (1) modifications to the criteria for acquiring citizenship by descent; (2) instituting mandatory registration of citizenship through documentary evidence; and (3) Adding religion as a criterion for certain pathways to citizenship.[13]

The laws and policies reordering Indian citizenship aggravate earlier efforts dating to the colonial and post/colonial period. In practice, the 'citizenship experiment' underscores two intersecting chronologies: the exclusionary amendments to the law; and the implosive situation on the ground driven by Hindu/far-right nationalists.[14] While some of the above changes were facilitated by the Indian National Congress Party, the present BJP government is primarily responsible for the thrust to base citizenship on descent and religion.

The law requires individuals to prove that they are citizens through an arduous process that is heavily weighted against Assam's sizeable Muslim population.[15] The assertion is that a large number of Muslims are residing in India 'illegally', and are not Indian. Individuals who are incriminated as 'illegal' and as 'foreigners' are mostly local inhabitants who are socially and economically marginalised. Bangla-descent Muslims, who are unable to meet the burden to prove their citizenship, or whose documentary evidence is rejected, are faced with the threat of expulsion, exile and statelessness.

The modalities for safe harbour that apply to other communities exclude Muslims. Bangla-descent Muslim inhabitants of Assam, fabricated as 'foreigners' and 'outsiders', are the primary targets. Bangla-descent Muslims are Bangla origin Assamese (Oxomiya)-speaking Muslims of Assam, many among whom self-identify as 'Miya' Muslims. The exclusion of a community based on their faith is a contravention of India's constitutional and juridical structure. The most recent update to the NRC was published on 31 August 2019. At that time, approximately 1.9 million persons were excluded from the published list. Reportedly, from a total of 700,000 excluded Muslims, 486,000 Bangla Muslims were excluded.[16]

[11] See Amnesty International, 'Designed To Exclude: How India's Courts are Allowing Foreigners Tribunals to Render People Stateless in Assam' (2019) 18, 22, available at web.archive.org/web/20201003054807/https://amnesty.org.in/wp-content/uploads/2019/11/Assam-Foreigners-Tribunals-Report-1.pdf, accessed 28 May 2025.

[12] Chatterji (n 9).

[13] ibid 5.

[14] ibid 2.

[15] ibid 4.

[16] ibid 7.

The Assam Foreigners Tribunal(s), created under the Foreigners Act, 1946, are the state mechanism of appeal for persons excluded from the NRC. While on 16 March 2021, the Lok Sabha recorded 300 Foreigners Tribunals in Assam, in February 2024, only 100 tribunals were operational. Individuals who receive an unfavourable judgment from a tribunal have the sole option of appealing to the Assam High Court (unaffordable for many), followed by a (small) possibility of approaching the Supreme Court.

Prevalently, persons among Assam's diverse Muslim communities possess documentary records that corroborate their claims to inhabitancy and citizenship and/or evidence based in oral history and customary practice. Frequently, proof of belonging rendered by individuals to the stipulated state institutions is discredited, dismissed, or deemed inadmissible. Of those declared 'foreigners', community leaders say, reportedly, above 70 per cent are Muslims, and among them, 90 per cent are Bangla-descent Muslims. As of 2023, of those adjudicated 'foreigners', reportedly 40 per cent were stipulated through ex parte proceedings, with judgments issued in the absence of the accused.[17]

Excluding subaltern individuals and groups and instigating extreme xenophobia are fundamental to fostering a polity based on Hindu supremacy. Muslims of Assam have been declared 'foreigners' without their knowledge; families have been forcibly separated; and those who experienced the risk of expulsion have been detained in makeshift 'internment' camps.[18] Some have committed suicide.[19] While it may be practically impossible to put all those that are declared to be 'foreigners' in detention camps, Assam is witnessing a new social order of forcibly separated families, broken communities and forced labour – a mass of repeatedly displaced individuals and peoples without rights or legal protections, refugees in their own land.

III. The Siege on Indian-administered Kashmir | Fragment 2

Kashmir is gripped by the Indian state's restructuring of its land and populations, further divaricating Muslim and Pandit. Kashmir, where Muslims are in a majority, is a monument to enforced disappearances, gendered and sexualised violence, displacement, torture, extrajudicial executions, psychological operations (psyops), and the burial of civilians in unknown, unmarked, and mass graves. Impunity laws – including the Armed Forces Special Powers Act (1990); Jammu and Kashmir

[17] ibid 8.
[18] ibid 4.
[19] ibid 11.

Public Safety Act (1978, amended 2012); and Jammu and Kashmir Disturbed Areas Act (1998) – offer de facto immunity to state forces personnel.[20]

The disintegration of the non-military political economy has exacerbated class and gender inequalities. Since 1990, heightened militarisation has been a prolonged political strategy formative of social isolation. The armed militancy of the 1990s, which reportedly received support from Pakistan, abated during the years 2002–2004. The 1990s also deeply impacted the minority Hindu Pandit population of Kashmir, tens of thousands of whom were displaced at the time. Concomitantly, the project of religionisation devised the Hinduisation of Kashmiri Pandits to fabricate Kashmiri Muslims as internal and external enemies of majoritarian India.

The Shri Maharaja Hari Singh Hospital in Srinagar reportedly records that, between mid-2016 and 2018, 1,253 persons were blinded by metal pellets used by state forces. According to the US State Department, in 2018, approximately 160 civilians were killed extrajudicially, the most in over a decade.

On 5 August 2019, Kashmir's partial autonomy was countermanded by the Indian government's revocation of Article 370. The Indian Constitution, adopted in 1949, extended special status to Jammu and Kashmir through Article 370. Article 370 prescribed Jammu and Kashmir's association with India, symbolising the contract between the two entities.

Following August 2019, various areas across Kashmir were placed under curfew. The government used surveillance, threats, and drastic repressive measures to contain civilian movement and civil disobedience, endangering freedom of assembly and speech, including through control over communication and information and heightened cyber surveillance.

The State Human Rights Commission was disbanded by New Delhi in October 2019 with over 639 cases of enforced disappearances pending before it. An equivalent body has not been established in its place. By March 2020, with the advent of Covid-19, state forces were given extended jurisdiction during the health emergency, further expanding their reach over civilian life. Persons detained without warrant were not released. Health services, already strained, reached breaking point.

In May 2020, the Indian government removed certain legal barriers to permanent residency for non-Kashmiris in Kashmir to potentially reconstitute its demographic makeup and render Muslims a minority. Two new decrees; the Jammu and Kashmir Reorganisation (Adaptation of State Laws) Order, 2020, and the Jammu and Kashmir Grant of Domicile Certificate Rules, 2020, expanded the parameters for residency. Following this, the powers conferred by Article 35A on the Jammu and Kashmir legislature to determine and guarantee rights and privileges to permanent residents were transferred to the government of India. These

[20] Amnesty International, 'India: The Government Must End the Repression of Rights in Jammu and Kashmir' 2 September 2022, available at www.amnesty.org/en/latest/news/2022/09/india-the-government-must-end-the-repression-of-rights-in-jammu-and-kashmir/, accessed 28 May 2025.

extend to the right to acquire immovable property, reside lawfully in Jammu and Kashmir, and seek employment in the public sector.

These laws and policies have raised public outcry from Kashmiris and their allies. These changes provoked Kashmiri concerns of 'demographic flooding' of the region and land grabs by non-Kashmiris. The proposed deprivation of the right to land is intensified by the reported seizure of land, including private property, by Indian forces in Kashmir.

Contemporaneously, many in Kashmir understand themselves to be under Indian occupation, living in contexts akin to collective internment. The state and its armed forces subdue the appearance of political conflict in Kashmir by rearranging 'facts on the ground', while dispersing movements for freedom, justice, and accountability. In October 2021, following the reported militancy-related killings of four Kashmiri Pandits and a Kashmiri Muslim, the Modi government sought to reposition official discourse, warning of present-day militancy threat-levels in Kashmir that were apparently analogous to the 1990s, without evidence. Human rights defenders and journalists have been arrested under terror laws, despite global outcry.

Kashmir's population lives with recurrent psychosocial trauma and social death and with a very high rate of suicidal behaviours. Individual and collective mourning is truncated, forcing loss and trauma to be internalised. In the context of India's emergence as a global player, institutionalised violence in Kashmir is presented as inevitable and necessary to national security, and crises and militarisation as propitious to national enterprise.

IV. Uttar Pradesh, Hindu Nationalist Heartland | Fragment 3

Uttar Pradesh, India's largest State, has a population of over 200 million, of whom approximately 38 million are Muslims. The twice-elected, incumbent head of state of Uttar Pradesh, Yogi Adityanath, has supported and directed various political, extra/legal and social campaigns to weaken and override the rights of Muslims and other communities.[21] In a video that surfaced in 2014, Adityanath reportedly stated that: 'If [Muslims] take one Hindu girl, we'll take 100 Muslim girls. If they kill one Hindu, we'll kill 100 Muslims'.[22]

On being elected, the Adityanath government began a process to withdraw 131 criminal cases against alleged perpetrators in the Hindu-directed mass violence

[21] AP Chatterji, 'Remaking the Hindu/Nation: Terror and Impunity in Uttar Pradesh' in Chatterji et al (n 2) 397.

[22] AP Chatterji, 'Election in India's Largest State Accelerates Anti-Muslim Hate Speech and Violence' *Just Security*, 14 February 2022, available at www.justsecurity.org/80203/election-in-indias-largest-state-accelerates-anti-muslim-hate-speech-and-violence/, accessed 28 May 2025.

against Muslims in Muzaffarnagar in 2013.[23] In 40 of 41 Muzaffarnagar cases, including in four gang-rape cases, the accused were acquitted.[24] In January 2019, the prime accused and 16 others out on bail for the 2015 lynching of Mohammad Akhlaq were seen cheering at the front of an Adityanath rally.

As many as 23,612 riots/events of organised violence were reported in Uttar Pradesh during 2017–2019, while 6,126 such events were reported in 2020, and 5,302 in 2021. The Rashtriya Swayamsevak Sangh (RSS), a leading Hindu nationalist organisation, reportedly operated 8,000 shakhas or branches in Uttar Pradesh in 2017. The RSS and other Hindu nationalist organisations are widely operational. Sections of these organisations operate as militias.

In December 2018, four United Nations Special Rapporteurs wrote to the government of India regarding extrajudicial killings by police officers in Uttar Pradesh between March 2017, when the BJP government took power, and June 2018. Extrajudicial killings and custodial torture from 19 March 2017 to 28 September 2021, include 'encounter' cases where police reportedly shot individuals in street protests and enacted custodial deaths, victimising individuals because of their religion and caste. Women experienced violence, including in police custody. There is no reporting on LGBTQ+-identified persons. Uttar Pradesh officials with alleged direct responsibility for extrajudicial killings and/or torture of civilians that took place between March 2017 and September 2021 include police personnel at the rank of Deputy Superintendent of Police, district level Superintendent of Police and Constable.

In Uttar Pradesh, 166 people were reportedly killed and more than 4,453 injured in encounters between March 2017 and October 2022. As of August 2020, about 37 per cent of the victims were Muslims. Between 24 November 2020 and 31 August 2021, at least 189 people were arrested in Uttar Pradesh for violating the anti-miscegenation 'love jihad' law. Uttar Pradesh reportedly witnessed 451 custodial deaths in 2020 and 501 in 2021. In May 2022, a 22-year-old man detained by Uttar Pradesh police in Lucknow on speculation of cattle slaughtering was reportedly tortured with electric shocks and violated with a stick. The extrajudicial killing and custodial torture of Bahraichi, a Dalit man, reportedly took place in July 2021. He was allegedly tortured in police custody, leading to his death.

In September 2017, Uttar Pradesh police increased 'award money' for arresting criminals at different police ranks, and authorised police chiefs to 'announce rewards of up to Rs. 1 lakh for a team that carries out an encounter'.[25] In March 2018, Adityanath reportedly gave special awards to police officers with high 'encounter' killing numbers. In October 2021, Adityanath highlighted encounters deaths and injuries as an achievement of his government at a police parade.

Extrajudicial killings reportedly took place during the December 2019 protests against the Citizenship Amendment Act, 2019. Police attacked civilians in

[23] ibid.
[24] Chatterji (n 22).
[25] Roughly equivalent to £870 at May 2025 exchange rates.

Uttar Pradesh, including with lethal force. Reportedly, 23 persons died, 21 of them due to bullet wounds. Three police personnel were alleged to be direct accused – a Station House Officer, the city in-Charge, and a Constable. Criminalising peaceful assembly, police opened fire with live bullets, and more than 700 people were detained. The Uttar Pradesh government sought to blame the violence on Muslims. Approximately 3,000 persons of predominantly Muslim descent were reportedly arrested under false charges across Uttar Pradesh and 350 First Information Reports were allegedly filed against 5,000 'named individuals' and 100,000 unnamed persons.

The extrajudicial killing of Mohammad Suleiman (Muslim descent, age 20) reportedly took place in December 2019. His family reported that he was picked up by police while returning from a mosque, taken to Mohallah Shekhan, and shot to death on 20 December. The police file reportedly stated that Suleiman had taken an officer's pistol and shot at a Constable, who shot back and killed Suleiman. In July 2020, the Special Investigation Team looking into Suleiman's case found the six police officers accused in his killing to be innocent, alleging that Suleiman had taken part in protests.

In 2022, Prime Minister Modi attended Adityanath's swearing-in ceremony. In December 2022, Adityanath reportedly asserted that opposition parties, the Congress and Aam Aadmi, 'should be hanged' as they were impediments to India's progress. In February 2023, Adityanath reportedly claimed that: 'India is a Hindu Rashtra [nation], because every citizen of India is a Hindu'.

V. India in Crisis | Fragment 4

Majoritarian dominance has been integral to nation-formation in India since 1947 and its secularity is steeped in oppressive histories. These histories are characterised by the absence of caste-reparations and economic restructuring; massive displacement of Adivasis and chronic conditions akin to bondage of Dalits; radical and legal gender inequities; a heteronormative body politic; the failure to address repeated, mass violence of Hindus against especially Muslims, Sikhs and Christians; maldevelopment based on deep corruption that has systemically seized resources from the margins and marginalised across society; and the debacle of land reforms and persistent nationalisation of common-community lands critical to the well-being of those who are economically dispossessed.

The Hindu Right, vociferously, and the larger dominant population through both indifference and complicity, have marshalled these inequities in the assemblage of the Indian nation since its inception. Protracted political conflict and iniquitous governance have facilitated the rapid consolidation of power by the Hindu Right. This trajectory derives from colonial and pre-and post/colonial imaginations, ideologies and desires. The cultural dominance of nationalist Hinduism in India emerged through the alignment of disciplinary forms of power with the technologies of governmentality.[26] Seven decades later, the Modi-led government's aggressive minoritisation is made synonymous with national security, making Hindu nationalism the *sine qua non* of nation-building in India.

Since its inception, movements in Nazi Germany and Italian fascism have been formative to Hindu nationalism. MS Golwalkar, an early ideologue of the RSS, professed admiration for Nazi Germany, noting:

> To keep up the purity of the Race and its culture, Germany shocked the world by her purging the country of the semitic [sic] Races – the Jews. Race pride at its highest has been manifested here … the non-Hindu … may stay in the country, wholly subordinated to the Hindu nation, claiming nothing, deserving no privileges … not even citizen's rights.[27]

Hindutva, Hinduness, is not an ideology, Hindu nationalists say, but integral practice, a lifestyle for nationhood. The partisan state unfolds in varying registers, constitutive of states of exception without end. The racialisation of the 'other' targets the material culture and psychosocial well-being of minority/marginalised communities.[28] The racialisation of Muslims creates pejorative representations and ascribes revisionist identities. The racialisation of difference by the Hindu Right is pertinent beyond the colonial and Western context, to understanding its contemporaneous and post-colonial constructions. Hindu nationalist racialisation reinforces unequal relations of power between the dominant and subordinate and enforces assimilation on the latter.

The BJP-led state weaponises the turbulent markers of religion, ethnos and identity to depict dominant Hindus as the national race and 'authentic citizens'.[29] Race and nation are rendered synonymous, and violence is used to relay political signals to trigger and heighten vigilantism. The idea of 'Hindus' as a unitary majority is vigilantly enforced to domesticate myriad communities across vast differences of culture, language, region, history and religious beliefs and practices. Simultaneously, fault lines between minority and majority are fomented across the body politic, to engineer difference as conflict and pose the minority/'Other' and allies as parasitic, dangerous, as India's adversaries, anti-national, seditious.

The resistance of the survivors of the Gujarat pogrom of 2002, Odisha 2007 and 2008, and Muzaffarnagar 2013, of women dissenters in Shaheen Bagh 2019 have been met with force. The January 2023 ban of the BBC documentary on Mr Modi's role in Gujarat 2002 by the Indian government reflects its stance on the freedom of the press and of free speech. Hindu nationalists exact vengeance for imagined wrongs using bulldozers to raze property and evict Muslims.

[26] AP Chatterji, *Violent Gods: Hindu Nationalism in India's Present: Narratives from Orissa*, 1st edn (Gurgaon, Three Essays Collective, 2009) 40–77.
[27] Chatterji (n 7); Chatterji (n 10).
[28] Chatterji (n 26) 42–44.
[29] Chatterji (n 9) 27.

In 2018, an RSS leader stated that the organisation was positioned to mobilise an army within three days. Between 2018 and 2021, 2,185 events of mass and religionised violence, 2,335 incidents of caste-related violence, and 4,695 'political riots' were recorded by the government agencies. In 2021, 6,753 dowry-related deaths of women were reported.[30] It must be noted that statistics pertaining to gendered, sexualised, political and caste, sexuality and religion-based violence are routinely unreliable due to underreporting for fear of social ostracisation and retaliation, and lack of police ministrations.

In 2023, India's press freedom ranked at 161 out of 180 countries.[31] In 2023, India's Internet freedom score was 50 of 100.[32] The escalated targeting of independent media, political and vigilante violence, massive corporate and economic corruption, large-scale disintegration of law and order, disintegration of judicial autonomy, and the vengeful circulation of nationalist propaganda and hate speech attest to this illiberal turn, collapsing an already conflicted democracy. The government of India opposed marriage rights for same-sex couples before the Indian Supreme Court in March 2023, terming same-sex marriage to be an urban and elitist notion.[33] Driving nationalist propaganda, human rights defenders and allies and alliances for social justice are demonised, as dissent is criminalised as anti-national.

Political majoritarianism advances the subjugation and economic ghettoisation of caste-oppressed groups, the minoritisation of non-Hindu communities, and the politicisation of religion. Repeated calls to genocidal violence via the extermination of Muslims, reverberate. The rule of law is subverted through securitisation and arbitrary governance that operates in the name of national well-being, spurring immense political violence, social upheaval, and new forms of partition and erasure. This new authoritarianism unfolds, unchecked by international attention or consequences. The construction of a prerogative state saturates the everyday with precarity for hundreds of millions in India today, prompting widespread foreboding and social and spiritual breakdown. Targeted communities say that only the groundswell of principled civil society dissent and political transformation, together with concerted and responsible global reaction, can repudiate the intensification of absolute nationalism in India.

[30] Press Trust of India, '35,493 Dowry Deaths Reported Between 2017-21: Government' *NDTV*, 14 December 2022, available at www.ndtv.com/india-news/35-493-dowry-deaths-reported-between-2017-21-government-3607608, accessed 28 May 2025.

[31] 'India Slips in World Press Freedom Index, Ranks 161 out of 180 Countries' *The Hindu*, 3 May 2023, available at www.thehindu.com/news/national/india-slips-in-world-press-freedom-index-ranks-161-out-of-180-countries/article66806608.ece, accessed 28 May 2025.

[32] 'India: Freedom on the Net 2023 Country Report,' Freedom House, available at freedomhouse.org/country/india/freedom-net/2023, accessed 28 May 2025.

[33] G Ananthakrishnan, 'CJI Chandrachud: No Data from Govt That Same-Sex Marriage Elitist Idea' *Indian Express*, 20 April 2023, available at indianexpress.com/article/india/cji-chandrachud-no-data-from-govt-that-same-sex-marriage-elitist-idea-8565721/, accessed 28 May 2025.

5

Democratic Crisis in South America? Ten Points for Debate[1]

PEDRO RUBIM BORGES FORTES[2]

I. Introduction

This chapter is based on my lecture delivered for The Putney Debates 2023,[3] which aimed to present an overview of the state of democracy in ten countries and to raise ten points for debate. In this written piece, in addition to this introduction, I will describe facts related to the South American countries and provide a discussion of ten relevant themes for reflection on the state of our democracies. Because of space limitations, we will not be able to provide fully detailed analyses of each country but will only mention more prominent recent events. Our point of departure will be Venezuela, the notable exception in South America because it used to be a beacon of democracy while the continent was under military dictatorships and currently provides an example of an authoritarian regime in contrast to all nine other regional democracies. Importantly, democratic credentials also vary across the other countries, with some considered partially free – Paraguay,

[1] This chapter is based on a lecture delivered as part of The Putney Debates 2023. I am grateful to Professor Denis J Galligan for the kind invitation to present the lecture and to write this book chapter. As part of this research project, I also taught an elective course on the 'Democratic Crisis in South America' at the State University of Rio de Janeiro (UERJ) in the first semester of 2024, when I had the opportunity to discuss various issues related to this text and I am grateful to all my students for the interesting classroom discussions. I am also thankful to Professor Jane Reis for her support for this research project. Importantly, this chapter was finalised on 19 July 2024 and the author could only make minor changes to the text subsequently. Therefore, except for this footnote, the reader will find no mention in the body of the text of the presidential elections in Venezuela on 28 July 2024, of the presidential elections in Uruguay on 24 November 2024, and of the indictment of former President Jair Bolsonaro and the preventive arrest of his running mate for vice-presidency, General Braga Netto, for an attempted coup d'état in Brazil. Errors are all mine.

[2] Adjunct Professor of Constitutional Law at the State University of Rio de Janeiro (UERJ), Professor of Law and Development at the Postgraduate Program in Law at the University Cândido Mendes (UCAM), and Public Prosecutor at the Attorney General Office of Rio de Janeiro. DPhil (Oxford), JSM (Stanford), LLM (Harvard), MBE (COPPE-UFRJ), BA in Business Administration (PUC-Rio), and LLB (UFRJ).

[3] 'Democratic Crisis in South America? Ten Points for Debate', published by Oxford Global Society, available at www.youtube.com/watch?v=8YwuxIFKJxQ&t=390s, accessed 31 May 2025.

Bolivia, Colombia, Ecuador, and Peru – and others considered completely free – Argentina, Chile, Uruguay, and Brazil.

The chapter consists of four substantive section. After this brief introduction, Section II provides an overview of the state of democracy in South America, describing the undemocratic exception (Venezuela), the partially democratic states (Peru, Paraguay, Bolivia, Colombia, and Ecuador), and democratic states (Argentina, Chile, Uruguay, and Brazil). Importantly, these levels of democracy are not arbitrarily defined by the individual researcher but are based on the reports of Freedom House in monitoring freedom and democracy across the world.[4] Section III of this chapter presents the ten points for debate:

1. the low visibility of South America as a forgotten continent for comparative studies of constitutional law;
2. the problem of concentration of powers in the Executive Branch and how it may affect the protection of fundamental constitutional rights;
3. the model of 'presidentialism of coalition' is considered problematic because it tends to produce high levels of political instability;
4. impeachment procedures are more common in the political setting of South America than in other presidential systems;
5. the transformation of the judicial branch and supreme courts means that political conflicts are often solved through judicial intervention and decision-making mediated by law;
6. the establishment of electoral courts as an important institutional mechanism that is relevant for the control of political activity;
7. the need for regulation of the internal organisation of political parties;
8. the lack of dense social integration that could facilitate socioeconomic development;
9. institutional fragility, characterised by the low quality in the provision of public services and infrastructure; and
10. the need to consider the multiple roles of constitutions and how they enable governments, empower institutions, collaborate for the promotion of social welfare, function as expressions of value, manifestations of power, and mechanisms of social coordination.

Section IV provides the final remarks.

II. An Overview of the State of Democracy in South America

One of the challenges of this research project is to provide a comprehensive overview of the current state of democracy in South America, a continent with ten different states, each with its own political organisation, electoral systems, and

[4] See freedomhouse.org/, accessed 31 May 2025.

societal characteristics. Interestingly, there is a certain homogeneity in terms of political systems, as all states are organised as republics, are governed by a president, and employ voting mechanisms for electing political leaders. However, there are several nuances related to their constitutional experiences, institutional qualities, and electoral competitiveness, which result in heterogeneities and different levels of political freedom among South American states. According to Freedom House reports from 2023, which served as a reference for my lecture and for this chapter, Venezuela is currently undemocratic; Peru, Paraguay, Bolivia, Colombia, and Ecuador are partially democratic states; and Argentina, Chile, Uruguay, and Brazil are democratic states.

A. The Undemocratic Exception: The Case of Venezuela

Venezuela was a democratic exception in South America during the Cold War because of a decisive political agreement called the *pacto de punto fijo* or *fixed point pact*. After a very unstable year with attempted coups d'état against President Marcos Pérez Jiménez, the three major political parties signed this agreement in 1958 with a strong commitment to respect electoral results, secure political stability, and facilitate alternation of power in Venezuela.[5] The proscription of the Communist Party and the electoral victories of moderate leaders from the centre-left and centre-right created a stable tradition of political democracy until the promotion of neo-liberal reforms by Carlos Andrés Pérez in 1989, which led to a strong popular revolt and the subsequent rise of populist leader Hugo Chávez.[6] After attempting an unsuccessful coup d'état in 1992 against Carlos Andrés Pérez, Hugo Chávez was elected President of Venezuela in 1998 and ended 40 years of the *pacto de punto fijo*.[7] Reversing neo-liberal measures, redistributing wealth through cash transfers, and reducing economic inequality and poverty, Hugo Chávez gained and retained popularity among the working class. Unifying left-wing political parties around his leadership, nominating political allies to key positions in the bureaucracy and judicial branch, transforming the constitution, and reducing the capacity of the opposition, Hugo Chávez ensured his perpetuation in the presidency for 15 years until his death in 2013. Under the pretext of promoting a Bolivarian revolution, the government captured the judiciary, reduced mechanisms for checks and balances on power, destroyed the autonomy of political institutions, and eliminated the democratic rule of law in Venezuela. Benedict Bull and

[5] RJ Alexander, 'Democracy in Venezuela' (1980) 15(2) *Latin American Research Review* 241.

[6] S Ellner, 'Political Party Factionalism and Democracy in Venezuela' (1996) 23(3) *Latin American Perspectives* 87.

[7] AR Brewer-Carías, *Dismantling Democracy in Venezuela: The Chávez Authoritarian Experiment* (Cambridge, Cambridge University Press, 2010); S Ellner and M Tinker Salas (eds), *Venezuela: Hugo Chávez and the Decline of an 'Exceptional Democracy'* (Lanham, Rowman & Littlefield Publishers, 2006).

Antulio Rosales refer to this process as a 'hijack of democracy'.[8] His Vice-President, Nicolás Maduro, succeeded him and inherited eroded political institutions that facilitated continuous re-elections and the demise of democracy in Venezuela. Constitutional law scholar Allan Brewer-Carías explains the collapse of the rule of law between 1999 and 2019 as a process of concentration of power by a populist leader, the use of constitutional mechanisms to undermine the Constitution, and the denial of fair, regular, and democratic elections.[9] A remarkable episode was the 'tale of two presidents' after the National Assembly considered the election of Nicolás Maduro in 2018 to be fraudulent, declared the vacancy of the presidency, and announced that the president of the National Assembly, Juan Guaidó, should become interim president according to the Venezuelan Constitution.[10] Because Nicolás Maduro fought against this decision with the support of the military forces and the judiciary, he retained control of the public administration, his de facto authority, and the force of law, even though part of the international community supported the National Assembly in this episode. Nicolás Maduro perpetuated himself in power, and the leaders of the opposition are unlikely to become competitive contenders in presidential elections because the judiciary typically prohibits candidates from opposition parties through restrictive judicial bans that exclude their names from the voting ballots. For these reasons, contemporary Venezuela is not a democratic country.

B. The Partially Democratic States: Peru, Paraguay, Bolivia, Colombia, and Ecuador

Five countries in South America may be considered partially democratic: Peru, Paraguay, Bolivia, Colombia, and Ecuador. Peru experienced periods of democracy and authoritarianism in the twentieth century. In 1968, General Juan Velasco Alvarado became Peru's 86th President through a coup d'état and remained in power until 1975, when another general, Francisco Morales Bermúdez, led another coup d'état and replaced Velasco as Peru's president until 1980. After the restoration of democracy and a few democratic elections, in 1992, the democratically elected president, Alberto Fujimori, promoted an institutional move later classified as a 'self-coup' – a rupture of government against its own institutions – when the President dissolved the parliament and judiciary, concentrating all powers in the executive branch with military support.[11] After reforming the Constitution to

[8] B Bull and A Rosales, 'The Crisis in Venezuela' (2020) 109 *European Review of Latin American and Caribbean Studies/Revista Europea de Estudios Latinoamericanos y del Caribe* 1.

[9] AR Brewer-Carías, 'The Collapse of the Rule of Law in Venezuela 1999–2019' (2019) 52 *New York University Journal of International Law and Politics* 741.

[10] A Boersner, 'Venezuela 2019: Un Relato de Dos Presidentes' (2020) 40(2) *Revista de Ciencia Política (Santiago)* 539.

[11] S Levitsky, 'Fujimori and Post-Party Politics in Peru' (1999) 10 *Journal of Democracy* 78.

increase his powers and permit reelections, Fujimori remained President until 2000, when he resigned and sought asylum in Japan.[12] Even if Peru restored democracy again and holds regular democratic elections with alternation of power, multiple corruption scandals reduce social trust on politicians and extremist discourses of populist leaders related to '*fujimorismo*' and other ideologies continue to pose risks to the Peruvian democratic stability.[13] For instance, in 2020, Martin Vizacarra left the presidency due to an impeachment because of corruption charges related to his previous mandate as a state governor in 2014.[14] Subsequently, in 2022, Pedro Castillo attempted to promote a self-coup, but Parliament fought against it and managed to approve his impeachment with a strong majority of 101 votes out of a total of 127 votes.[15] Vice-President Dina Boularte assumed the presidency but suffers with low approval rates and political turbulence, as Peru had six different heads of government since 2017.[16]

Paraguay experienced the longest presidential mandate by one authoritarian leader in South America during the military dictatorship of General Alfredo Stroessner between 1954 and 1989.[17] After the deposition of the dictator by General Andrés Rodriguez, he remained as interim President for a couple of months, restored the legality of political parties and called democratic presidential elections, which he won with 74.3 per cent of votes as the candidate of the traditional 'Colorado Party'. During his government, the democratic rule of law was re-established, with the new Constitution of Paraguay approved in 1992 and the election of Juan Carlos Monti in 1993 as the candidate of the 'Colorado Party' and the first civilian to become a President after five decades of military rulers in Paraguay.[18] However, even if Paraguay has held regular presidential elections since this period of transition to democracy, Paul Sondrol considers it to be a case of semi-authoritarianism, in which democratic institutions are in operation, but elections do not transfer significant political power and institutions operate weakly providing a believable democratic disguise to regime incumbents.[19] The long dominance of the 'Colorado Party' and the characterisation of Paraguay as a one-party regime are also essential factors for analysis of the state of democracy in this country, as only Fernando Lugo has been elected for the presidency

[12] GD Schmidt, 'Delegative Democracy in Peru? Fujimori's 1995 Landslide and the Prospects for 2000' (2000) 42(1) *Journal of Interamerican Studies and World Affairs* 99.

[13] S Levitsky and A Vergara, 'Trumpian Tactics Threaten to undo Democracy in Peru' *International New York Times*, 23 June 2021.

[14] P Muñoz, 'Peru Goes Populist' (2021) 32 *Journal of Democracy* 48.

[15] I García Marín, 'Two Decades of Politics Without Parties, Growing Tensions Between Powers, and the Risk of Democracy in Peru' (2023) 13(1) *Revista Andina de Estudios Políticos* 18.

[16] J Carrión and P Zarate, 'Peru: Deep Political Dissatisfaction Weakens Support for Democracy' (2023) *Revista Latinoamericana de Opinión Pública* 1.

[17] P Lambert and A Nickson (eds), *The Transition to Democracy in Paraguay* (New York, Springer, 2016).

[18] P Lambert, 'A Decade of Electoral Democracy: Continuity, Change and Crisis in Paraguay' (2000) 19(3) *Bulletin of Latin American Research* 379.

[19] PC Sondrol, 'Paraguay: A Semi-Authoritarian Regime?' (2007) 34(1) *Armed Forces & Society* 46.

for another party – Christian Democrats in 2008 – since the restoration of democracy.[20] Remarkably, Fernando Lugo was subjected to an expedited process of impeachment in 2012, which removed him from the presidential office within a couple of days and only gave him a couple of hours to prepare his defence before the Senate.[21] This extraordinary procedure of removal of a President from the head of government by the Senate without the opportunity for a formal defence was condemned by other countries in South America that deemed it equivalent to a coup d'état, but the Supreme Court of Paraguay validated it and confirmed the transfer of power to his Vice-President, Federico Franco.[22] According to the Freedom House Report, Paraguay remains partially free, because democracy is dominated by the Colorado Party and fundamental rights are negatively affected by corruption, organised crime, pollution, poverty, and discrimination.[23]

Bolivia provides another example of a country in which a military leader promoted a coup de État to remove a leftist political from the presidential office, as Hugo Banzer led a revolt against socialist leader Juan José Torres, who was forced to abandon power and seek refuge in Buenos Aires, Argentina. Between 1971 and 1978, Bolivia experienced severe violations of fundamental rights through the elimination of freedom of expression, widespread physical torture of political dissidents, and a complete ban on political opposition. The transition into democracy was complicated by attempts to manipulate electoral results in favour of the military candidate officially supported by President Hugo Banzer, who was overthrown as part of democratisation process.[24] Interestingly, Hugo Banzer would return to the presidential office after winning the democratic elections in 1997. After two decades of alternation of power, the election of Evo Morales in 2006 represented a turning point for democracy in Bolivia, especially because the leader of the cocaleros (coca-leaf growers) and of the leftist political party 'Movement to Socialism' attempted to perpetuate himself in the presidential office by winning three consecutive reelections. After three weeks of strong protests in 2019 following another reelection, Evo Morales renounced the presidency.[25] Following Evo Morales, the Vice-President, the President of the Senate, and the President of the House of Representatives also renounced their positions, giving the opportunity to the Vice-President of the Senate, Jeanine Añez, to proclaim herself as the Interim President in charge of organising new presidential elections in 2020. Even if Evo Morales was prohibited from running as the official candidate, his political party

[20] D Abente-Brun, 'Paraguay: The Unraveling of One-Party Rule' (2009) 20 *Journal of Democracy* 143.

[21] L Marsteintredet et al, 'Paraguay and the Politics of Impeachment' (2013) 24 *Journal of Democracy* 110.

[22] R Szucs, 'A Democracy's Poor Performance: The Impeachment of Paraguayan President Fernando Lugo' (2013) 46 *George Washington International Law Review* 409.

[23] See Freedom House, 'Paraguay', available at freedomhouse.org/country/paraguay, accessed 31 May 2025.

[24] W Queiser Morales, 'Bolivia Moves Toward Democracy' (1980) 78(454) *Current History* 76.

[25] J Wolff, 'The Turbulent End of an Era in Bolivia: Contested Elections, the Ouster of Evo Morales, and the Beginning of a Transition Towards an Uncertain Future' (2020) 40(2) *Revista de Ciencia Política* 163.

'Movement to Socialism' won.[26] After the inauguration of new President, Luis Arce, in November 2020, the former Interim President Jeanine Añez was investigated, detained, convicted and sentenced to ten years in prison for conspiracy against the presidency of Evo Morales. In June 2024, the Commander of the Army, General Juan José Zuñiga, mobilised military troops for a coup d'état, but President Luis Arce resisted, dismissed him, and managed to imprison him. The current situation remains unstable, as former President Evo Morales announced his wish to return to the presidency and accused President Luis Arce of promoting a self-coup d'état.

Colombia also experienced an authoritarian regime during the Cold War, as Gustavo Rojas Pinilla ruled the government through a military dictatorship between 1953 and 1957, when he was forced to step down as part of the transition into democracy.[27] After one year under a military junta, since 1958 Colombia has held regular democratic elections and experienced several periods of alternating power between presidents from different parties, mostly between liberals and conservatives.[28] Importantly, Colombia provides an important counterexample to the democratic crisis related to the perpetuation of power in the presidency. Alvaro Uribe was elected President of Colombia in 2002 with 53 per cent of the valid votes in the first electoral round, becoming the first candidate to be elected directly after the constitutional reform of 1991 that established two electoral rounds in Colombia. Subsequently, Alvaro Uribe managed to change the Constitution to allow his reelection in 2006. However, when President Álvaro Uribe amended the Constitution to run for a second reelection, the Colombian Supreme Court considered that continuous reelections violated the democratic principle of the Federal Constitution.[29] Even if the project for another reelection started with five million popular signatures, was approved by the Colombian Parliament, and would lead to the victory of a widely popular presidential candidate, on the other hand, it would lead to the concentration of powers and perpetuation of the presidency. In contrast to the Bolivian experience with Evo Morales, the Colombian Supreme Court preserved the institutional rules of the game and protected democracy in Colombia. Current political challenges and democratic dilemmas are related to fundamental rights and transitional justice after the peace treaty between the government and the FARC.[30]

Like many countries in South America, Ecuador experienced a military government between 1972 and 1979 but has held regular elections since then, and

[26] CM Cunha Filho, '¿Qué pasa en Bolivia? De las elecciones fallidas del 2019 al regreso triunfal del MAS en el 2020 y más allá' (2023) 137(2) *Debats. Revista de Cultura, Poder i Societat* 41.

[27] O Scarpetta, 'Political Traditions and the Limits of Democracy in Colombia' (1991) 5(2) *International Journal of Politics, Culture, and Society* 143.

[28] RH Dix, 'Consociational Democracy: The Case of Colombia' (1980) 12(3) *Comparative Politics* 303.

[29] E Posada-Carbó, 'Latin America: Colombia after Uribe' (2011) 22(1) *Journal of Democracy* 137.

[30] The *Fuerzas Armadas Revolucionarias de Colombia– Ejército del Pueblo* (Revolutionary Armed Forces of Colombia – People's Army). See L Gamboa, 'Latin America's Shifting Politics: The Peace Process and Colombia's Elections' (2018) 29(4) *Journal of Democracy* 54.

democratic institutions have displayed greater political independence.[31] Various political parties from contrasting ideologies represent different stakeholders in national politics. Ecuador has provided a competitive electoral system in which politicians may run for presidential office and be elected, even if personal leadership and charisma are more decisive than political programs.[32] One of the prominent political leaders from this period was President Rafael Correa, a democratic socialist elected in 2007, who was reelected twice, remained in power for ten years, and managed to elect his Vice-President Lenin Moreno as his successor in the presidency in 2017.[33] Importantly, Rafael Correa aligned himself politically with other Latin American leaders like Hugo Chávez and Evo Morales and opposed neo-liberal measures associated with the Washington Consensus, increasing governmental spending, raising minimum wages, and reducing poverty. However, in contrast to the Venezuelan and the Bolivian Presidents, Rafael Correa voluntarily left the presidency after completing his cycle of government. During Lenin Moreno's four-year mandate, some illiberal measures – like unlimited presidential reelections, restrictive financial regulations on banks and private wealth, and trade control – adopted by Rafael Correa were reversed.[34] In 2021, when Lenin Moreno did not present himself as a candidate for reelection, the conservative politician Guillermo Lasso won the presidential elections and governed with a traditional economic liberal agenda.[35] In 2023, Guillermo Lasso adopted the institute of 'crossed death', a constitutional mechanism in which the President may dissolve the National Assembly, but only at the price of also submitting the presidential seat for general election on the same date for the remaining time of the mandate.[36] After Guillermo Lasso announced that he would not run for his presidential seat, another right-wing politician, Daniel Noboa, presented himself as a candidate and won the presidential elections. Current political challenges and democratic dilemmas are related to corruption and violence.

[31] JD Martz, 'The Quest for Popular Democracy in Ecuador' (1980) 78(454) *Current History* 66.

[32] C de la Torre, 'Populism and Democracy: Political Discourses and Cultures in Contemporary Ecuador' (1997) 24(3) *Latin American Perspectives* 12.

[33] CM Conaghan, 'Delegative Democracy Revisited: Ecuador under Correa' (2016) 27(3) *Journal of Democracy* 109.

[34] JC Calzavara Alves, 'Ideias Políticas e História do Tempo Presente no Equador: Uma Análise dos Discursos Políticos de Rafael Correa e Lênin Moreno' (2021) 10.06 *Boletim do Tempo Presente* 28.

[35] J Polga-Hecimovich and F Sánchez, 'Latin America Erupts: Ecuador's Return to the Past' (2021) 32(3) *Journal of Democracy* 5.

[36] GM González Orna, 'La Inestabilidad Hispanoamericana: La "Muerte Cruzada" en Ecuador' (2023) *Boletín del Departamento de América Latina y El Caribe*; M Michelle Guevara-Cunalata et al, 'Efectos y Consecuencias Jurídicas del Mecanismo Constitucional de la Muerte Cruzada en el Ecuador' (2024) 10(1) *CIENCIAMATRIA* 719; LF Guevara Mena, 'La "Muerte Cruzada" en la Constitución del Ecuador: Disolución de la Asamblea Nacional y Elecciones Anticipadas' (2023) 8(11) *Polo del Conocimiento: Revista Científico-Profesional* 405; P Medina and R Dandoy, 'Presentación: Las Elecciones Anticipadas de 2023 y las Consecuencias de la Muerte Cruzada en Ecuador' (2024) 1(12) *Democracias* 3.

C. Democratic States: Argentina, Chile, Uruguay, and Brazil

During the Cold War, Argentina also experienced a military dictatorship, which was comparatively shorter – seven years (1976–1983) – and more violent (tens of thousands of deaths of political dissidents) – than the authoritarian rule in other South American states.[37] After the Argentinian surrender in the Falklands War, the collapse of the military regime resulted in the democratic election of President Raul Alfonsin in 1983.[38] In the last four decades, the Argentinian alternated elections of Presidents from different political parties, like the Radical Civic Union Party, the Justicialist Party (Peronist), and the Advance of Liberty Party (right wing). Even if political instability correlated with economic crises during the great economic depression (2001–2002) resulted in several interim presidents with short-lived terms as head of state, constitutional institutions and legal rules of the game solved the political disputes.[39] Because political elites avoided the authoritarian temptation of governing without democratic elections, continuous electoral competition for the presidency with regular alternation of power in the middle of severe economic difficulties provides evidence of democratic strengthening rather than democratic decay.[40] In this context, the growth of right-wing political parties implies that economic elites needed to organise themselves politically and that a coup d'état is not an available option. Even if Peronism remains a very strong political force in Argentina[41] and elected former Presidents Carlos Menem, Nestor Kirchner, Cristina Kirchner, and Alberto Fernandez,[42] people also voted and democratically elected conservative Mauricio Macri in 2015 and current President Javier Milei, a right-wing populist politician in 2023.[43] Contemporary problems of Argentine democracy are not related to elections and civic participation, but more a question of improving institutional quality in terms of provision of public services, reduction of public debt and monetary inflation, and promotion of economic development.[44]

Chile experienced a very long presidential mandate by one authoritarian leader during the military dictatorship of General Augusto Pinochet between 1973

[37] E Jelin, 'The Politics of Memory: The Human Rights Movement and the Construction of Democracy in Argentina' (1994) 21(2) *Latin American Perspectives* 38.

[38] AM Garro, 'Nine Years of Transition to Democracy in Argentina: Partial Failure or Qualified Success' (1993) 31 *Columbia Journal of Transnational Law* 1.

[39] HE Schamis, 'Argentina: Crisis and Democratic Consolidation' (2002) 13(2) *Journal of Democracy* 81.

[40] S Levitsky and MV Murillo, 'Argentina: from Kirchner to Kirchner' (2008) 19(2) *Journal of Democracy* 16.

[41] LE Anderson, 'The Problem of Single-Party Predominance in an Unconsolidated Democracy: The Example of Argentina' (2009) 7(4) *Perspectives on Politics* 767.

[42] MV Murillo and R Zarazaga SJ, 'Argentina: Peronism Returns' (2020) 31(2) *Journal of Democracy* 125.

[43] Á Perényi et al, 'Institutional Transformation and Development from an Economic Transition Perspective: The Case of Argentina' (2020) 16(1) *Journal of Institutional Economics* 83.

[44] ibid.

and 1990.[45] During the 1980s, political mobilisation of the opposition parties and civil society groups led to a series of political protests and to the defeat of the dictator in a 1988 plebiscite that could eventually have extended his presidency for a period of eight years with the support of the popular vote.[46] After the democratisation, the Christian Democratic Party elected Presidents Patricio Alwyn and Eduardo Frei, but subsequently the Chilean people voted for and elected Presidents from political parties of various ideological perspectives, like Ricardo Lagos from the Party for Democracy, Michelle Bachelet from the Socialist Party, and Sebastian Piñera, from the National Renewal Party.[47] Currently, the President of Chile is Gabriel Boric, who was elected by a leftist coalition in 2021. Democratic strengthening is demonstrated by continuous electoral competition for the presidency, with regular alternations of power between the right and the left. Contemporary problems of Chilean democracy are more related to the question of designing a new democratic constitution, as the government is still based on a constitution established in 1980 by General Augusto Pinochet during his authoritarian regime. The Constitutional Convention started deliberating in 2021 with some popular support, but opinion polls after the election of Gabriel Boric indicated that a majority of the people would reject it, and 62 per cent per cent voted against the draft Constitution in a plebiscite on 4 September 2022.[48] The fact that this draft was produced by a group of independents without representation from right-wing politicians in a highly decentralised and public writing process may provide explanations for the crisis of representation and the failure to produce a politically acceptable constitutional text.[49] The current constitutional crisis, the ideological polarisation between right and left, and the difficult search for a political compromise and the definition of a new constitutional identity are some of the current challenges of Chilean democracy.[50]

Uruguay also experienced a military dictatorship during the Cold War, but for a relatively short period of eight years (1975–1983). Traditionally, democratic politics were divided between the nationalist party (or white party) and the

[45] P Constable and A Valenzuela, 'Chile after Pinochet: Democracy Restored' (1990) 1(2) *Journal of Democracy* 3.

[46] P Oxhorn, 'Where Did All the Protesters Go? Popular Mobilization and the Transition to Democracy in Chile' (1994) 21(3) *Latin American Perspectives* 49.

[47] P Navia, 'Top-Down and Bottom-Up Democracy in Latin America: The Case of Bachelet in Chile' (2008) 3 *Stockholm Review of Latin American Studies* 119; P Vidal et al, 'Neoliberalismo y Neodesarrollismo en Latinoamérica: Encuentros y Desencuentros Ideológicos entre los Gobiernos de Bachelet-Piñera y Lula-Dilma Rousseff (2005–2013)' in *Neoliberalismo, Neodesarrollismo y Socialismo Bolivariano: Modelos de Desarrollo y Políticas Públicas en América Latina* (2019) 162, 174–81; C Heiss, 'Latin America Erupts: Re-Founding Chile' (2021) 32(3) *Journal of Democracy* 33.

[48] E Alemán and P Navia, 'Chile's Failed Constitution: Democracy Wins' (2023) 34(2) *Journal of Democracy* 90.

[49] G Larraín et al, 'How Not to Write a Constitution: Lessons from Chile' (2023) 194(3) *Public Choice* 233.

[50] R Hirschl and Y Roznai (eds), *Deciphering the Genome of Constitutionalism: The Foundations and Future of Constitutional Identity* (Cambridge, Cambridge University Press, 2024).

liberal (or red party).[51] In the twenty-first century, the 'Broad Front' – a coalition of socialists, communists, social democrats, and Christian democrats – emerged as a new powerful electoral actor, being responsible for the election of President Tabaré Vazquez in 2004, José Mujica in 2009, and again Tabaré Vazquez in 2014.[52] In 2019 the candidate of the National Party, Luis Lacalle Pou, defeated the socialist candidate, Daniel Martinez, and the conservatives regained the presidency of Uruguay.[53] Considered to be the strongest democracy in contemporary South America, current challenges are mostly related to socio-economic development and inequality reduction.

Like most other South American states, Brazil also experienced a military dictatorship between 1964 and 1985, with the power as head of state alternating between five different unelected generals (Castelo Branco; Costa e Silva; Médici; Geisel; Figueiredo).[54] In the 1980s, after a strong social mobilisation for 'direct elections now' (*diretas já*), Congress frustrated civil society by defining that democratisation would initially happen through the indirect election of the new civil President and elected Tancredo Neves. After his dramatic disease and subsequent death, Vice-President José Sarney took office as the new President in 1985.[55] As part of the transition into democracy, the National Congress received the mission to elaborate the new Constitution promulgated in 1988.[56] Direct elections for the presidency have occurred regularly in Brazil since 1989. By then, Fernando Collor de Mello had been elected but governed weakly and was politically isolated in a presidency that was abbreviated by an impeachment process in 1992 based on corruption charges. Vice-President Itamar Franco assumed the presidency and managed to promote an economic plan and a new currency that brought stability to the country and stimulated the election of the Minister of Economy, the Social Democrat Fernando Henrique Cardoso, as the new President in 1994.[57] A change of power occurred again in 2002, with the election of Lula, leader of the Workers' Party, who managed to get his former Minister, Dilma Rousseff, elected to the presidency in 2010 and reelected in 2014. However, her second term was abbreviated by an impeachment process in 2016 based on charges of fiscal fraud, which was very politically divisive and paved the way for the strong ideological polarisation between right and left that affects Brazilian politics today.

Under pressure caused by the evidence of widespread political corruption revealed by the 'Car Wash Operation', Vice-President Michel Temer assumed

[51] J Lanzaro, 'Uruguay: Persistence and Change in an Old Party Democracy' (2010) 1 *Political Parties and Democracy* 195.

[52] A Garcé, 'Uruguay 2009: De Tabaré Vázquez a José Mujica' (2010) 30(2) *Revista de Ciencia Política (Santiago)* 499.

[53] L Nocetto et al, 'Uruguay 2019: Fin del Ciclo Progresista y Reestructura del Sistema de Partidos' (2020) 40(2) *Revista de Ciencia Política (Santiago)* 511.

[54] E Gaspari, *A Ditadura Acabada*, Vol 5 (São Paulo, Editora Intrínseca, 2016).

[55] P Fraga, *Tancredo Neves, o Príncipe Civil* (Rio de Janeiro, Objetiva, 2017).

[56] A Pilatti, *A Constituinte de 1987–1988: Progressistas, Conservadores, Ordem Econômica e Regras do Jogo* (Rio de Janeiro, Editora PUC-Rio, 2008).

[57] FH Cardoso, *A Arte da Política: A História que Vivi* (Rio de Janeiro, Editora José Olympio, 2015).

the presidency with very low levels of popular support and decided not to run for reelection.[58] Presenting himself as an independent and antisystem candidate, right-wing Jair Bolsonaro was elected by the end of 2018 and became President in 2019. During his presidency, Jair Bolsonaro attempted to weaken the constitutional mechanisms for checks and balances and Brazilian democratic institutions, trying to change well-established electoral procedures, to exercise direct control over the Federal Police and the Federal Prosecutors Office, and to delegitimate the other branches of the state and the opposition as 'enemies' of his government.[59] Jair Bolsonaro lost his reelection in 2022 to Lula, who had been convicted of corruption in 2017 and imprisoned for 580 days but was rehabilitated after his conviction was nullified by the Supreme Court in 2021. After the inauguration of Lula, thousands of right-wing militants invaded the buildings of the Presidency, Supreme Court, and National Congress at Plaza of Three Powers in Brasilia, calling for military intervention, a coup d'état, and the restoration of the presidency of Jair Bolsonaro. Since the invasion on 8 January 2023, police have investigated a few thousand individuals, and the Supreme Court has already convicted a few hundred defendants for crimes against the state. In June 2023, the Superior Electoral Tribunal ruled that Jair Bolsonaro was ineligible for reelection for eight years because of the dissemination of fake news and attacks against the Brazilian electoral system.

In the last 40 years, Brazilian constitutional democracy has managed to solve political conflicts according to the institutional rules of the game and has been resilient in resisting calls for authoritarian solutions. Current challenges include socio-economic development, inequality reduction, public safety, and political reforms.

III. Democratic Crisis in South America? Ten Points for Debate

The theoretical discussion on the democratic crisis in South America provides a series of relevant points for our debate. During my lecture at The Putney Debates 2023, I highlighted ten of these points for analysis and discussion. One first point was related to the fact that the continent is often forgotten in comparative studies, and there are interesting lessons to be learned about constitutional law, institutional mechanisms, and political dynamics. Therefore, I mentioned the provocative statement made by journalist Michael Reid from *The Economist*, that our continent is a forgotten one and that it should not be, because of its cultural

[58] MM Prado et al, 'Uso do Direito Penal para Combater a Corrupção: Potencial, Riscos e Limitações da Operação Lava Jato' (2021) 17(2) *Revista Direito GV*.

[59] O Vilhena Vieira et al, *Estado de Direito e Populismo Autoritário: Erosão e Resistência Institucional no Brasil (2018–22)* (Rio de Janeiro, Editora FGV, 2023).

wealth, ecological capital, and laboratory for democracy.[60] Importantly, a few recent works of comparative constitutional law focus on Latin American countries and bring important lessons from our continent to a broader global audience.[61]

Second, Argentine constitutional scholar Roberto Gargarella presented a metaphor of the 'Engine Room of the Constitution' to criticise the problem of concentration of powers in the executive branch, suggesting that there are contradictory arrangements in most South American constitutions because of a combination of progressive social rights that are frustrated by political decisions.[62] This theory may be considered a further development of a previous insight from Argentine legal theorist Carlos Santiago Nino, who argued that a strong concentration of power in the presidency in South America is a specific feature of our constitutional design that characterises our system as a 'hyper presidentialism'.[63] In contrast with US presidentialism, there is a strong concentration of power for lawmaking through direct initiative and direct power to enact provisory norms for congressional approval.[64] Importantly, the theoretical argument made by Roberto Gargarella depends on empirical evaluation, and the gradual implementation of educational rights and healthcare rights may reveal that governments need to promote progressive social rights to remain competitive in democratic elections.[65]

A third point, also related to the power structure and the relationship between the executive branch and the legislative branch, consists of a model of 'presidentialism of coalition', a concept developed by Brazilian political scientist Sérgio Abranches.[66] According to him, some states are governed by an elected president, but the political environment of the state is not limited to two major parties, unlike in the US. Therefore, in a setting of fragmented political parties in which the National Congress is composed of various political parties and none have an overall majority of representatives, the President must engage in constant negotiation with several political parties to be able to form a multipartisan coalition that makes government viable. In countries like Brazil, for instance, the cabinet is formed by Ministers from the political parties that support the governmental coalition; their presence in the Cabinet normally guarantees votes for governmental policies

[60] M Reid, *Forgotten Continent: The Battle for Latin America's Soul* (New Haven, Yale University Press, 201).

[61] C Hübner Mendes at al (eds), *The Oxford Handbook of Constitutional Law in Latin America* (Oxford, Oxford University Press, 2021); R Dixon and T Ginsburg, *Comparative Constitutional Law in Latin America* (Cheltenham, Edward Elgar Publishing, 2017); P Fortes et al (eds), *Law and Policy in Latin America: Transforming Courts, Institutions, and Rights* (Cham, Springer, 2016).

[62] R Gargarella, *Latin American Constitutionalism, 1810–2010: The Engine Room of the Constitution* (Oxford, Oxford University Press, 2013).

[63] C Santiago Nino, 'Hyperpresidentialism and Constitutional Reform in Argentina' in A Lijphart and CH Waisman (eds), *Institutional Design in New Democracies* (London, Routledge, 2018) 161.

[64] C Merlin Clève, *Medidas Provisórias* (São Paulo, Max Limonad, 1999).

[65] MP Dallari Bucci and C Seixas Duarte, 'Judicialização da Saúde: A Visão do Poder Executivo' (2017); PR Borges Fortes, 'De Graça Até Injeção na Testa? Dez Mitos da Literatura Crítica e uma Defesa da Judicialização da Saúde Baseada em Evidências' (2021) 7(1) *REI-Revista Estudos Institucionais* 226.

[66] S Abranches, *Presidencialismo de Coalizão: Raízes e Evolução do Modelo Político Brasileiro* (São Paulo, Editora Companhia das Letras, 2018).

and legislative projects in the National Congress. This model of 'presidentialism of coalition' is considered problematic because it tends to produce high levels of political instability.

On the other hand, however, this complex political equation between politicians, political parties, and branches of the state explains the fourth point: impeachment procedures are more common in the political setting of South America than in other presidential systems like in the US, for instance.[67] Once a President becomes politically weak and loses support in the national Congress in countries like Brazil, the support of one or two major parties may not be sufficient to preserve the presidential mandate and to protect the President from being impeached, as evidenced by the impeachments of former Presidents Fernando Collor de Mello in 1992 and Dilma Rousseff in 2016.[68] This point is not limited to Brazil, as evidenced by the relevant episodes of the 'expedited impeachment' of Fernando Lugo in Paraguay, the adoption of the 'crossed death' by Guillermo Lasso in Ecuador to prevent his own impeachment, and the recurrent use of impeachment in Peruvian politics too. One point related to these political dynamics is the independence of the police, the public prosecutors, and the judiciary in the investigation, persecution, and conviction of politicians for crimes related to corruption. A prodigious example comes from the 'Car Wash Operation' and its impact on various political leaders across the continent.

Fifth, the conception of the rule of law and the juridical control of political activity in the past few decades involves a significant transformation in the role of the judicial branch and supreme courts over power dynamics, because political conflicts are often solved through judicial intervention and decision-making mediated by law. Particularly in Brazil, the prominence of the Supreme Court was even characterised by constitutional law scholar Oscar Vilhena Vieira as a 'supremocracy', because the Brazilian 'Supremo Tribunal Federal' has taken several major political decisions that would normally be taken by other branches of the state.[69] Some commentators have criticised the concentration of power by the Brazilian Supreme Court and also eventually by one single Justice, especially because a few selected decisions made by rapporteurs in some particular cases may have strong political consequences.[70] In recent years, the National Congress and the presidency have attempted to reduce the powers, prerogatives, and jurisdiction of the Brazilian Supreme Court.[71] Importantly, some critiques of the Brazilian Supreme

[67] P Brossard, *O Impeachment: Aspectos da Responsabilidade Política do Presidente da República* (São Paulo, Saraiva, 1992); L Tribe and J Matz, *To End a Presidency: The Power of Impeachment* (London, Hachette UK, 2018).

[68] R Mafei, *Como Remover um Presidente: Teoria, História e Prática do Impeachment no Brasil* (São Paulo, Editora Schwarcz-Companhia das Letras, 2021).

[69] O Vilhena Vieira, *A Batalha dos Poderes: Da Transição Democrática ao Mal-Estar Constitucional* (São Paulo, Editora Companhia das Letras, 2018); O Vilhena Vieira, 'Supremocracia' (2008) 4 *Revista Direito GV* 441.

[70] D Werneck Arguelhes and L Molhano Ribeiro, 'Ministrocracia: O Supremo Tribunal Individual e o Processo Democrático Brasileiro' (2018) 37 *Novos Estudos CEBRAP* 13.

[71] R Glezer and O Vilhena, 'A Supremocracia Desafiada' (2024) 10(2) *Revista Estudos Institucionais* 248.

Court are based on a perfectionist perspective and may demand an idealised institutional perfection that one may not find in the real world of political experience.[72]

Sixth, an important institutional mechanism that is relevant for the control of political activity consists of the establishment of electoral courts, an institutional innovation pioneered by Chilean constitutionalism in 1823.[73] The lack of a unified federal body to oversee US elections may be considered a weakness of the electoral system, because of the reduced capacity of the judicial branch to respond to political conflicts between presidential candidates, as evidenced by the US Supreme Court decision in *Bush v Gore*.[74] In contemporary Brazil, the Superior Electoral Tribunal was a major political player in the protection of democracy, because of its responses to challenges posed by some politicians on the regularity of the electoral process and its capacity to demonstrate the integrity of the electronic ballots.[75] The establishment of electoral tribunals transformed the institutional quality of democratic elections in some South American states, especially in Chile and Brazil.

The seventh point consists of the regulation of the internal organisation of political parties. One seminal lesson from the German political scientist Robert Michels consisted of a critique that the major political body of the democratic political process (the political party) could have an oligarchical internal structure that concentrated power on one member (its President) or a few members (its Executive Committee).[76] Paradoxically, the most important political decisions – especially related to the selection of political candidates – could be taken by only one or a few individuals and are crucial for the democratic experience.[77] Importantly, most South American states defined a legal framework for the internal organisation of political parties to guarantee its internal democracy, but Brazil remains a notable exception in the region and political candidates may be chosen directly by the party leader or by an Executive Committee without internal elections or primaries between party potential candidates.

Our eighth point is a serious problem in contemporary South American states that consists of the lack of 'social glue', that is, the absence of a dense social integration that could facilitate socioeconomic development.[78] In contrast to the horizontal society pursued by republicanism, with reduced social distinction

[72] PR Borges Fortes, 'A Crítica Ilusionista: Uma Defesa de "A Razão Sem Voto"' (2023) *Revista da AGU*.

[73] Hübner Mendes at al (n 61); V Nunes Leal, *Coronelismo, Enxada e Voto: O Município e o Regime Representativo no Brasil* (São Paulo, Editora Companhia das Letras, 2012).

[74] *Bush v Gore*, 531 US 98 (2000).

[75] PR Borges Fortes, 'Crises da Democracia e de Governo: Um Ensaio de História Constitucional Brasileira em Defesa da Constituição-Cidadã e da Cidadania Emancipada' (2023) *Passagens: Revista Internacional de História Política e Cultura Jurídica* 4.

[76] R Michels, *Political Parties: A Sociological Study of the Oligarchical Tendencies of Modern Democracy* (New York, Hearst's International Library Company, 1915).

[77] M Duverger, *Political Parties: Their Organization and Activity in the Modern State* (London, Methuen & Co Ltd, 1959).

[78] JE Stiglitz, 'Formal and Informal Institutions' in P Dasgupta and I Serageldin (eds), *Social Capital: A Multifaceted Perspective* (Washington, DC, World Bank, 2000) 59.

among individuals of different classes, South American states are characterised by socioeconomic inequality and a concentration of wealth and power among the elites.[79] This great social divide requires the special attention of our institutions, policymakers, and our peoples, because of the negative influence on social life in general and democratic promises in particular. In extremely unequal societies, excluded individuals may eventually not be able to develop themselves to exercise their full academic and professional potential to achieve positions of leadership, change their social status, and accumulate economic wealth.[80] When opportunities are not really available for talented individuals because of forms of direct and indirect discrimination, members of minority groups may not be able to exercise their political capacity as active citizens.[81] Moreover, this great social divide may be translated into an ideological polarisation between right and left, in which each side perceives the other side as an 'enemy' that should be eliminated and not simply an adversary that could be engaged in political dialogues.[82] Particularly in the twenty-first century, the emergence of new leftist political leaders was followed by the appearance of extreme right-wing politicians in the political landscape too.

The ninth point comes from another difficulty of South American states: institutional fragility, characterised by low quality in the provision of public services and infrastructure. In some states, progressive social rights to education and healthcare are not delivered by the state to the people because the state needs to build its organisational capacity to produce and maintain well-equipped schools and hospitals and provide continuous training to teachers and medical doctors. This same process of state building is necessary to improve the quality of organisations, train public agents, and establish the institutional rules of the game for the regular functioning of the institutions of market, society, and democracy.[83]

One final and tenth point for our debate is related to the full understanding of the role of constitutions and of constitutional law. In the twenty-first century, South American states experienced the growth of importance of Supreme Courts and of the effectiveness of constitutional law as positive law that should be applied to solve political disputes between branches of power and the socioeconomic elites.[84] Even if this new development is remarkable and demonstrates the institutional maturity

[79] L Meir Friedman, *The Horizontal Society* (New Haven, Yale University Press, 1999); P Pettit, *Republicanism: A Theory of Freedom and Government* (Oxford, Oxford University Press, 1997).

[80] R Mangabeira Unger, *The Self Awakened: Pragmatism Unbound* (Cambridge, MA, Harvard University Press, 2007).

[81] W Corbo, *Discriminação Indireta: Conceitos, Fundamentos e Uma Proposta de Enfrentamento à Luz da Constituição de 1988* (Rio de Janeiro, Lumen Juris, 2024); B Crick (ed), *Active Citizenship: What Could It Achieve and How?* (Edinburgh, Edinburgh University Press, 2010).

[82] C Schmitt, *The Concept of the Political: Expanded Edition* (Chicago, University of Chicago Press, 2008); C Mouffe, *Agonistics: Thinking the World Politically* (London, Verso Books, 2013).

[83] DC North, 'Institutional Change and Economic Growth' (1971) 31(1) *The Journal of Economic History* 118; F Fukuyama, *State-Building: Governance and World Order in the 21st Century* (Ithaca, Cornell University Press, 2019).

[84] LR Barroso, *O Direito Constitucional e a Efetividade de Suas Normas: Limites e Possibilidades da Constituição Brasileira* (Rio de Janeiro, Renovar, 2009).

of South American states, we should also consider the multiple roles of constitutions and how they habilitate governments, empower institutions, collaborate for the promotion of social welfare, function as expressions of value, manifestations of power, and mechanisms of social coordination.[85]

IV. Conclusion

The subject of 'democratic crisis' became one of the most relevant themes for discussion in contemporary constitutional law, leading to various reflections being made by renowned scholars in the last few years, based on the experience of democratic erosion in Eastern European states and democratic decay in the US and Central Europe.[86] In this setting of growth of democratic deficit related to the increase of populism, ideological polarisation, and dissemination of fake news, we need to revisit concepts of 'militant democracy' and 'defensive democracy' to preserve constitutional democracy and prevent movement towards democratic erosion.[87]

Particularly in the South American states, the role of the judicial branch in protecting constitutional democracy has become very important in recent decades, especially in the Supreme Courts and Electoral Tribunals. Concrete episodes in Colombia, Brazil, and Peru demonstrate that strong institutions may provide checks and balances over a strong presidency. Future research should also further investigate these points beyond the doctrinal view of positive law and examine the democratic crisis through the perspectives of institutional theory, of legitimacy, of representation, of communication, and public policy.[88] This chapter provides a comprehensive overview of the democratic crisis in South American states and ten points for discussions on the future of democracy in the continent as part of The Putney Debates 2023.

[85] DJ Galligan and M Versteeg (eds), *Social and Political Foundations of Constitutions* (Cambridge, Cambridge University Press, 2013). I thank editor Zim Nwokora for reminding me of the potentials for abuse of constitutionalism.

[86] KL Scheppele, 'Autocratic Legalism' (2018) 85(2) *The University of Chicago Law Review* 545; KL Scheppele, 'The Opportunism of Populists and the Defense of Constitutional Liberalism' (2019) 20(3) *German Law Journal* 314; KL Scheppele, 'How Viktor Orbán Wins' (2022) 33(3) *Journal of Democracy* 45; A Przeworski, *Crises of Democracy* (Cambridge, Cambridge University Press, 2019); S Levitsky and D Ziblatt, *How Democracies Die* (New York, Crown, 2019); A Voßkuhle, *IDP-Linha Direito Comparado: Defesa do Estado Constitucional Democrático em Tempos de Populismo* (São Paulo, Saraiva Educação SA, 2020).

[87] K Loewenstein, 'Militant Democracy and Fundamental Rights, I' (1937) 31(3) *American Political Science Review* 417; K Loewenstein, 'Militant Democracy and Fundamental Rights, II' (1937) 31(4) *American Political Science Review* 638; D Sarmento and JG Madeira Pontes, 'Democracia Militante e Imunidade Material dos Parlamentares: Limites Constitucionais aos Discursos de Deputados e Senadores' (2020) 47(149) *Revista da AJURIS* 67.

[88] LR Barroso, 'Populismo, Autoritarismo e Resistência Democrática: As Cortes Constitucionais no Jogo do Poder' (2023) 14 *Revista Direito e Práxis* 1652.

6

Leadership in Democratic Systems

I. Leadership and Democracy – Ritual Performance versus Substantive Aspiration and Achievement: Some Reflections[1]

FUI S TSIKATA

'The seventeenth century was a tough time to be alive.' Thus opens Jonathan Healey's *The Blazing World: A New History of Revolutionary England*.[2] 'Life was capricious and uncertain', he goes on to say on the same opening page. He provides us with an account of the sources of dissatisfaction and the upheavals to which they led, the political struggles which characterised that century, as well as the changes in material conditions which facilitated or accompanied them. The contribution of the 1600s, particularly the mid-century, to the articulation and implanting of ideas of freedom, equality and institutions of representative government constrained by law is not in doubt. Healey describes the original Putney Debates, held in late October and early November 1647, as 'one of the most remarkable meetings in the whole of English history …, in which soldiers [of the New Model Army] and civilians argued about the future of the constitution, the nature of sovereignty and the right to vote'.[3]

For students of constitutional law brought up on the typical diet of ideas expressed in more or less abstract, idealised form, an appreciation of social context – of the real-life issues of the day and the battles around them – is critical for enabling us to move beyond mere invocation of handed-down notions. To that end, the primary objective of this chapter is limited and pedagogical. We can formulate it in the form of a number of questions. Beyond texts articulating principles and institutional arrangements, what sorts of materials and tools would assist us to respond with more than bewilderment to the deficits in performance

[1] I am grateful to the following, who have provided me with material or comments or both as I worked on this paper: Theophilus Acheampong, Hakeem Belo-Osagie, Kofi Gunu, Elizabeth Nwarueze, Thomas Stephens, Dotse Tsikata and Tsatsu Tsikata. Edinam Cofie served as an engaged and assured research assistant. However, none of them has responsibility for anything I say in the paper.

[2] J Healey, *The Blazing World: A New History of Revolutionary England* (London, Bloomsbury, 2023)1.

[3] ibid 231.

we are experiencing in many parts of the world, even in those countries typically regarded as role models?[4] How might the signs of their fragility in our supposed exemplars assist us in transcending tendencies to deploy them merely as weapons in contests between grand ideological camps? How does an awareness of history and social context make us sensitive, whether as intellectuals or activists, to the opportunities for and constraints in the way of furthering the multiple values and aspirations embedded in any project for democratic achievement?

As we have said elsewhere, '[t]he elaboration of ... rights and freedoms in relation to each other has occurred not merely or even principally on the basis of the mental exertion of intellectuals, but as part of the historical experience of definite societies'.[5] To make an impact, the efforts of the most formidable intellectuals have to find plausibility (if not viability), even as ideals, in the context of definite societies. For, after all, they offer recommendations for social conduct, whether or not the time frames in which their substantial attainment is proposed to be achievable are tied to them.

In an article on the Nigerian presidential elections of February 2023, titled 'Nigeria's Hollow Democracy', the writer Chimamanda Adichie refers to an editorial in *The Washington Post* which opines:

> that 'much good' came from the Nigerian elections, which are worth celebrating because, among other things, 'no one has blocked highways', as happened in Brazil after Jair Bolsonaro lost his reelection bid. We are also told that 'it is encouraging ... that losing candidates are pursuing their claims through the courts ...'[6]

Chimamanda describes the reactions of *The Washington Post* and the U.S. State Department as those of 'cordial condescension.'

> Has the United States, she asks, once again decided that what matters in Africa is not democracy but stability? ... Or is it about that ever-effulgent nemesis China, as so much of U.S. foreign policy now invariably seems to be?

What her comments point to is the potential for using apparent measures of 'democratic' practice as an indicator of approval or disapproval, rather than a genuine assessment of substantive performance. The conclusion that 'the elections fell short of Nigerian citizens' legitimate and reasonable expectations'[7] appears to represent a more credible attempt at genuine evaluation. Even where the objective

[4] B Fogel, 'The Future Starts in South Africa' *The New Statesman*, 18 May 2024.

[5] FS Tsikata, 'Towards an Agenda for Constitutional Discourse' in K Arhin (ed), *The Life and Work of Kwame Nkrumah* (Accra, Sedco, 1991) 211, 212. The title in the book is mis-rendered, presumably by an over-enthusiastic editorial assistant, as 'Towards an Agenda of Constitutional Issues Under the Kwame Nkrumah Regime'.

[6] C Adichie, 'Nigeria's Hollow Democracy', *The Atlantic* (28 April 2023), available at www.theatlantic.com/ideas/archive/2023/04/nigerias-hollow-democracy/673647/, accessed 31 May 2025.

[7] Final Report of the Joint Observation Mission of the International Republican Institute and the National Democratic Institute, available at www.ndi.org/sites/default/files/IRI_NDI%20Final%20Report_2023%20Nigeria%20IEOM.pdf, accessed 31 May 2025; see also European Union Election Observation Mission, *Nigeria 2023, Final Report.*

of optimistic public statements goes beyond merely cynical exercises in realpolitik and rather aims to encourage by acknowledging what are perceived to be advances in performance, however limited, it is important to recognise the risk of contributing to legitimising what are essentially power grabs, with little or no commitment to the principles or ideals that are invoked. If the shortcomings noted in the reports of the Joint Observation Mission of the International Republican Institute and the National Democratic Institute, as well as the European Union Election Observation Mission and by Chimamanda engender cynicism and demoralisation rather than active 'quality engagement' of the citizenry the next time round, it would be hard to agree with *The Washington Post* that much good came from those elections.

The level of abstraction in the articulation of key elements of the ideas of freedom and equality, as well as representative and accountable government, means that they tend to qualify, if not tussle with, each other. Indeed, Simon Reid-Henry posits '[t]he struggle between equality and liberty, and the form of government that struggle has bequeathed' as defining in the latter part of the West's twentieth century and the early years of its twenty-first.[8]

In his classic text *Constitutionalism and the Separation of Powers*, Maurice Vile takes us on an elaborate journey tracing the evolution of the main theories and institutional arrangements which Western political thought has proposed to make for representative and accountable government consistent with values of liberty and equality.[9] He cites 'An Agreement of the People', a document which featured prominently in The Putney Debates, as proposing that Parliament 'intermeddle not with the execution of laws, nor give judgment upon any man's person or estate, where no law hath been before provided'.[10] He quotes John Lilburne, a leader of the Levellers and a significant influence at Putney, as referring to 'complaints of oppression' from committees of Parliament 'determining particular matters, which properly appertains to the cognisance of the ordinary Courts of Justice' and to his contention that 'Parliament had the power to set up courts of justice, but only "provided that the Judges consist of persons that are not members of … [Parliament], and provided that the power they give them be universal," not a power directed at particular individuals.'[11]

These proposals bear a striking resemblance to those of others who, according to Vile, were concerned that 'the legislature will, or may, be taken over entirely by the democratic element, and that checks upon "mob rule" will therefore have to be applied by branches of government largely or wholly outside the legislature'.[12] The tensions that Vile presents in the design of institutional arrangements that allow

[8] S Reid-Henry, *The Empire of Democracy: The Remaking of the West since the Cold War: 1971–2017* (New York, Simon & Schuster, 2019) 11.

[9] MJC Vile, *Constitutionalism and the Separation of Powers*, 2nd edn (Indianapolis, Liberty Fund, 1998). The original edition was published by Oxford University Press in 1967.

[10] ibid 48. See also Healey (n 2) 230–32.

[11] Vile (n 9) 48–49.

[12] ibid 37.

for expressions of popular will while imposing constraints to safeguard fundamental values have remained at the heart of much constitutional law discussion.[13]

The political party is a key feature of modern contests for political power, though operating largely outside formal constitutional structures. For many developing countries, it was an important vehicle for mobilising for independence and has remained significant. Constitutional doctrines of separation of powers and checks and balances have to reckon with the capacity of the party machine to override or modify their operation by uniting, often in subterranean activity, though at other times openly, power structures whose separation or combination those doctrines express themselves as prescribing or constraining. The avenues for access to power that they provide mean that the political party can be a vehicle for mobilising for social change or primarily for individual or factional self-advancement. Indeed, the expression 'state capture' has gained popularity as shorthand for the corrosion of public purpose and its replacement by decision-making in the interests of a narrow band of businesspeople who manage to exercise overwhelming influence over the executive and other public sector institutions.[14] This is, of course, not coextensive with that of influence through the machinery of the party, though there is much room for overlap.

Attempts to constrain the combination of power in an elected executive and legislature belonging to the same political party have at least heightened the desire for independent institutions that are not beholden to either. In the traditional doctrines of constitutional democracy, the independence of the judiciary has been a central tenet to that end. The Constitution of Ghana, for example, grandly proclaims in Article 125(1) that 'Justice emanates from the people and shall be administered in the name of the Republic by the Judiciary which shall be independent and subject only to this Constitution.' In several constitutions, other institutions, such as the Electoral Commission, have been designed with that aim in view. The fundamental assessment to make is how independent are those who populate these bodies in their performance, what commitment to respect their capacity for independence is shown by other organs of governmental power, and how much does it matter to other elements of society that those who are supposed to be independent act independently? Indeed, criticisms of the conduct of Nigeria's Independent National Electoral Commission (INEC) in the 2023 elections were a central element in the scepticism about their outcome. That scepticism was deepened to some extent by the judgments of the Presidential Election Petition Court and the Nigerian Supreme Court in upholding the results declared by INEC. Among the criticisms was that while acknowledging non-compliance with elements of the regulations and guidelines published by INEC and much touted as

[13] B Nwabueze, *Constitutional Democracy in Africa*, Vol 1 (Nigeria, Spectrum Books, 2003), especially Chs 9–14.

[14] *The Commission of Inquiry into State Capture, Part VI, Vol II* (2022), available at www.gov.za/sites/default/files/gcis_document/202206/electronic-state-capture-commission-report-part-vi-vol-ii.pdf, accessed 31 May 2025.

critical to the transparency of the elections, both courts determined that as those provisions were not in the Electoral Act 2022 itself, they could not form the basis for challenging the validity of the elections.[15]

US Senator Sheldon Whitehouse and Representative Jamie Raskin have provided much material in support of their contention that the current majority of the US Supreme Court is acting at the behest of wealthy vested interests in pursuit of pre-determined doctrinal positions.[16]

Even more serious is the suggestion that the performance of the Court has, on critical occasions, been skewed to achieve ad hoc outcomes, with no regard to principle, whether ideological or otherwise.[17] If that were shown to be consistently the case with the judiciary or other institutions in any country, the invocation of its independence would be no more than a cynical mask covering a lack of commitment to substantive principles.

Simon Reid-Henry takes us beyond the traditional tripartite division of governmental authority in his observation that 'institutions of the market' have, in the countries on which he focuses, taken 'their place alongside parliaments, the executive branch and the judiciary' as 'a fourth pillar of political authority'.[18] He identifies 'a program of political minimalism that reduced state capacity and amplified market freedoms'.[19]

In *No Ordinary Time*, the historian Doris Kearns Goodwin gives us an instructive and fascinating account of the skills, energy and passion that Franklin and Eleanor Roosevelt deployed in galvanising the transformation of what FDR had

[15] *Judgment of the Presidential Election Petition Court*, available at drive.google.com/file/d/1da6I0w6k3HIFcCyAVLgvO6Lj0W1lBpLY/view, accessed 31 May 2025; 'Supreme Court Delivers Final Judgement on Tinubu's Election Today: Live Updates' *Premium Times*, 26 October 2023, available at www.premiumtimesng.com/news/headlines/637115-supreme-court-delivers-final-judgement-on-tinubus-election-today-live-updates.html, accessed 31 May 2025; 'Critical Appraisal of Supreme Court Judgment on Presidential Election Petition Judgment Appeal', *The Nigerian Lawyer*, 5 November 2023, available at thenigerialawyer.com/critical-appraisal-of-supreme-court-judgment-on-presidential-election-petition-judgment-appeal/, accessed 19 November 2024.

[16] S Whitehouse, 'The Supreme Court Has Become Just Another Arm of the GOP', available at: www.whitehouse.senate.gov/op-eds/the-supreme-court-has-become-just-another-arm-of-the-gop/, accessed 31 May 2025; S Whitehouse and J Mueller, *The Scheme: How the Right Wing Used Dark Money to Capture the Supreme Court* (The New Press, 2023); 'US Supreme Court Ethics Democrats Hearing' *The Guardian*, 12 June 2024, available at www.theguardian.com/law/article/2024/jun/11/us-supreme-court-ethics-democrats-hearing, accessed 31 May 2025.

[17] S Wilentz, 'The "Dred Scott" of Our Time' *New York Review of Books*, 15 August 2024; L Litman, 'Something's Rotten About the Justices Taking So Long on Trump's Immunity Case' New York Times, 19 June 2024, available at www.nytimes.com/2024/06/19/opinion/supreme-court-trump-immunity.html, accessed 31 May 2025; Ranking Member Raskin, 'Opening Remarks at Roundtable on Supreme Court Ethics Crisis', available at www.youtube.com/watch?v=8f3vTzGQYLc, accessed 31 May 2025; 'The Delay in Trump's Immunity Case Shows What's at Stake in November' *The Hill*, 20 May 2024, available at thehill.com/opinion/judiciary/4673692-the-delay-in-trumps-immunity-case-shows-whats-at-stake-in-november/ accessed 31 May 2025.

[18] Reid-Henry (n 8) 6.

[19] ibid 738. For a discussion of the tension between democratic aspirations and market-enhancing reforms in the context of developing countries, see R Idrissa, 'Weakened States and Market Giants: Neoliberalism and Democracy in Niger and West Bengal' (2018) XLIII(3) *Africa Development* 25.

described as a significantly 'ill-housed, ill-clad, ill-nourished'[20] country into a nation in which substantial progress had been made in quality of life, social mobility and economic revitalisation.[21] The underlying premise was, of course, that indicia of material welfare of the majority of the population were as much a part of the democratic project as were institutional, governmental arrangements reflective of staple constitutional doctrines and that active governmental intervention was not, by itself, inconsistent with democracy. The Roosevelts exhibited impressive capabilities in gathering and distilling information and perspectives from a broad range of sources, making informed and conscientious judgements and taking hard decisions. The resolution in concrete situations of the tension between Franklin's sensitivity to what was politically realisable and Eleanor's doggedness in bringing the marginalised into view, as well as their mutual commitment to social progress, appear to have been important contributors to their achievements.

It does not take much imagination to transpose the challenges that the Roosevelts confronted with those faced by leaders of anti-colonial movements when they took over the institutions of government upon independence. Yearnings and projects for social change were evidently central to anti-colonial movements. However, certain differences in context must be noted. In the first place, the constitutions under which those leaders achieved office typically stood historical practice on its head: liberal constitutions reflecting different aspirations from the authoritarianism of immediately preceding governmental practice. Second, some of these constitutions contained strong provisions aimed at protecting advantages procured by ruling groups who were becoming minorities in the transition to governments elected through one person one vote processes.[22] Third, the starting point of significant constituencies of the Roosevelts (and, indeed, of the Levellers' demands in the mid-seventeenth century) was for greater inclusion in the polity.[23] The central demand of the anti-colonial struggle was not for the rulers to bring us into their rule; if anything, in many instances the demand was for them to 'leave and leave us alone'.

In sum, the context in which the Roosevelts mobilised support and sought to obstruct, marginalise, or co-opt representatives of vested interests opposed to their projects for change had some similarities to, but was rather different from and perhaps somewhat less complicated than, that of those who led popular nationalist

[20] FDR, Second Inaugural Address, 20 January 1937, available at www.fdrlibrary.marist.edu/_resources/images/msf/msf01059, accessed 31 May 2025.

[21] D Kearns Goodwin, *No Ordinary Time: Franklin & Eleanor Roosevelt: The Home Front in World War II* (New York, Simon & Schuster, 1994).

[22] J Dugard, 'Unpacking Section 25: Is South Africa's Property Clause an Obstacle or Engine for Socio-Economic Transformation', available at www.wits.ac.za/media/wits-university/faculties-and-schools/commerce-law-and-management/law/documents/constitutional-court-review-program/Potenial%20and%20Limits%20of%20Section%2025_CCR.pdf, accessed 31 May 2025; B Mabasa et al, 'The Legal and Philosophical Dichotomy between Land and Property: A Transformative Justice Approach to the Rights and Wrongs of South African Property Law', available at www.cambridge.org/core/books/beyond-expropriation-without-compensation/legal-and-philosophical-dichotomy-between-land-and-property/AFBF297BECBB7B650AF6CFC1602CE35F, accessed 31 May 2025.

[23] See Healey (n 2) especially 230–35.

movements into government in much of Africa and the rest of the developing world. Pankaj Mishra expresses the context tellingly thus in relation to India:

> Social change was what India needed above all .... For as Ambedkar warned in 1951 in resigning from Nehru's cabinet, 'to leave inequality between class and class, between sex and sex ... and to go on passing legislation ... is to make a farce of our Constitution and to build a palace on a dung heap.'[24]

The risks to the projects for change in the developing world ranged from regime destabilisation, by external and internal forces, through to a descent into authoritarian, demagogic and/or essentially parasitic rule. Perhaps the most dramatic instance of destabilisation in the latter part of the twentieth century was that of attempting to prevent the election of Salvador Allende in Chile and then overthrowing his government in a military coup, which much evidence shows was orchestrated by US government agencies under the active leadership of Henry Kissinger as Secretary of State.[25]

The recognition that popular mobilisation may be required for projects for change to advance democracy is in tension with an acknowledgement of the risks of a concentration of power resulting, on the contrary, in undermining democratic prospects. In *Days and Nights of Love and War*, Eduardo Galeano narrates sobering conversations with Juan Domingo Perón, under whose leadership significant mobilisation and social change had occurred in Argentina in the mid-twentieth century. The words of Peron, in whom popular forces in Argentina had invested so much hope, dramatically exemplify the manipulative tools available to a leader to perform at communicating empathy and solidarity with the aspirations and values on which he rides to power:

> One morning, during the first days of exile, the caudillo had explained to his host in Asuncion, Paraguay, the political importance of the smile.
>
> 'Do you want to see my smile,' he had asked.
>
> And he put his false teeth in the palm of his hand.[26]

This chapter attempts to focus our attention on the phenomenon of rhetorical expressions and rituals deploying the language of democratic principles to mask genuflection in the direction of power, vested interest, and prejudice. It also seeks to remind especially students of constitutional law of the risk that a certain focus on constitutional texts can lead to paying insufficient attention to deep-rooted constraints to the possible realisation of the aspirations these texts articulate.[27]

[24] P Mishra, 'God's Oppressed Children' *New York Review of Books*, 21 December 2017, available at www.nybooks.com/articles/2017/12/21/dalits-gods-oppressed-children/, accessed 31 May 2025.

[25] See 'Henry Kissinger: The Declassified Obituary', available at nsarchive.gwu.edu/briefing-book/chile-cold-war-henry-kissinger-indonesia-southern-cone-vietnam/2023-11-29/henry; see also history.state.gov/historicaldocuments/frus1969-76v21/ch2, both accessed 31 May 2025.

[26] E Galeano, *Days and Nights of Love and War* (Monthly Review Press, 2000) 30.

[27] S Hahn, 'The Deep Tangled Roots of American Illiberalism' *New York Times*, 4 May 2024; A Hochschild, *American Midnight: The Great War, a Violent Peace and Democracy's Forgotten Crisis* (Boston,

II. Same Old or Something New? The Leadership Crisis and Political Reconciliation in Contemporary Democracies

ALEXANDRA IANCU AND BOGDAN IANCU

A. Democratic Erosion (Decline, Backsliding, etc)

To paraphrase a recent book title, it is commonly agreed today that 'democracy erodes from the top'.[28] The democratic decline is heavily embedded in a profound leadership crisis. Unexpected alliances recently surfaced. Steve Bannon, for instance, once said that Victor Orbán, the Hungarian Prime Minister, was a 'Trump before Trump'. Tucker Carlson repeatedly went to Budapest, in a strange reverse trek to the fortress of the defender of the 'true' populist faith. Before the 2024 Republican Party presidential primaries, in 2023, Hungarian President Katalin Novák (as she then was) paid an official visit to Governor Ron DeSantis, in what was widely read as a form of endorsement or at least proxy hedge-betting by the true Hungarian kingmaker, Prime Minister Orbán.[29]

As we revised this chapter for print, an unexpected invalidation by the Romanian Constitutional Court of the ongoing Romanian presidential elections immediately elicited feverish global networking. Elections were stopped in their tracks by the ruling, just as voting abroad had commenced. The frontrunner of the first round, Mr Georgescu, an ethnonationalist, was instantly defended by Donald Trump Jr. The latter attacked the presumably 'globalist' court on X, accusing it of nefarious, Soros-beholden motives: '[a]nother Soros/Marxist attempt at rigging the outcome and denying the will of the people'.[30] An accolade by Elon Musk followed shortly after. These reactions appeared to confirm, or at least lend credence to, Mr Georgescu's allegations and allusions of connections with notabiles in Trump's inner circle; he frequently dropped the name of Robert Kennedy Jr as a close friend and ally. The runner-up, Ms Lasconi, presumably the progressive defender of democracy against Mr Georgescu, tweeted an open letter to Donald Trump Sr, the President-elect. She asked for a meeting to prove that she was a true leader of people, like Trump himself (and no Soros stooge).[31]

Mariner Books, 2022); LA Villalón, 'The Politics of Democratization and State Building in the Sahel' in LA Villalón and R Idrissa (eds), *Democratic Struggle, Institutional Reform, and State Resilience in the African Sahel* (Lanham, MD: Rowman & Littlefield, 2020); A de Waal, 'The Deluge Facing Africa's Leaders is Going to Get Worse' *New York Times*, 14 August 2023, available at www.nytimes.com/2023/08/14/opinion/niger-sahel-military-rule.html, accessed 31 May 2025.

[28] L Bartels, *Democracy Erodes from the Top: Leaders, Citizens, and the Challenge of Populism in Europe* (Princeton: Princeton University Press, 2023).

[29] 'Viktor Orbán's Support for Trump Seems to Wane as Ally Meets with DeSantis' *The Guardian*, 12 April 2023, available at www.theguardian.com/world/2023/apr/12/viktor-orban-ron-desantis-trump-hungary (all links last accessed on 31 May 2025).

[30] At x.com/DonaldJTrumpJr/status/1865160362988826986.

[31] At x.com/ElenaLasconi/status/1865501542888976665.

From an Eastern European perspective, such developments are extraordinary. Thirty-five years ago, there was nothing to anticipate such moves, namely, that the leader of the most powerful country in the world (the oldest continuing democracy), also the leader of one of the two American mainstream parties, would take cues from the Hungarian Prime Minister (the leader of a peripheral country whose GDP is about 7–8 times smaller than that of Florida). Orbán's close ties with Georgia Meloni, Robert Fico, or, more recently, Herbert Kickl, Geert Wilders, or Andrej Babiš, were less striking but equally creative and evocative of this global networking trend. In the US and the EU, populist leaders cooperate transnationally across former central-periphery divides.

The junction between the success of 'populist' leaders and the citizens' mistrust of political representatives constitutes the most visible manifestation of the current crisis. Once in power, populist leaders systematically reshape institutions and boost polarisation, encouraging copycat attacks on liberal constitutionalism. However, the potential dangers of elites' abusiveness and instrumentality are not new to Western democracies. Early on, post-war scholars warned about the propensity and ability of leaders to abuse legal frameworks for political gains, particularly in contexts marked by the decline of party representation. In Western Europe, the professionalisation of politics and the personalisation of power, which gradually emerged in the 1950s–1960s, entailed the structural transformation of political regimes by narrowing the ideological salience of party competition.[32] New forms of judicialisation or managerialism took the upper hand, in sync with the reduction in the scope of old-fashioned majoritarian politics. In the US, personalisation of politics was actively shaped through decentralisation reforms – misguided steps in the search for democratisation (ie party primaries, direct leadership selection, etc).[33] Such reforms eventually backfired, increasing voters' alienation from politics and party decline. Decades later, authors such as Manin continued to outline the revival of the 'aristocratic' forms of representation colliding with the democratic ethos.[34]

Contrasted with such a long history of individualisation of politics, contemporary phenomena of rampant 'backsliding,' 'democratic decline,' or 'authoritarianism' remain without answer. Why now? What has fundamentally changed to explain the political convergence of the transnational democracy crisis?

We argue that, differently from the past, leadership contestation became legitimised due to the more profound structural predicament of 'mediating institutions'.

[32] See, for instance, O Kirchheimer, 'The Transformation of the Western European Party Systems Political Parties and Political Development (SPD-6)' in J La Palombara and M Weiner (eds), *Studies in Political Development* (Princeton, Princeton University Press, 1966) 177; RS Katz and P Mair, 'Changing Models of Party Organization and Party Democracy: The Emergence of the Cartel Party' (1995) 1(1) *Party Politics* 5.

[33] F McCall Rosenbluth and I Sapiro, *Responsible Parties. Saving Democracy from Itself* (New Haven, CT, Yale University Press, 2018) 2.

[34] B Manin, *Principles of Representative Government* (Cambridge, Cambridge University Press, 1997) 134.

We attach to mediating institutions a broader sense than the original meaning (confined to parties, social movements, or interest groups acting to integrate citizens in political processes and policymaking[35]) to include a more comprehensive array of agents linking citizens and the state (eg tertiary education, contextualised informal agents supporting social mobility – ie welfare programmes, media outlets, etc).

Such agents stabilised political action in different contexts and historical periods, sometimes in a less formalised manner, normalising the inherent tensions in the contemporary regimes' power articulation. We argue thus that recently, the mediating institutions – meant to smooth the conciliation processes between elitism as a by-product of liberal constitutionalism and democracy – started to systematically and simultaneously fail to secure democratic integration. This failure would thus not be univocally connected to idiosyncratic shortcomings pre-existent in most post-war Western societies but rather is the outcome of the synchronicity of malfunctioning of intermediary institutions on the politics/policy/polity dimension.

B. Liberal Constitutionalism vs Democracy: Shallow Pacification Through Mediation

For most contemporary scholars, liberal constitutionalism goes hand in hand with democratic ethos. However, it is essential to remember that adopting universal suffrage or the displacement of census-based representation was not a sudden historical shift, but a gradual process often animated by anti-reformist movements and political struggles. While the ideal of democracy is about equal leadership, liberal constitutionalism is about elite enlightenment and lawful rule. The merit-based selection of liberal constitutionalism was somewhat compatible with the Ancien Régime proto-forms of representation. The passage from ascription (wealth and family ties) to a merit-based selection was, in most cases, incomplete in displacing former strategic elites from positions of power.[36] For example, university education offered legitimacy badges and political know-how that smoothed the transition from old to new elites. The elite replacement was continuous and, more importantly, partial, as – for instance – high-quality university education traditionally replicated social status inequities. In this context, the political establishment amply rejected and criticised the disruptive attempts to blur the meritocratic principle by introducing a new referential of equality and inclusion.

Two primary forms of opposition came to the fore. First, classic constitutionalism was reluctant to endorse the democratic principle in decision-making

[35] C Wolbrecht, 'Mediating Institutions' in C Wolbrecht and RE Hero (eds), *The Politics of Democractic Illustion* (Philadelphia, PA, Temple University Press, 2005) 103.

[36] S Keller, *Beyond the Ruling Class. Strategic Elites in Modern Society* (New York, Random House, 1963) 59.

processes, and second, more importantly, political leaders opposed the extension of the franchise by outlining the dangers posed by looser selection criteria.

It is thus not surprising that Walter Bagehot wrote his classic *The English Constitution* in response to the Reform Act of 1867, which moderately extended suffrage. His fears about the effects of this modest extension of the franchise inform and pervade the entire book. From the 70-page introduction (written later but expressive of the main tenets of the argument), the following passage bears somewhat longer quotation:

> *The Reform Act of 1867 did not stop at skilled labour; it enfranchised unskilled labour too. No one will contend that the ordinary working man who has no special skill and who is only rated because he has a house can judge many intellectual matters. The average can only earn very scanty wages by coarse labour. They have no time to improve themselves, for they are labouring the whole day through, and their early education was so small that in most cases, it is dubious whether, even if they had much time, they could use it to good purpose. We have not enfranchised a class needing to be guided by their better than the old class; on the contrary, the new class needs it more than the old. The real question is, Will they submit to it, will they defer similarly to wealth and rank, and to the higher qualities of which these are the rough symbols and the common accompaniments?*[37]

While the electoral reforms only enfranchised 60 per cent of English males, Bagehot considered it a mortal danger to the system. Dicey outlined a similar position when he wrote his *Law and Public Opinion* lectures, believed by the author to be his true, most mature work. Dicey commented in the additional manuscript of the Macmillan papers:

> I have no belief myself that England will, in the long run, be converted into a socialistic state. The rich and the educated will somehow get the upper hand.[38]

According to Dicey, the modernity dilemma would be solved by 'democracy tempered by snobbishness'. The belief that Englishmen, even if they had the right to vote, would defer to their 'natural' social superiors (ie obey the traditional merit-based social distinctions) somewhat allayed his fears about the havoc this new role was to wreak on the system.

The argument of 'the ignorant poor' corrupting the ideal of good government was widespread in the nineteenth century. In France, institutional choices often justified the twisted history of universal suffrage. In 1830, Guizot famously argued in favour of one nation without classes, claiming at the same time that census-based selection did not alleviate rights or liberties.[39] Similar forms of opposition

[37] W Bagehot, *The English Constitution*, 2nd edn (London, Macmillan, 1884) xv.

[38] AV Dicey, *Lectures on the Relation Between Law and Public Opinion in England During the Nineteenth Century* (London, Macmillan, 1905); Macmillan Papers, Add Mss 55085, 24 February 1914.

[39] 'Freedom produces the separation of powers and deference of such powers towards one another. A great society of industrious owners, different from each other in their respective degrees of education and and ownership, this is the true meaning of the word democracy' ('La liberté a pour résultat le partage des pouvoirs et le respect qu'ils se portent les uns aux autres …. Une grande société de propriétaires laborieux, à des degrés très différents de fortune et de lumières, voilà le sens du mot

contaminated peripheral countries. In Romania, male universal suffrage had been primarily opposed by citing the people's ignorance. By the end of the nineteenth century, even the more progressive elites mooting for universal suffrage, such as the liberal CA Rosetti, stated that literacy increase and taming governmental abuses of power should have preceded the extension of voting rights. As Ziblat pointed out, the expansion of the franchise, even when accepted as an overarching political principle or as a political necessity facilitating national integration – indemnifying by plebiscite autocratic rules – has traditionally been tamed by other institutional devices (ie the weakening of the parliament, electoral law reforms) meant to downsize the political impact of the massification of politics.[40]

In the passage from liberal constitutionalism to democracy, the party's prominence as a mediating institution became the primary political device in safeguarding regimes from significant shifts and political chaos. Party functions were well-defined in ensuring candidate selection, political education, citizens' integration, or providing citizens with symbolic functions. Mass parties successfully incorporated active membership, focused on interest representation, and defined strong party ideology. Due to their hierarchical structures, such parties consolidated leadership selection at the central level and imposed clear lines of discipline within party organisation, which were then replicated in public offices. In contemporary imagination, such parties are still considered, following the Weberian quip, the genuine 'children of democracy', the well-desired forms of civic participation. While mass parties had indeed an essential quality of encapsulating new electorates, they were not necessarily democratic political structures. The massification of politics also encouraged Panopticon forms of political integration of the masses in politics. Such organisations' autocratic/oligarchic decision-making processes rapidly solidified. The high membership figures did not stand for knowledge or ideological deliberation. As Michels pointed out, the trade unions/party affiliates on the left were:

> Quite young men [who] find other ways of employing their leisure; they are heedless, their thoughts run in erotic channels, they are always hoping that some miracle will deliver them from the need of passing their whole lives as simple wage-earners, and for these reasons, they are slow to join a trade union. The men over forty, weary and disillusioned, commonly resign their membership (unless retained in the union by purely personal interest, to secure out-of-work pay, insurance against illness, and the like).[41]

Analyses of the rank and file suggested volatile membership structures. Members were little involved in political activities and focused on the structure of incentives

démocratie'): F Guizot, 'L'esprit d'insurrection est un esprit radicalement contraire à la liberté' (29 December 1830), available at www2.assemblee-nationale.fr/decouvrir-l-assemblee/histoire/grands-discours-parlementaires/francois-guizot-29-decembre-1830 (authors' translation).

[40] D Ziblatt, *Conservative Parties and the Birth of Democracy* (Cambridge, Cambridge University Press, 2017) 7.

[41] R Michels, *Political Parties. A Sociological Study of Oligarchic Tendencies of Modern Democracy* (New York, Hearst's International Library Co, 1915) 78.

offered to them by party organisations. At the beginning of democratisation, as today, members were not angels, as their internal participation was driven by particular sets of expectations of 'personal compensation from the victory of their leader, that is, offices or other advantages'.[42]

Irrespective of grassroots-level political practices, the initial pacification between liberal constitutionalism and democracy came through politics. Mass parties ensured membership commitment through the political insulation of newcomers and the distribution of a wide range of public services at ancillary levels (commercial, educational, leisure).

Political parties also became the primary agents of governability, reshaping the functioning of liberal constitutionalism through the principles of majority and party discipline. Nevertheless, mass parties were far less liberal in their views and practices than the founding fathers of liberal constitutionalism. Ideological rigidity and the lack of intraparty competition and deliberation brought political closure and excessive bureaucratisation. As Weber puts it, leadership selection highlights the importance of party organisational activities and increases the leaders' demagogical capacity. Nevertheless, after adopting universal suffrage, party politics became quintessential to the regime's routinisation. Political parties remained the sole formal and informal agency that offered political coordination for a while.

C. Systemic Failures of Mediating Institutions: Politics/Policy/Polity and the Populist Turn

It is difficult to point out when the political economy behind the conciliation of constitutional liberalism and democracy started to go on a downward trend. Nevertheless, the question is less: 'Why is democracy in decline nowadays?' as it is, and perhaps more so, 'Why has democracy lasted so long?' If intermediary institutions had a role in maintaining the political systems' functionality by encouraging citizen integration, their constant reshuffling stopped at a certain point. In wilful blindness, populist parties today seem more to aim at restoring some of the traditional mediating institutions (albeit preferably under their control) than at their political demolishment.

The most visible sign of the democracy crisis has been the erosion of politics. Immediately after the Second World War, the ideological convergence towards centrist positions and the parties' inability to control the underlying social structures gradually eroded the linkage function. Partyness and the ascent of leader-centred politics alienated the masses from politics. Today, party organisations are merely an extension of the political class, more akin to the central civil service party. High levels of incumbency, intensive professionalisation, and mediatisation of politics

[42] M Weber, 'Politics as a Vocation' (1919) in HH Gerth and C Wright Mills (trs and eds), *From Max Weber: Essays in Sociology* (Oxford, Oxford University Press, 1946) 25.

animate more extensive processes of delegitimating traditional elites. The gradual demise of political parties as agents of representation and the colonisation of state resources continuously haunt all political processes. Political closure is at its peak, amplifying the structural decoupling between governmental accountability/effectiveness, political pluralism, and liberal values. The 'retribalisation of politics', forging opponents as political enemies, replaces political activists and citizen encapsulation with new forms of social identity.[43]

However, the gradual demise of democratic party politics had variable speeds. While parties rapidly disconnected from society at an organisational level, they pushed forward a welfare-state agenda three decades after the Second World War. In Europe, the social-democratic project implied economic safeguards: a social security system (access to public education, healthcare, unemployment benefits, family allowances, etc), the fight against unemployment, and robust public services. Although based on different policy sets, the economic boost and the creation of public services in Europe and the US became instruments of broader political integration.[44] The policy connection to the citizens made authors such as SM Lipset consider that the conflict between different social groups continued to be expressed through political parties.[45] Social and economic factors such as wealth, literacy, and urbanisation highly predicted democracy's quality in the long run. However, the political shift from politics to policies as a means of conciliation reconfigured the role of mediating institutions. Intermediary public and private agencies directly involved in policymaking, such as trade unions, NGOs, schools, and public healthcare systems, contributed to social mobility and integration. Parties pushed the agenda but were no longer the main avenues of public expression.

Endogenous and international factors (ie US hegemony, the Cold War, etc) contributed to the ascent of public policies as conciliatory mechanisms of liberalism and democracy in a post-war consensus. The economic crisis in the 1970s and the wave of the 80s neo-liberal ended the role of solidarity as a substitute for politics. The change of context particularly impacted the political left. As Piketty famously put it, contemporary social democracy resembles 'Brahmin parties' by its inherent choice to outstrip the more traditional social-economic dimension. Demobilising the working class or abandoning traditional trade unionism became a conscious choice of the left despite being detrimental to the conventional loyal constituencies. In this context, the masses tend to retreat altogether from politics. Abstentionism became the primary expression of dealignment as a new form of a revived class distinction. In the 2000s, electoral results in Great Britain

[43] EA West and S Iyengar, 'Partisanship as a Social Identity: Implications for Polarization' (2022) 44 *Political Behaviour* 807.

[44] JE Cronin, *Fragile Victory: The Making and Unmaking of Liberal Order* (New Haven, CT, Yale Univeristy Press, 2023) 7.

[45] SM Lipset, *Political Man: The Social Bases of Politics* (Washington, DC, Library of Congress, 1960) 83–90.

and the US showed, for example, that well-off classes participated in the electoral processes twice as much as unskilled workers. Such political contraction echoes the contemporary intellectual criticisms and public statements dubbing the electorate incompetent and ignorant. In a way, the demise of mediating agencies of the welfare state revamped the elitist drive of census-based politics. The political retreat from policy dimension hallowed even further the legitimatory mechanisms of institutional conciliation between democracy and constitutionalism.

Last but not least, the political stability in post-war Europe was also granted by continuities in the polity dimension. Nonetheless, the process of denationalising democracies produced, in the long term, numerous grievances and social distress and amplified political alienation. For a while, increasing institutional safeguards within nation-states in terms of new regulations and good practices obfuscated or at least slowed down the polity change. The substitution from inter-state to infra-state definition of boundaries brought looser forms of political survival by offering a symbolic redemption to the active citizen. Mass participation has been reduced to the ability to oversee the political scene closely, examine the activity of political leaders, and denounce the excesses of power. A transparent state became a moral requirement. Constitutional courts' adjudication, rule of law, and integrity-related standards were substitutes for the lack of direct forms of accountability towards the public. However, in the long run, such arrangements could not replace the challenges to intermediary institutions necessary to survive in the globalised environment – eg restrictions to mobility (restrictions to freedom of circulation), unequal access to education or other public services, etc. While political accountability was secured through autonomous institutions, substantive accountability refers to direct forms of benefits that did not find alternative channels of expression. As Kriese et al noted, '[as] a consequence of globalization, nation-states are losing part of their problem-solving capacity and scope of action, which means that the citizens' political rights, which are mainly tied to the nation-states, are hollowed out'.[46] In this vein, the lack of systemic solutions to replace former mediating institutions with effective political agents created a political backlash. All empirical studies outline the reconfiguration of political space dominated by a neo-nativist/globalist tension. Polity, as such, lost its unifying force of conciliation.

Throughout the twentieth and twenty-first centuries, the politics/policy/polity dimensions remained highly intertwined, forming substituting dynamics to pacify the centrifugal tendencies between liberal constitutionalism and democracy. In doing so, democratic decline became a gradual process often obscured by the intensive action of mediating institutions. Mass parties had been primarily in charge of social and political integration. Public policies took the floor with the demise of politics in post-war Europe, offering positive or negative incentive

[46] H Kriese et al, 'Globalization and its Impact on National Spaces of Competition' in H Kriese et al, *West European Politics in the Age of Globalization* (Cambridge, Cambridge University Press, 2008) 7.

for social integration. Mediating agents multiplied to ensure social mobility and political integration. However, the economic crisis in the mid-70s and the decline of solidarity reshuffled the traditional agencies of integration once more. In this context, the polity devices remained the ultimate frontier in ensuring systemic legitimacy. Limiting government and increasing expectations linked to downsizing the public sector could create a virtual community of citizens. However, due to intensive transnationalisation, what had initially constituted a source of cohesion became the main principle of political discrimination.

Political cleavages and polarisation manifestly mobilise the politics-policy areas less as they focus more on the contestation of polity re-articulation. Neo-nativism, sovereigntist, and nationalistic parties seek revival by politicising the globalist/anti-globalist divide. In this context, populists can thus be seen as clinging to the last dimension of politics-as-we-used-to-know-it by trying to restore the political dimension by manipulating polity tropes. Their political success is often linked to the activation of the new political cleavage and the attempt to instrumentalise the historical policy dimension – bringing back the redistributive dimension of policymaking. In this context, populist leaders' prominence is only partially related to their contentions, demagogical skills, or social media presence. Their contemporary prevalence is riding on more structural determinants of modern democracies. Nostalgia as a hidden mechanism of restoration of political routines lies at the heart of their immediate ascent.

D. Conclusion: Populism as Unmediated Democracy

The current crisis of democracy emerged in a context of all-encompassing phenomena modifying contemporary politics, policy, and polity levels symmetrically. All the mechanisms that temporarily pacified the institutions of liberal constitutionalism with democracy face today a chronic legitimacy crisis. In this context, the predominance of populist leaders/movements seems intransigently linked to political nostalgia – as populist leaders seem to embrace distorted restorative attempts of some of the previous pathways of pacification: sovereignty, redistribution, and activation of salient ideologies shaped as (neo-)conservative values. Populist leadership becomes, in this way, a secondary means of expression of more profound structural crises.

We contended that the populist ascent is not accidental or a simple pathology of recent politics. Instead, we argued that the two elements of contemporary political systems – the rule by elites and democracy as an aspiration for equality – were not reconciled by universal suffrage but by the advent of the mediating institutions that made universal suffrage function. Such informal devices of consensus were less stable and context-dependent. Their political nature allowed them to metamorphose by shifting from politics to policies and polity dimensions. The three main stages of survival of democratic regimes thus emerged. If the initial forms of conciliation took the form of the political side, through the articulation of mass parties, after the war, other mediating institutions took upon them this task. In the post-war decades, welfare state major institutions ensured that policy support for elitism and democracy coexisted. While the erosion of solidarity was unavoidable, the polity level remained the ultimate substitute for citizens' compliance with traditional politics. Finally, globalisation and de-nationalisation challenged the last resorts of consensus-based political regimes. The lack of reshuffling of the politics/policy/polity dimensions ended in a political deadlock, leading to the ascent of illiberal values. Populist parties, in this vein, are forcing the rebooting of the polity dimension into a return to politics. Nevertheless, in doing so, they question the principles that politics and policy dimensions from the past tended to protect, namely the values of liberal constitutionalism.

Unsurprisingly, contemporary democracy crises blur the lines between central and peripheral societies. With the decline of mediating institutions in the West, old democracies have increasingly resembled their younger counterparts, who had never experienced a fully-fledged process of democratic mediation. In this vein, it is unsurprising that Donald Trump is turning to relatively small new democracies to grasp their functioning or that former political divisions are erased in the name of illiberal values. In fact, in old and new democracies alike, the political downfall of mediating institutions brought the prevalence of elitism, leaving it far from the gaze of the public and creating new potential forms of expression of democratic pathologies.

7

Institutions of Government and their Role in Democracy

I. The Administrative State: Friend or Foe of Representative Democracy?

RICHARD W CLARY

Different countries have different constitutional schemes (written or unwritten) that establish the basic core for their form of representative democracy. The US, for example, in its written constitution has a tripartite form of government, with three branches – the executive, the legislature, the judiciary – having a separation of powers designed to serve as checks and balances on each other. The UK, in contrast, in its largely unwritten constitution, has a model based on parliamentary sovereignty, with the executive drawn from the Parliament itself; the courts, originally drawing their authority from the Crown, sit somewhat to the side. Other countries have their own structures.

What these representative democracies have in common, at a level separate from the elected representatives, is what can loosely be called the 'administrative state': the institutions of government, such as the civil service, independent agencies, and regulatory authorities. These institutions are the machinery of government, essential because elected officials cannot run the country entirely on their own.

The institutions of government vary by country. In the UK, the Civil Service is divided into government departments, agencies, and non-departmental government bodies. Day-to-day running of the departments is the responsibility of the relevant permanent secretaries, who in turn support and report to the government Ministers officially heading each department. The government Ministers are political actors appointed by the Prime Minister, members of the Cabinet (and of Parliament), accountable to the Prime Minister and Parliament, whereas the permanent secretaries and the work force below them are career civil servants.

In the US, there are 15 Departments of the executive branch staffed by public servants whose tenure (at least in theory) survives changes in the administration, but who ultimately report to political appointees selected by the President (the Secretaries, who form the President's Cabinet, subject to legislative confirmation by the Senate). In the US there are also independent executive agencies (such as the Environmental Protection Agency) and independent regulatory agencies (such as the Securities and Exchange Commission and the Federal Reserve). Independent executive agencies have a single leader appointed by the President and serving at the President's pleasure, whereas independent regulatory agencies are generally led by commissions or boards, the members of which are appointed by the President for a set term and can only be removed for cause. Many of the independent regulatory agencies are subject to statutory bipartisan requirements that the commissioners or board members reflect both major political parties. For both types of agencies, the employees are public servants.

Whatever the particular model chosen by a given country, the theory is the same: these institutions are repositories of experience and expertise useful to the functioning of government, ultimately subject to the control of some duly elected political actor. The talents of these experts are available to support whatever elected officials have taken the reins of leadership, however the political winds may be blowing at a given time. These experts also serve as checks on the legality and fiscal sustainability of the policies and plans of the elected officials.

As previewed in Chapter 1, there is a growing controversy over the proper balance between the elected political actors – particularly the executive – and the unelected actors of the administrative state. Is the theory as described above still working?

It has become increasingly common for the institutions to be cast in a very different light: that they have their own political agendas, acting as an unelected fourth 'branch' of government that is independent of the will of the people as embodied in the elected representatives, particularly the executive. Some argue that the rise of administrative expertise reflects the outsourcing of decision-making. Taken to its extreme, this view suggests that while elections may change the government, they will not necessarily translate into changed national policy, thus undermining faith in elections and the proper functioning of representative democracy. Professor Smilova's essay in this chapter (see Section IV below) analyses this argument in scholarly terms. Elected politicians holding this viewpoint often substitute derogatory terms: unelected actors in the administrative state standing in the way of representatives' plans are the 'Mandarins', the 'blob', the 'deep state', a 'swamp' that needs to be 'drained' to return power to the people's elected representatives. Several recent UK Prime Ministers, such as Boris Johnson and Liz Truss, were especially vocal in advancing this theory, and President Trump in his second term is actively taking an axe to large swathes of the administrative machinery of government in the name of restoring electoral power.

Taking a very different perspective on the same conflict, the attack on an impartial civil service can be viewed as overreach by the executive, part of an ongoing trend – in both the UK and the US – of expanding the role of the executive, in this case by substituting partisan players for non-partisan institutions. The trend of executive expansion and its impact on various forms of checks and balances is analysed in the essay by Professor Douglas-Scott in Section III of this chapter. From this perspective, it can be argued that the various government institutions are part of the checks and balances inherent in the proper functioning of an elected government, part of the protection from what some scholars have described as the imperial presidency.

So what should be the interrelationship in a representative democracy between elected officials and the unelected administrative state? Does the civil service provide essential, impartial expertise that serves as a useful check and balance on elected officials – especially the executive – or has the administrative state become fundamentally undemocratic, or even anti-democratic? Has government decision-making been outsourced to technocrats beyond the reach of the electorate, or does the administrative state provide essential guard rails to help elected actors govern in a responsible manner consistent with the constitutional scheme? Perhaps there is a middle ground: public policy should be decided by the people's elected representatives, but those representatives' short-term electoral considerations are tempered by the knowledge and experience of relevant experts, as Frank Vibert analyses in his contribution to this chapter (see Section V below). If constitutions are not good at defining the scope of executive power, as Professor Craig argues, and if executive overreach and dominance over the legislature is an expanding problem, as Professor Douglas-Scott argues, then perhaps a new regime of checks and balances, described by Vibert, is the solution: a replacement of the old legislative/executive/judiciary model with a new elected officials/judiciary/independent experts model using cross-connections as mutual limitations. But where is that division of powers, checks and balances found in the constitution (written or unwritten)?

Relatedly, how should one view the role of the judiciary in a representative democracy?[1] Here too there is a contrast between the courts seen as a check and balance against government overreach by the executive or the legislature (the model found in the US Constitution), and the courts seen as unelected, undemocratic institutions standing in the way of the will of the people as expressed by their elected representatives. Political undermining of the perceived legitimacy of the US Supreme Court as a neutral arbiter is discussed in Chapter 1. Professor Craig, in Section II of this chapter, notes that challenging judicial independence is a common initiative in democratic backsliding. Professor Douglas-Scott addresses recent attacks on the role of the courts in the UK. Attacking the independence – and even the role – of the judiciary has become a prominent part of President Trump's second term.[2]

The fundamental question becomes: do these institutions of government – the administrative state and the judiciary – serve an essential role in representative democracy, or are they part of why representative democracy is now in crisis? Where

[1] A deeper dive into that question was undertaken in The Putney Debates 2019, 'The Courts and the People: Friend or Foe', and the subsequent volume of published essays of the same name (Oxford, Hart Publishing, 2021).

[2] On 15 February 2025, President Trump posted as a response to critics questioning the legality of his executive orders that 'He who saves his Country does not violate any Law'.

do they sit in the relevant constitutional scheme, which often did not contemplate their existence or at least the evolution to their current roles? The essays in this chapter take very different perspectives in addressing that basic question.

II. The Impact of the Constitution

PAUL CRAIG

It was a great pleasure to take part in The Putney Debates 2023, concerning the important topic of institutions of government and their role in democracy. We were asked to focus on the legislature, executive, judiciary and the administration. The focus of the ensuing analysis is directed towards the impact of the constitution in addressing this inquiry.

Constitutions have existed for a very long time. This is a trite proposition. The relative provenance of the 'modern' written constitution is, however, contested, as are the criteria that should count in this respect, and the cause of its emergence. This is not the place for exegesis on this issue, which could well occupy an article or book. Some sense of the argumentation is, nonetheless, helpful for the ensuing analysis.

Dieter Grimm's account is helpful in this regard.[3] He argues that the modern written constitution should be dated from the American and French revolutions and the subsequent constitutional settlements. The term 'constitution' can be found earlier, but it generally denoted 'the condition or situation of a state', as shaped by 'historical development, natural features and legal order'.[4] In this sense, 'every state was in a certain "constitution", and where no constitution could be identified, no state existed'.[5] This older conception of the constitution was thus principally empirical, by way of comparison to the modern constitution that was normative, insofar as it prescribed how state power should be established. The modern constitution thus 'constituted' rule; it was 'comprehensive' in the sense of regulating the entirety of rule, and also 'universal' in that it benefited all persons subject to rule.[6] For Grimm, the distinguishing feature of the American and French revolutionaries was that their discontent was 'not limited to the person of the ruler but encompassed the system of rule'.[7] The forces that shaped the modern constitution appear from the following passage:[8]

> Historically, constitutions are a product of the conflict between the liberal bourgeoisie and the absolute monarchy. The bourgeoisie was seeking to emancipate the production

[3] D Grimm, *Constitutionalism: Past, Present, and Future* (Oxford, Oxford University Press, 2016).
[4] ibid 44.
[5] ibid 44.
[6] ibid 43.
[7] ibid 6.
[8] ibid 128–29.

> and commercial sphere from hierarchical direction and to guarantee the predictability of state power. To this end, it demanded the limitation of princely competence to questions of security and order as well as participation in state decision-making concerning issues of freedom and property. These demands were justified on the basis of natural law and were to be secured through positive law. The means was the constitution, which regardless of how it came to be in each individual case had a contractual character. It typically contained basic rights to re-define the social sphere of freedom, on the one hand, and rules regulating the holders and modalities of the exercise of state power on the other. In particular, it provided for representational bodies to communicate civic interests to the state, a guarantee that the state complied with the decisions of these bodies, together with the establishment of independent courts as a complementary safeguard.

For Dieter Grimm, the single biggest challenge to this conception of the constitution has been the changing nature of state obligations, principally, albeit not exclusively, through the emerging conception of the social state, with the consequence that the 'constitution can no longer restrict itself to organising the state apparatus and limiting state power', but must 'order not only the state, but society as well'.[9]

The role of the respective governmental institutions in relation to democracy will perforce be shaped by the constitution of the particular polity. It will stipulate with varying degrees of specificity the horizontal division of power as between executive, legislature and courts, as well as the vertical division, insofar as the latter captures the relation between individual and state, as exemplified by Bills of Rights.

Constitutions vary significantly in terms of the topics covered and the depth of the coverage. This heterogeneity should not, however, conceal the commonality of subject-matter as between written constitutions, and this is so notwithstanding the obvious fact that different polities may choose to address such issues in different ways. The common core consists of constitutional provisions that are horizontal, vertical and structural in nature.

The ***horizontal dimension*** speaks to the procedural and substantive rules that establish and regulate the principal organs of government, their structure and powers. These rules classically relate to the legislature, executive and judiciary. They will identify the respective organs and specify their powers. Procedural norms will, for example, specify how legislation is to be passed, whether special majorities are required and the like. Substantive norms will, for example, denominate the legislature and the nature of its power, the same being true for the executive and the judiciary. There can be difficulties in defining the institutions that exercise certain types of power, and there can also be difficulties in deciding on the precise powers that a certain institution should have. This is especially so in relation to executive power. Constitutions are, in general, not good at defining the executive or the scope of its powers.[10] This is so for a concatenation of reasons, a principal

[9] ibid 135.

[10] P Craig and A Tomkins (eds), *The Executive and Public Law: Power and Accountability in Comparative Perspective* (Oxford, Oxford University Press, 2005).

cause being the duality in the meaning of the term executive. It can mean the body charged with developing policy and the legislative agenda; it can also connote the body charged with implementing legislation. The increased use of agencies that exercise executive powers, and operate outside the strict confines of departmental structures, has exacerbated the difficulties in identification of the executive and the delineation of its powers. Constitutional uncertainty concerning the location and scope of executive power then generates rival theories that give diverse answers to these issues, which play out not just in law review exchanges but in high-level politics.

The ***vertical dimension*** of the constitution traditionally captures constitutional rules that regulate the interrelationship between citizen and state. The paradigm situation is rights-based constraints on government action, through a Bill of Rights enshrined in the constitution. This may form part of the initial constitution, as is commonly the case with constitutions created after 1945. It may be added later through constitutional amendment, as with the US Constitution. There will then be a range of second-order issues that must be resolved, most prominently the rights to be included in the constitutional document. There is significant choice in this respect, ranging from the traditional focus on civil and political rights to more expansive documents that also include social and economic rights, such as the EU Charter of Rights. The other central issue concerns the reach of the Bill of Rights, whether it operates only on a vertical plane, or whether it also has a horizontal impact as between private parties. This choice may be made explicitly in the Bill of Rights, but where there is uncertainty, it falls to the courts to make the interpretive choice.

The ***structural dimension*** of the constitution in nation-states that are federal is concerned with the division of power between the federal and State levels. A written constitution may also contain analogous provisions that demarcate the boundaries between central power and that of regions where there is a measure of devolution. The constitutional criteria used for such division or demarcation of power are varied, including specification of subject matter and impact across intra-State territorial boundaries. The criteria often lack pristine clarity, thereby sowing the seeds for contestation as to the boundaries of power that fall to be resolved in the courts. This uncertainty can impact diverse issues, including the allocation of regulatory authority as between the federal and State levels, and the federal constraints on State rules concerning who can vote in federal elections.

There will, however, always be an unwritten element in all written constitutions, even those that are more detailed. There may be issues that were never addressed in the constitution because they were never thought about by those who drafted the document. There may be certain constitutional provisions, whether horizontal or vertical, which are set at a high level of abstraction, thereby requiring further specification through legislation, judicial interpretation or administrative practice, or an admixture of all three.

Constitutions vary significantly when judged by a plethora of criteria. A significant factor in this respect is the constitution's relative breadth or narrowness, as judged by the range of its coverage and the detail thereof. To put the point more starkly, constitutions can be relatively fat or thin. There is no a priori reason to prefer one over the other. The choice between the two can be the result of conscious constitutional design, or adventitious historical circumstance flowing from the founding constituent moment. A range of considerations may well play into the option thus selected. The choice will have consequences. Thus, other things being equal, the greater the constitutional coverage, the more issues are taken off the agenda of normal politics, or the normal political process is circumscribed. This, in turn, prompts inquiry into the problem of over-constitutionalising.

This can be exemplified by discourse in the EU, most notably by Dieter Grimm.[11] His central thesis is that the EU Treaties are over-constitutionalised, with the consequence that issues are thereby taken off the agenda of normal politics, notwithstanding the fact that they might be regarded as within the province of ordinary law in Member States:

> In the EU the crucial difference between the rules for political decisions and the decisions themselves is to a large extent levelled.[12] It is inherent in the nature of constitutions that they function as the framework for political decisions, with the consequence that elections do not matter as far as constitutional law extends.[13] There may be too little constitutionalism, but there may also be too much, with the consequence that the democratic process is fettered.[14] While there are no universally applicable principles for determining the content of a constitution, the function of constitutions is to legitimise and to limit political power, not to replace it,[15] with the consequence that constitutions are a framework for politics, not the blueprint for all political decisions.[16]

For Grimm, the EU Treaties fulfil many functions of national constitutions, specifying matters such as the inter-institutional distribution of power, the mode of law-making, and the respective competence of the EU and Member States. They also go significantly beyond the remit of national constitutions, with the consequence that a wide range of matters becomes constitutionalised and taken off the agenda of normal politics. The effect of this is further enhanced by the constitutional doctrines of direct effect and supremacy, which transformed the four economic freedoms from 'objective principles for legislation into subjective rights of the market participants who could claim them against the Member States before the national courts'.[17]

This then meant that there were two modes of EU integration. The Treaty precepts could be advanced through legislation enacted by the EU institutions, or they could be taken forward through judicial decisions, which were imbued

[11] D Grimm, 'The Democratic Costs of Constitutionalising: The European Case' (2015) 21 *European Law Journal* 460.
[12] ibid 470.
[13] ibid 463.
[14] ibid 464.
[15] ibid 465.
[16] ibid 465.
[17] ibid 467.

with considerable force through direct effect and supremacy.[18] Member States had limited influence over the latter, and this was particularly important since the lack of differentiation between the constitutional law level and the ordinary law level meant that the 'constitutionalisation of the treaties immunises the Commission and particularly the European Court of Justice against any attempt by the democratically responsible institutions of the EU to react to the Court's jurisprudence by changing the law'.[19] For Grimm, the remedy was to limit the EU Treaties to their truly constitutional elements and downgrade other Treaty provisions that were not constitutional in nature to the status of secondary law.

The issue of constitutionalisation and over- and under-constitutionalisation is also relevant for unwritten constitutions, and the answer will depend on the relative breadth and depth of the constitution's coverage. It is possible in theory for an unwritten constitution to be relatively dense in terms of the mesh of rules that speak to constitutional issues. The empirical reality tends to the contrary, such that the constitutional frame is more skeletal in this respect. This is more especially so where the dominant constitutional principle is parliamentary sovereignty, which weakens the binding force of other constitutional constraints. There is then a greater danger of under-constitutionalisation. The UK is almost certainly one of the most under-constitutionalised countries in the world. It is a choice that we made since the seventeenth century when parliamentary sovereignty became a reality. The orthodox reading of parliamentary sovereignty is that Parliament is omnipotent and thus can be subject to no substantive or procedural limits. This precept is subject to one exception, which is that Parliament cannot bind its successors. The thesis is thus one of continuing parliamentary sovereignty, such that each successive Parliament is invested with the same omnipotence as its forebears, thereby reflecting the normative claim that each Parliament is entitled to the same authority flowing from the fact that it has equal democratic pedigree to the Parliaments that preceded it. The possible twin qualifications to this proposition are well-known and do not warrant detailed explication here. They relate to the possibility of procedural constraints on sovereignty, whereby Parliament would be bound by manner and form provisions contained in earlier legislation, unless and until they are altered; and to the possibility that the courts might, in extreme circumstances, refuse to apply legislation that is deeply problematic in terms of substance.

There are to be sure constitutional conventions and the like as to how power is used; there are constraints that flow from the rule of law; there are limits that flow from what is deemed to be politically acceptable. This does not alter the point being made here, which is that the very constitutional frame in the UK, which places parliamentary sovereignty centre stage, is in itself predicated on, and reflective of,

[18] J Weiler, 'The Community System: The Dual Character of Supranationalism' (1981) 1 *Yearbook of European Law* 267; J Weiler, 'The Transformation of Europe' (1991) 100 *Yale Law Journal* 2403, 2412–31; P Craig, 'Once Upon a Time in the West: Direct Effect and the Federalization of EEC Law' (1992) 12 *Oxford Journal of Legal Studies* 453.

[19] Grimm (n 11) 471.

a relationship between the institutions of government and democracy. It vests the choices as to the more particular modality that the democratic state should assume squarely in Parliament, the legislative output of which is not subject to constraint as to substance or form.

These possible qualifications should not mask the centrality of parliamentary sovereignty to the UK unwritten constitution or the contrast with the basic precepts of written constitutions. The foundational starting point of written constitutions is the distinction between ordinary politics and the constitution; the latter circumscribes the former, such that the terrain of ordinary politics is bounded by the constitution. The foundational starting point of the UK unwritten constitution is that parliamentary sovereignty is the principal constitutional principle; the terrain of ordinary politics is boundless and parliamentary sovereignty instantiates and elevates ordinary statute as the vehicle for its delivery.

The justifications proffered for the status accorded to parliamentary sovereignty have differed over the course of 400 years in the UK. For William Blackstone, the ascription of such sovereignty was expressly predicated on the idea of constitutional balance, whereby King, Lords and Commons, would act as a mutual check on each other. He was clear that in the absence of such balance, there would be a danger of tyranny. For Albert Venn Dicey, the ascription of such power was expressly predicated on the idea of self-correcting parliamentary democracy, which captured the idea that power vested in the people who elected the MPs, that the MPs controlled the executive, and hence because of this upward trajectory, neither the executive nor Parliament would hurt the body politic. Neither rationale is applicable in the modern day.

The modern case for parliamentary sovereignty rests squarely on its democratic legitimacy flowing from the extended franchise. There is undoubtedly normative force in this precept. It should nonetheless be acknowledged that there are limits to this foundational precept. This is in part because the same foundational precept has not been found conclusive by almost any other country in the world. It is in part because the executive continues to dominate the legislature, with the consequence that radical shifts in the direction of executive policy can have a very marked impact on the country in a very short space as time, as exemplified by experience over the last decade. It is in part yet again because the first-past-the-post electoral system, although based on universal franchise, repeatedly produces governments that have only secured a minority of the vote.

There is then a greater danger of under-constitutionalisation in the UK. Whether this would be alleviated by a written constitution depends in large part on the content thereof, and its animating principles. Thus, a UK written constitution crafted on the bedrock of parliamentary sovereignty could still be under-constitutionalised. Having said this, it should be acknowledged that the very ascription of the label under-constitutionalised to such a putative written constitution is predicated on certain normative assumptions, the principal one being that Parliament should not have such legal omnipotence. This assumption is normatively contestable, but so too is the contrary assumption.

It is clear from modern as well as past events that the existence of a written constitution which is founded on democratic impulses, and designed to protect democracy, may fail to do so. This is readily apparent from the extensive literature on democratic backsliding, exemplified by the situation in Poland and Hungary. It denotes, in the words of Bermeo, 'the state-led debilitation or elimination of any of the political institutions that sustain an existing democracy'.[20]

> Elected executives weaken checks on executive power one by one, undertaking a series of institutional changes that hamper the power of opposition forces to challenge executive preferences. Disassembling of institutions that might challenge the executive is done through legal channels, often using newly elected constitutional assemblies or referenda. Existing courts or legislatures may also be used, in cases where supporters of the executive gain majority control of such bodies. Indeed, the defining feature of executive aggrandisement is that institutional change is either put to some sort of vote or legally decreed by a freely elected official – meaning that the change can be framed as having resulted from a democratic mandate.[21]

If the governing party wishes to emasculate the constitutional status quo, it is techniques of this nature that it will resort to. Statal legitimacy generated by a constitution is undermined through the executive aggrandisement that is central to backsliding. Constitutions embody the horizontal structural attributes of the system, delineating the legislative, executive and judicial branches of government and their respective powers; they also commonly contain vertical provisions concerning the relation between citizen and state, as epitomised by rights-based protection against the government. The loss of independence, de facto and de jure, of key state institutions, such as courts, government agencies and the like, undermines the foundations on which the constitution was constructed and the legitimacy that is attendant thereon. Rather than overnight breakdown, 'democratic backsliding is a death by a thousand cuts, in which power-hungry executives slice away at fundamental institutional checks and balances in ways that ultimately distort pluralism and political competition'.[22]

Challenge to judicial independence is commonly in the forefront of such initiatives. This is exemplified by the situation in Hungary. During Hungary's transition from communism in 1989–1990, constitutional drafters sought to avoid a parliament in which small parties could not form stable majority coalitions and an entrenched constitution that would be too difficult to change. The election law thus favoured larger parties, and the new constitution could be amended by a single two-thirds majority of parliament. The election law enabled the Fidesz party in 2010 to secure 68 per cent of the seats in Parliament based on 53 per cent of the vote, thereby giving it the required two-thirds majority to amend the constitution, which it did 12 times during its first year in office. This included the removal of the constraint

[20] N Bermeo, 'On Democratic Backsliding' (2016) 27(1) *Journal of Democracy* 5, 5.

[21] ibid 10–11.

[22] L Cianetti and S Hanley, 'The End of the Backsliding Paradigm' (2021) 32(1) *Journal of Democracy* 66, 66.

concerning the writing of a new constitution and attacks on the judicial system. The Constitutional Court had for 20 years been an important check on government, and it was therefore important for the success of Fidesz initiatives that it should be disabled. The new Constitution duly provided that the governing party could nominate candidates to the Court, thereby obviating the need for multiparty backing. Fidesz increased the number of judges from eight to fifteen and installed its loyalists in the new positions. It also limited the Court's jurisdiction and, by constitutional amendment, repealed all Constitutional Court decisions prior to 1 January 2012, when the new Constitution entered into force, with the result that precedent from earlier decisions could no longer be invoked in new cases. There were, in addition, serious incursions on the independence of the ordinary judiciary.[23]

It is clear, moreover, that democracy can be undermined through weaknesses of constitutional design, which may not be apparent at the outset of the constitutional founding, but which become apparent later, more especially when everyday politics becomes more divisive. The dangers that currently beset US democracy can be taken by way of example. The electoral system is premised on State control of voting districts, coupled with State control over voting arrangements at the time of elections. There is room for contestation as to the historical rationale for this constitutional regime, but it lends itself not only to gerrymandering, but also as evident post the 2020 election, to attempts by State legislatures to frame voting rules in State legislation so as to favour their own party. The electoral regime is central to the democratic regime that emerges from the popular vote. If it is distorted in this manner, or if as in the case of Trump, there is repeated baseless claim that the election was stolen, then the democratic foundation for government is thereby severely shaken.

III. Dominance of the Executive[24]

SIONAIDH DOUGLAS-SCOTT

A. Introduction

The very topic of this panel – *Institutions of Government and Their Role in Democracy* – brings to mind so many questions and issues.

[23] KL Scheppele, 'Autocracy under Cover of the Transnational Legal Order' in G Shaffer et al (eds), *Constitution-Making and Transnational Legal Order* (Cambridge, Cambridge University Press, 2019) ch 7; L Sólyom, 'The Rise and Decline of Constitutional Culture in Hungary' in A von Bogdandy and P Sonnevend (eds), *Constitutional Crisis in the European Constitutional Area: Theory, Law and Politics in Hungary and Romania* (Oxford, Hart Publishing, 2015) Ch 1.

[24] This contribution was originally written in 2023 and provides a critique of executive governance in Britain in 2023 and in the five or so years before then. It does not examine events since the election of the Labour Government in July 2024, although – at least at time of writing – its argument remains relevant to the new administration.

A preliminary question might be why the focus on representative democracy (indicated by the panel title *Institutions of Government*), given the possibility of participatory or direct democracy becoming an institutional force in the UK – as, for example, raised by the Brexit referendum.[25]

There is also the question of how, institutionally, democracy can be said to work across the UK when, within large swathes of its territory, within its component nations and provinces, there are issues of a democratic nature. During 2023 (and many other periods of time), the Northern Ireland Assembly was not functioning, in that instance, because one party (the Democratic Unionist Party) refused to participate, given they would no longer occupy the role of First Minister. Furthermore, Scotland has been denied the possibility of holding a second independence referendum, an issue that has been cast by the Scottish National Party as one of democracy, of the Scottish people's right to choose.

Another issue stems from a major criticism of the EU, often made by eurosceptics, namely, that it contained a democratic deficit. However, we can turn this on its head and highlight that there also exist democratic deficits in British law and politics. All of Britain's major institutions – the Crown, Parliament, the Judiciary, the Civil Service, the Military, the Church, the Media – indeed the UK's basic constitutional order – were established in pre-democratic times, and it is a pertinent question how far some have adapted to democracy. Tony Wright noted how:

> In the First World War centenary commemorations, the fact that most of the men slaughtered on the Somme could not vote … went unremarked.[26] [However, after the Fourth Reform Act of 1918 and extension of women's franchise in 1928, most adults in Britain had the vote. Yet there still exist inequalities of wealth, race, gender and power in Britain.]

All of these issues raise the question of what we mean by democracy in the first place – it is 'a most promiscuous word', as Bernard Crick once wrote.[27] However, democracy is a concept too promiscuous for detailed consideration within the limited scope of this chapter, I'm afraid, and, as will be seen, I dodge this question and restrict myself to considering the ways in which the executive impacts democracy in the UK.

Therefore, putting these initial but salient questions aside, this contribution focuses on the dominance of the executive (more particularly, of the UK government) as a decisive feature of democracy, or not, in the UK today – because so many other problems for UK democracy seem to grow out of this dominance.

[25] A point made by, eg, Vernon Bogdanor in 'The EU Referendum Shows How the Sovereignty of Britain's People Can Now Trump Its Parliament' *The Daily Telegraph*, 26 June 2016.

[26] T Wright, 'Democracy in Britain: Retrospect and Prospect' in A Gamble and T Wright (eds), *Rethinking Democracy* (London, Wiley-Blackwell, 2019) 191.

[27] B Crick, *In Defense of Politics* (Chicago, University of Chicago Press, 1993) 56.

As a starting point, it is an intrinsic feature of democracy in the broad sense (and, of course, of key constitutional principles – the rule of law and separation of powers) that executive authority is not absolute. And so state constitutions have been crafted, or evolved, to ensure that a system of checks and balances applies to render executive authority less absolute. But have such checks and balances operated effectively in contemporary Britain?

This section highlights what I take to be some of the major problems of executive dominance in the UK in a very broad, general way, with the overall reflection that such problems are liable to cripple democracy in the UK.

B. Executive Dominance Over Parliament

Britain follows the parliamentary constitutional model. The government is drawn from and nested within Parliament. This means there exists no strict separation of powers, and although the government is supposedly responsible or accountable to Parliament, this arrangement has not always functioned effectively – which is why UK courts have increasingly, by means of judicial review, been looked to as a source of some sort of legal accountability for the government's actions.

The British tradition has been one of 'strong government', based on a first-past-the-post system, rather than pluralist power-sharing or participatory democracy. This situation might be summed up by saying that it features a powerful and predominant executive that dominates Parliament, and it is questionable whether there exist sufficient constitutional checks and balances.

One example of how the executive dominates Parliament is provided by events during the minority Conservative government from 2017–19, when Parliament sought to exert itself and MPs tried to take greater control of affairs to shape the form that Brexit took, most particularly after Theresa May's Brexit deal had been voted down (by the largest majority in parliamentary history, on 15 January 2019). Times of minority government are not usually cited as the best illustration of executive dominance. Nonetheless, even then, because the government controlled the agenda for Parliament, it was very hard for backbench MPs (ie majority party non-government MPs) to take action. As a result, some of the most crucial parliamentary happenings were forced to take place in the margins of parliamentary affairs – over procedures, motions, amendments to motions or even to amendments, 'humble addresses', and references to standing orders – which sidelined and obscured their impact. It is much easier for the government to control parliamentary processes than for backbench MPs to assert authority.

i. Executive Dominance of Legislation

Although the principle of parliamentary sovereignty applies in the UK, this usually takes the form of the government acting through Parliament to implement its programme of legislation, and so the Executive dominates. Apart from rare chances, such as Private Members' Bills, the legislative initiative lies with the executive, which has also striven to control the legislature through patronage or the party whipping system. The Elections Act 2022 (which requires photo identification to vote and may disproportionately impact democratic participation) was driven through Parliament in the face of objections from backbench MPs, and there were similar issues with the Police, Crime, Sentencing and Courts Act 2022, the Nationality and Borders Act 2022, the Illegal Migration Bill 2023, and the Public Order Act 2023. Without government support, it is very difficult for backbenchers, even with cross-party support, to curb any perceived government abuses, especially where the government has a large majority.

Moreover, (contrary to a strict theory of the separation of powers) the executive has considerable powers of its own to legislate. Delegated legislation (commonly taking the form of statutory instruments) is drafted by the executive and is now frequently used[28] for administrative convenience. Both the Covid pandemic and Brexit have been used by the UK government to justify the use of secondary legislation for wide-ranging purposes – even to limit fundamental rights without any parliamentary sanction. UK Ministers have increasingly attempted to use statutory instruments rather than Bills (ie primary legislation) to achieve their policy objectives, as these receive much less scrutiny than primary legislation and take up less parliamentary time. 'Henry VIII powers' – which enable Ministers to amend or repeal primary legislation by statutory instrument – are common, despite their potential for serious constitutional implications, and many Acts of Parliament crafted to effect Britain's departure from the EU were replete with such 'HenryVIII' clauses. Moreover, statutory instruments, with only a few exceptions, may not be amended by Parliament. In such circumstances, both Houses of Parliament are confronted with an uninviting 'take it or leave it' legislative measure, amounting to this: either accept a statutory instrument even if it appears deeply flawed or reject it entirely even if some elements are satisfactory. Such an approach does little to promote the effective scrutiny of secondary legislation.

Concerns regarding the anti-democratic nature of secondary legislation have been expressed by a variety of parliamentary committees, as well as by external experts such as the Hansard Society. The House of Lords Secondary Legislation Scrutiny Committee recently produced a critical report,[29] highlighting the constitutional implications of the government's heavy reliance on delegated legislation, 'skeleton' Bills lacking sufficient detail, and 'Henry VIII' powers. To

[28] According to Parliament UK in 2023, approximately 3,500 SIs are adopted every year.

[29] See eg House of Lords Secondary Legislation Scrutiny Committee 38th Report of Session 2021–22 'What Next? The Growing Imbalance between Parliament and the Executive: End of Session Report 2021–22', HL Paper 200.

be sure, this imbalance in legislative power is not new. However, Brexit and the Covid-19 pandemic have exacerbated problems with the secondary legislative system and, in spite of these shortcomings, the secondary legislative system has proved resistant to reform, so the Executive continues to dominate the process.

C. The Prerogative

Government Ministers also have many powers which are not statutory in nature but exercised under the royal prerogative, which is often vague and untransparent. This vagueness has provided further scope for Executive dominance. The royal prerogative is a form of legally binding, non-statutory law-making by the Crown, now usually exercised by government Ministers. Lord Roskill famously said that with prerogative, he could hear 'the clanking of medieval chains of the ghosts of the past'.[30] Prior to 2000, the executive's prerogative powers were not much questioned. However, this started to change with the publication of the 2004 report 'Taming the Prerogative'[31] by the Public Administration Committee led by Tony Wright, which provided a wide-ranging account and critique of prerogative powers. So far, however, attempts to put the prerogative on a codified statutory footing have been unsuccessful and so, in its very vagueness, it remains open to government abuse.

Nonetheless, Parliament's ability to curb the exercise of the prerogative is contentious. Even though there now may be a weak precedent (which some attempt to elevate to the status of constitutional convention) requiring that the government obtain parliamentary consent before committing British armed forces to military intervention overseas, this is not very well-established.[32] In 2018, (then) Prime Minister Theresa May committed UK forces to military action in Syria without first taking the matter to Parliament for a vote. This left the status of the war powers 'convention' ambiguous, which highlights the weakness of relying on convention in this respect.

Additionally, Britain's uncodified constitution leaves many key constitutional issues related to use of the prerogative unsettled. Brexit revealed the prerogative's status as particularly ill-defined and potentially wide-ranging in the UK. It is not unusual for the executive to control much of foreign affairs and, in the UK, treaty-making and foreign affairs more generally are usually managed by the executive,

[30] *Council of Civil Service Unions v Minister for the Civil Service* [1985] AC 374, 417 (Lord Roskill), quoting *United Australia Ltd v Barclays Bank Ltd* [1941] AC 1, 29 (Lord Atkin).

[31] House of Commons Public Administration Select Committee, *Taming the Prerogative: Strengthening Ministerial Accountability to Parliament*, Fourth Report of Session 2003–04.

[32] See Research Briefing, *Parliamentary Approval for Military Action*, House of Commons Library, 17 April 2018.

often by means of the prerogative, but also often with some sort of participation by the legislature. However, it took litigation to establish that the government could not use the prerogative to trigger Article 50 TEU (and so initiate the process of leaving the EU) without Parliament's consent – a principle established in the first *Miller* case.[33] *Miller I* also acknowledged the crucial role of Parliament in protecting rights, as well as underlining that a UK statute may not be repealed by prerogative alone.

After the *Miller* decision, Parliament enacted legislation consenting to Article 50 being triggered and the Brexit process was set in motion. This took the form of the EU (Notification of Withdrawal) Act 2017, a minuscule piece of legislation with only one brief provision: 'The prime minister may notify, under Article 50(2) of the Treaty on European Union, the United Kingdom's intention to withdraw from the EU.' This legislation has been subsequently criticised by Mark Elliott as giving the government 'a blank cheque',[34] so maybe the consequences of *Miller I* did not illustrate Parliament's victory over executive dominance through prerogative use.

i. Unlawful Prorogation of Parliament

An extreme example of the executive attempting to assert its power of Parliament took place in the autumn of 2019, when (then) UK Prime Minister Boris Johnson prorogued (ie suspended) Parliament for five weeks. This had the drastic result of closing down Parliament altogether at a crucial moment in UK affairs. During that time, Parliament could not sit. No legislation could be adopted, nor could Parliament call the government to account for any actions it was taking. The deadline under the Article 50 TEU process was soon to expire, and without a Withdrawal Agreement negotiated with the EU, there were fears that Britain would leave the EU with no deal at all, with all sorts of dire consequences. It was seen as essential that, in this crucial time, Parliament be able to sit, and call the government to account on Brexit. Many suspected the prorogation was an attempt by the Prime Minister to 'shut down Parliament' to prevent it from scrutinising his handling of Brexit.

The issue of the royal prerogative reared its head. The power to prorogue Parliament is a prerogative power exercised by the Prime Minister with the consent of the monarch, although it had never been exercised for such a long period of time.[35] A legal action was instituted,[36] to test the Prime Minister's ability to act by prerogative alone to shut down Parliament, which went to the UK Supreme Court.

[33] *R (Miller) v Secretary of State for Exiting the EU* [2017] UKSC 5.

[34] M Elliott, 'Why on Earth Didn't Parliament Take Control When It Had the Chance?' *Prospect*, 16 January 2019.

[35] It is usually just exercised to suspend Parliament briefly for agreed recesses, such as the summer vacation.

[36] *Miller/Cherry v Prime Minister* [2019] UKSC 41. Two separate actions were brought – one in the Scottish courts (by Joanna Cherry QC, then a Scottish National Party MP) and another in England (by

In a unanimous judgment (in itself striking), the UK Supreme Court held that the prorogation was unlawful. The first issue was whether the actual issue (of Prime Ministerial advice to prorogue) itself was justiciable – ie a matter that can be determined by a court, or instead a matter reserved for 'high policy and politics'. The UK Supreme Court found it justiciable and, as if to stress the orthodoxy of this holding, cited case law going back to 1610 in support ('the King hath no prerogative but that which the law of the land allows him'[37]). As was stated in the *Miller/Cherry* judgment:

> Although the courts cannot decide political questions, the fact that a legal dispute concerns the conduct of politicians, or arises from a matter of political controversy, has never been sufficient reason for the courts to refuse to consider it.[38]

The Supreme Court went on to find that this prorogation had the effect of frustrating or preventing Parliament from carrying out its constitutional functions. As the Court stated, 'The effect upon the fundamentals of our democracy was extreme', but 'No justification for taking action with such an extreme effect has been put before the court'. 'The Court is bound to conclude, therefore, that the decision to advise Her Majesty to prorogue parliament was unlawful.'[39] This meant that Parliament had to be recalled immediately, and it was as if Parliament had never been prorogued.

One might interpret *Miller/Cherry* as robustly upholding the UK Constitution, relying on old and venerated precedents. Judicial review proved to be an important check on an overreaching executive, which had exploited both its prerogative powers and populist sentiment to weaken Parliament. However, the Supreme Court judgment has also been attacked, and this will be considered below in the context of attacks on judicial review.

D. Unlimited Parliamentary Sovereignty

Both *Miller* judgments might seem to have checked executive overreach and reinforced parliamentary sovereignty, which is often seen as the key principle of the UK Constitution. If Parliament is sovereign, surely this can restrain the Government?

Not necessarily. It should be stressed that parliamentary sovereignty is not really the sovereignty of every MP, but legislative sovereignty, which is very often simply *executive* sovereignty, enabling a government (usually elected by a minority of the electorate) to enforce its legislative agenda through Parliament. This gives the government considerable power, because parliamentary sovereignty is

Gina Miller). Both actions were consolidated in the UK Supreme Court.

[37] This statement was famously made by Sir Edward Coke CJ, in *The Case of Proclamations* [1610] EWHC KB J22.

[38] *Miller/Cherry* at para 31.

[39] All extracts from *Miller/Cherry* [2019] UKSC 41.

interpreted in the UK as excluding the possibility of legal entrenchment. Any law, however, fundamental, is only as protective as the parliamentary majority of its day permits it to be. The British Constitution is often vaunted for its great flexibility. But flexibility is not always a good thing, as when it enables repeal or amendment of any provision with the ease of a parliamentary majority of one. Therefore, human rights, even those in primary legislation, have a precarious status, vulnerable to repeal by ordinary legislation,[40] which is what a former Lord Chancellor (in the last administration), Dominic Raab, had in mind for the Human Rights Act 1998. Another example is provided by the fact that the Scottish and Welsh Parliaments have been declared to be 'permanent' in devolution legislation,[41] but these provisions could be repealed by new legislation, given the absence of any *legal* entrenchment in the UK Constitution.

The government has also used parliamentary sovereignty as a shield in its attempts to violate international law by claiming, as then Attorney General Suella Braverman did, regarding the UK Internal Market Bill, that parliamentary sovereignty – ie the government's parliamentary majority – governed, rather than the international law to which the UK had already committed itself in treaties, and which the Bill appeared to violate. The Northern Ireland Protocol Bill[42] was also strongly criticised for violating international law at its second reading by senior backbenchers (including Theresa May – by then no longer Prime Minister) as well as by many external experts.[43] Indeed, (then) Northern Ireland Secretary Brandon Lewis actually acknowledged in Parliament that the Bill would break international law in a 'very specific and limited way' (by allowing the UK to override parts of the EU-UK Withdrawal Agreement). Such action led to the resignation of the then head of the Government Legal Department, and criticism from several former Prime Ministers and Conservative leaders, plus external expert bodies such as the Institute for Government and Public Law Project.

Yet the government continues to deploy the parliamentary sovereignty of UK Acts of Parliament as a defence and means to ignore the application of international law. The United Nations refugee agency raised similar anxieties about the (Conservative government, led by Rishi Sunak) government's policy of 'offshoring' asylum seekers to Rwanda – a policy containing measures considered illegal under international law, but legislated in domestic legislation and such a policy was actually found to be illegal by the UK Supreme Court.[44]

[40] Though the Human Rights Act has been classified as a 'constitutional statute' (*Thoburn v Sunderland CC* [2002] EWHC 195, per Laws LJ at para 62), namely one that may only be repealed by express and not implied repeal by the legislature.

[41] Namely Scotland Act 2016, s 1 and Wales Act 2017, s 1.

[42] This Northern Ireland Protocol was incorporated into the European Union (Withdrawal Agreement) Act 2020.

[43] See eg Bingham Centre for the Rule of Law, 'Northern Ireland Protocol Bill: A Rule of Law Analysis of Its Compliance with International Law', available at binghamcentre.biicl.org/publications/northern-ireland-protocol-bill-a-rule-of-law-analysis-of-its-compliance-with-international-law, accessed 31 May 2025.

[44] *R (on the application of AAA and others) v Home Secretary* [2023] UKSC 42.

In such an environment, where parliamentary sovereignty is used as a means to justify violations of international law and human rights, there exists a need for checks and balances, and the judiciary has been seen as a potential important element of these checks, as indeed it was in the challenge to the Rwanda asylum policy.

E. Attacks on Judicial Review

However, one result of the *Miller/Cherry* prorogation judgment was an increase in the calls for curbs on judicial review, something which had already occurred after the first *Miller* case[45] (which concerned the government's capacity to trigger Article 50 without parliamentary consent). Limiting judicial review would, of course, restrain an important check on the government. After *Miller/Cherry*, attacks on the judiciary increased exponentially. Johnson proclaimed that the UK Supreme Court got it 'wrong'. (Compare this to President Trump's tweets attacking 'so-called judges'.[46]) Courts have found against governments before in the UK, but never previously found a Prime Minister's advice (to the Queen) to be unlawful, as it was in *Miller/Cherry*. Yet the principles on which the Court relied to make its judgment in *Miller/Cherry* could not be more central – parliamentary sovereignty, accountability, control of the exercise of the prerogative. If the Courts are not able to police and uphold these, who else could, given that Parliament was then disabled? In upholding the fundamental principle of parliamentary sovereignty in *Miller/Cherry*, the Court was hardly setting itself up as a proponent of some new judge-made constitution.

To be sure, attacks on the judiciary, whether from the press or politicians, are not new. There are many examples from the 1990s and also from Home Secretaries of Labour governments in the 2000s.[47] One further well-known example was provided by Theresa May, who, while Home Secretary, famously misrepresented a judicial ruling in 2011 when she blamed a judge for blocking the deportation of a Bolivian citizen 'because he had a pet cat'. In spite of clear criticism of May's deceptive account of the case, the press continued to perpetuate the misrepresentation.[48] Nonetheless, attacks on the courts continued to increase. For example, the UK Judicial Power Project (JPP) has been particularly active in its critique of judicial review. The JPP is part of Policy Exchange, a right-wing UK think tank. On its website, the JPP claims to focus on 'the proper scope of the judicial power within

[45] *Miller v Secretary of State for Exiting the EU* [2017] UKSC 5.

[46] DJ Trump, 'The opinion of this so-called judge, which essentially takes law-enforcement away from our country, is ridiculous and will be over-turned!' (4 February 2017), x.com/realdonaldtrump/status/827867311054974976?lang=en.

[47] See eg 'Judges are failing to do their jobs, says Blunkett' *The Times*, 8 May 2003.

[48] See further, 'Catgate: Another Myth Used to Trash Human Rights' *The Guardian*, 4 October 2011, available at www.theguardian.com/law/2011/oct/04/theresa-may-wrong-cat-deportation, accessed 31 May 2025.

the constitution', contending that 'Judicial overreach increasingly threatens the rule of law and effective, democratic government'.[49]

In 2019, the then Conservative government set out specific plans (many in its 2019 election manifesto[50]) to reduce the influence of the courts. These included the proposed replacement of the Human Rights Act 1998 with a Bill of Rights (which was, however, never adopted). In addition, there were attempts in two specific areas to reduce the ability of the judiciary to act as a check on executive power – ouster clauses, and the increasing use of policies, guidance and advice rather than primary or secondary legislation. This resulted in the adoption of some actual legislation. In both the Dissolution and Calling of Parliaments Act 2022 and the Judicial Review and Courts Act 2022, ouster clauses were employed to prevent judicial review. Notably, in both statutes, the clauses are worded so as to evade the impact of the *Anisminic* judgment.[51] As for the government's increasing use of policies, guidelines and advice rather than binding legislation, this makes a government action much harder to legally challenge. This is because the adoption of what is in practice a decision through 'advice' is a means to limit judicial review, as 'advice' is not capable of having legal effect.

Politicians have also suggested the instigation of US-style political vetting for senior judges. After the prorogation decision, Iain Duncan-Smith, former Conservative party leader, was quoted in the *Daily Telegraph* saying of Lady Hale (then President of the UK Supreme Court that delivered the judgment), 'Given the radical judgment she's just made – inventing a law – if we're going to get this kind of stuff from her, is it not time for parliament scrutinise appointments to the Supreme Court?'[52] Geoffrey Cox, (then) Attorney General, also suggested overhauling the appointment process to resemble something like the US system.

An article in *The Daily Telegraph*, commenting on the *Miller/Cherry* judgment, stated: 'The very title [Supreme Court] implies ultimate judicial power of a sort that refashions our constitution along continental or American lines incompatible with our own belief in the supremacy of the voters' elected representatives.'[53] This is incorrect. The UK Supreme Court has no power of 'hard judicial review' to strike down legislation and does not function in the same way as the US Supreme

[49] Judicial Power Project, 'About the Judicial Power Project', at judicialpowerproject.org.uk/about/. For a critique, see P Craig, 'Judicial Power, the Judicial Power Project and the UK' Oxford Legal Studies Research Paper No 68/2017.

[50] The Conservative Party, *Election Manifesto 2019*, available at cchq2019.webflow.io/our-plan, accessed 31 May 2025.

[51] In the famous *Anisminic v Foreign Compensation Commission* [1969] 2 AC 147 case, the House of Lords held that a clause purporting to oust the jurisdiction of the courts to review any 'determination' was ineffective if that determination were tainted by legal error.

[52] 'Lady Hale "Revelling" in Supreme Court Judgment, Say Critics, in Row over "Girly Swots" Remark' *Daily Telegraph*, 4 October 2019.

[53] C Moore, 'Fixing the Supreme Court Should Be Boris Johnson's Constitutional Priority' *Daily Telegraph*, 8 February 2020.

Court. Judicial review in the UK does not permit courts to replace government decisions with their own; instead, it is a supervisory mechanism that reviews the lawfulness of decisions made by public bodies. This, however, has not stopped the attacks on judicial review.

The 2019 Conservative manifesto proclaimed that 'Our independent courts and legal system are respected throughout the world.' However, judicial independence was afforded little respect when Johnson openly disagreed with the Supreme Court's prorogation judgment in September 2019, nor was it in *Miller 1* in 2016, when the UK Divisional Court were declared 'enemies of the people' by the *Daily Mail*. Judicial independence continues to be under attack across the world by authoritarian regimes such as the former administration in Poland and Orban's Hungary. Majoritarian democracy will continue to be pitted against supposedly elitist, anti-majoritarian judges. Britain is not immune.

Justice Suzanne Baer, formerly of the German Constitutional Court, issued a timely reminder of the many threats to judicial independence and the rule of law that currently exist across Europe and North America when she wrote that:

> constitutionalism connects democracy and human rights, by the rule of law, and installs courts as the backup to make it work if all others do not comply anyway. Courts, then, do not replace politics but are the safety belts for democratic politics that do not hurt anyone.[54]

F. Civil Service, Regulators and the Media

Another check, or balance, to executive overreach might be provided by impartial officials, such as within the UK's Civil Service. This is a contrast to some more politicised civil service systems, such as that in the US.[55] However, within the UK, the appointment of political candidates has increased, sometimes illustrating a close association between senior officials and specific Ministers, thus making it less likely that officials counsel against controversial policies. For example, on becoming Prime Minister, Liz Truss dismissed the experienced Treasury Permanent Secretary, at an especially vulnerable time during a cost-of-living crisis,[56] apparently finding his views unamenable.

A further check on government is that provided by independent regulators and advisory bodies. Such bodies may cultivate good practice and pinpoint misconduct within government. For example, the Advisory Committee on Business

[54] S Baer, 'The Rule of – and Not by Any – Law. On Constitutionalism' (2018) 71(1) *Current Legal Problems* 339, 357.

[55] See eg P Kopecky et al, 'Party Patronage in Contemporary Democracies: Results from an Expert Survey in 22 Countries from Five Regions' (2016) 55(2) *European Journal of Political Research* 416.

[56] See eg 'Truss and Kwarteng Sacking of Top Civil Servants "Damaged Government"' *The Guardian*, 26 April 2023.

Appointments[57] may highlight or constrain potential corruption where ministers or senior officials have been appointed to new posts. Yet the last government also showed itself willing to ignore the advice of bodies regulating conduct in public office, as when Priti Patel breached the Ministerial Code.[58]

Regulators also play an important role where they formulate policies which may have a direct democratic impact, independent of ministerial control. For example, the Boundary Commission for England[59] (and its counterparts in Scotland, Wales and Northern Ireland) independently reviews parliamentary constituency boundaries – in contrast to eg the US, where the drawing of parliamentary constituencies is usually the province of state legislators and has given rise to some very contentious case law on gerrymandering.[60] Nonetheless, the last government was accused of limiting the independence of important regulators. For example, the former Commissioner for Public Appointments, Peter Riddell, criticised the last government for overtly recommending its political allies for central public appointments, as well as for attempting to 'pack' appointment interview panels. The last Government also appeared to undermine the independence of the media, by for example, attacking the BBC, discrediting its neutrality, sapping its funding, and making a controversial appointment as BBC Chairman in Richard Sharp, who was later forced to resign.

G. Direct Mandate?

Critics of the *Miller/Cherry* judgment attacked it as a check on executive power that thwarted the will of the people that Brexit be delivered. As stated, among these critics were the JPP. Although the JPP claims to emphasise the importance of parliamentary sovereignty in the British Constitution, stressing that courts have no place to question Parliament's decisions, critics of the JPP argue that its thrust is rather to strengthen the executive. Thomas Poole for example, argued that:

> … its targets seemingly include any institutional check on executive power, political as much as legal … Authoritarian rather than conservative in disposition, it treats established constitutional forms and norms as fungible, even disposable, and presses exceptional moments in the direction of a central authority delivering the 'will of the people.[61]

Such an image of a strong executive presence, delivering on the 'will of the people' was further emphasised in Boris Johnson's first statement after the General

[57] Further information is available at www.gov.uk/government/organisations/advisory-committee-on-business-appointments, accessed 31 May 2025.

[58] See 'Bullying Allegations, the Home Secretary and the Ministerial Code' (House of Lords Library, 29 October 2020).

[59] See boundarycommissionforengland.independent.gov.uk, accessed 31 May 2025.

[60] Eg 'Gerrymandering Explained' *Brennan Centre for Justice*, 9 June 2023.

[61] T Poole, 'The Executive Power Project' *LRB blog*, 2 April 2019.

Election in December 2019, in which he referred to 'members of our new one nation government – a people's government'.[62]

The suggestion that the government has a free-standing mandate from the people is redolent of the populism of a Carl Schmitt or Viktor Orban. When government Ministers find their policies constrained by the judiciary, civil service or House of Lords, they often argue such resistance is illegitimate because these are unelected institutions. The inference is that only executive government has legitimate political power because it enjoys popular democratic endorsement. Yet this is an untenable argument. Only a minority of the population votes for the government at general election, very often not on the basis of its manifesto, so this is a very limited understanding of democracy. (In any case, other institutions, such as the courts, contribute to democracy, by for example, upholding human rights.) It also replaces parliamentary sovereignty with executive sovereignty without any grounding.

H. Conclusion

Not all the issues addressed above are singular to Britain. Executive overreach is evident in many jurisdictions. However, there exist too many recent examples whereby the mechanisms of executive accountability have been weakened in the UK.

The UK has often relied on a theory of the 'political constitution'.[63] The essence of the British Constitution has long been characterised as resting on the sovereignty of Parliament, as unwritten, flexible, uncodified in nature, with political conventions and ministerial accountability often taking the place of hard law or a Constitutional Court. These accompanying political checks are, however, frequently lacking. As British Prime Minister, William Ewart Gladstone, said back in 1879, the British Constitution 'presumes more boldly than any other the good sense and good faith of those who work it'.[64] This is because the UK has no codified constitution, and relies greatly on political conventions and understandings. It also relies on the fact that those who work within politics – civil servants, politicians and their special advisors – operate with self-restraint; that, in the words of Hennessey and Blick, they 'behave themselves'. Hennessey and Blick further write:

> in the UK, we have trusted politicians to behave themselves. We have long assumed that those who rise to high office will be 'good chaps', knowing what the unwritten rules are and wanting to adhere to them, even if doing so might frustrate the attainment of their policy objectives, party political goals, or personal ambitions … A

[62] Available at www.gov.uk/government/speeches/pm-statement-in-downing-street-13-december-2019, accessed 31 May 2025.

[63] JAG Griffith, 'The Political Constitution' (1979) 42 *Modern Law Review* 1.

[64] WE Gladstone, *Gleanings of Past Years 1843–78*, Vol 1, 243.

> government-of-the-day is its custodian but not its sole owner. The constitution is a shared possession of the nation as a whole which imposes a special duty of care on Prime Ministers, Cabinets, and Parliament too.[65]

That self-restraint has now vanished. The trust in politicians has been lost. The remainder of the Hennessey and Blick article contains a long list illustrating the many ways (mostly relating to Brexit) in which those running the show are no longer 'good chaps' (or 'chapesses'). If 'good chaps' can no longer be trusted to observe unwritten conventions and understandings, political constitutionalism cannot work effectively and there is a greater need for more secure constitutional checks and legally enforceable constitutional principles. Otherwise, the UK Constitution becomes ever more susceptible to manipulation by those who are definitely not 'good chaps'.

The examples given herein of potential abuse by the executive have included the widespread use of secondary legislation with minimum scrutiny, which compromises the rule of law and sidelines Parliament; use of the prerogative to sideline Parliament; the absence of any possibility of legal entrenchment which allows government to push through major constitutional change (eg Brexit by ordinary legislation alone); an interpretation of parliamentary sovereignty which strengthens executive sovereignty, and also enables the government to ignore international law to press through domestic legislation where it has the majority to do so; the attempted weakening of judicial review; members of the executive continuing in office despite a general deterioration in standards (eg Partygate); and the politicising of formerly independent and/or neutral officials.

What, if anything, is to be done? And will the existence of a new Labour administration since July 2024 make any difference? Time will tell. However, the introduction of more trenchant enforceable procedures – those that go beyond mere customs and conventions – in some areas would help. This does not necessitate a full-scale codified Constitution, but reform to ensure the possibility of legal entrenchment of certain key issues – the field of human rights, and certain devolved powers, might be obvious areas, as well as codification of some prerogative powers.

Constitutional principles are under attack. The attacks on judicial review, as well as attempted sidelining of Parliament accompanied by a growing reliance on executive sovereignty, lead to a diminishing of the rule of law. Where will this lead? Predicting the future is challenging. But within that 'Mother of all Parliaments', it might seem we can no longer rely on the 'good chaps,' or 'chapesses', to see us through.

[65] A Blick and P Hennessy, 'Good Chaps No More? Safeguarding the Constitution in Stressful Times' (London, The Constitution Society, 2019), available at https://consoc.org.uk/wp-content/uploads/2019/11/FINAL-Blick-Hennessy-Good-Chaps-No-More.pdf, accessed 31 May 2025.

IV. Liberal Democracy and the Dangers of Meritocratic Depoliticisation

RUZHA SMILOVA*

A. Tensions in Liberal Representative Democracy

Processes of de-democratisation, observed globally in the last two decades, have triggered panic in the pro-democracy camps worldwide.[66] Explaining democracy's recurrent crises has long been a major preoccupation of political theorists. Many find the key in inherent tensions in liberal representative democracy. These tensions have been identified differently. For Margaret Canovan, the tension is between redemptive (helping constitute a people that can act together) and pragmatic (delivering good, changeable government) aspects of democracy.[67] For Jürgen Habermas it is between popular sovereignty – exercised directly or through representatives – on the one hand and rule of law and respect for individual/minority rights on the other.[68] Yascha Mounk has also argued that contemporary liberal democracies are in crisis because the balance between their constitutive elements – individual rights and rule of law, on the one hand, and democratic rule, on the other – has been lost.[69]

I will argue that the central tension underlying democracy's crisis is between equality – the fundamental value and a necessary presupposition of democracy – on the one hand, and the growing inequalities and asymmetries of power under representative government, on the other. Yet my focus is not on the tension between democracy and capitalism, often presented as a primary source of the crisis of representative democracy.[70] Rather, I identify what I believe is an even more fundamental tension. It is between the meritocratic ideal for selecting ruling elites, and for attributing value and prestige in Western liberal democracies, on the one hand, and the democratic requirement for equality – for equal participation in the democratic process, on the other.

* This study is financed by the European Union-NextGenerationEU, through the National Recovery and Resilience Plan of the Republic of Bulgaria, project No BG-RRP-2.004-000, coordinated by Sofia University St Kliment Ohridski.

[66] *Freedom in the World 2021: Democracy under Siege* (Freedom House, 2021).

[67] M Canovan, 'Trust the People! Populism and the Two Faces of Democracy' (1999) 47(1) *Political Studies* 2; M Canovan, *The People* (Cambridge, Polity Press, 2005).

[68] J Habermas, 'Constitutional Democracy: A Paradoxical Union of Contradictory Principles?' (2001) 29(6) *Political Theory* 766.

[69] Y Mounk, *The People vs Democracy* (Cambridge, MA, Harvard University Press, 2018).

[70] W Streeck, 'The Crisis in Context: Democratic Capitalism and Its Contradictions' (2011) Max-Planck-Institut für Gesellschaftsforschung, Discussion Paper 11/15; W Streeck, *Buying Time: The Delayed Crisis of Democratic Capitalism* (London, Verso Books, 2014); W Merkel, 'Is Capitalism Compatible with Democracy?' (2014) 8(2) *Zeitschrift für Vergleichende Politikwissenschaft* 109.

B. The Meritocracy Problem for Liberal Democracy

This fundamental tension, which I call the meritocracy problem for liberal democracy, helps turn representative democracy into a regime where unelected, democratically unaccountable technocratic experts uphold individual and minority rights at the expense of the popular will. This is achieved through various institutional mechanisms and practices, such as agencification, judicialisation, constitutionalisation, globalisation of decision-making, etc. The result of the mass spread of such practices is that even though meritocracy promises fair, merit-based elite recruitment and competent rule, aimed at bringing about better-results democracies, it breeds inequality, distrust, and dissatisfaction instead.

The asymmetries of power that ensue from meritocracy – most characteristically when its promises fail, but even when they are kept – open a widening gap between citizens and the governing elites. Democracy is gradually eroded, fuelling citizen resentment. The growing gap opens space for populists, who promise to restore democracy yet create deeper problems, often delivering what Yascha Mounk has aptly termed 'democracy without rights'.[71]

Many authors find the source of the current crisis of representative democracy in the many failures of meritocracy.[72] Probably the crucial shortcoming of meritocratic elite recruitment and rule in electoral democracies is that it inadvertently promotes *depoliticisation*: important aspects of the political process are increasingly insulated from democratic say, and decision-making is gradually transferred from the citizens to credentialed elites, to experts. The promise is that electing representatives based on personal merit – or transferring more power to non-elected experts – will contribute to better-quality government. However, this promise not only turns our democracies into a non-representative 'diploma democracy',[73] but, and even more importantly, is in tension with the fundamental democratic right to participate on equal terms in decision-making. The right to democratic say includes the 'right to be wrong', as Jeremy Waldron has put it.[74] People have a democratic right to oust even their 'best' representatives, even when this ousting would threaten to bring about worse quality government.

[71] Y Mounk, *The People vs Democracy* (Cambridge, MA, Harvard University Press, 2018).

[72] C Hayes, *Twilight of the Elites: America After Meritocracy* (New York, Crown Publishing Group, 2012); N Fraser, 'The End of Progressive Neoliberalism' *Dissent* (2 January 2017); I Krastev, *After Europe* (Philadelphia, University of Pennsylvania Press, 2017); M Sandel, *The Tyranny of Merit: What's Become of the Common Good?* (London, Penguin, 2020); D Goodhart, *Head Hand Heart: The Struggle for Dignity and Status in the 21st Century* (London, Penguin, 2020).

[73] M Bovens and A Wille, *Diploma Democracy: The Rise of Political Meritocracy* (Oxford, Oxford University Press, 2017).

[74] J Waldron, 'Participation: The Right of Rights' (1998) *Proceedings of the Aristotelian Society* 307.

This right of democratic say is threatened by diverse mechanisms of depoliticisation, introduced with the benign intent to insulate quality governance from the pressures and likely mistakes of popular majoritarian politics. Rights-protecting institutions such as courts are among the counter-majoritarian institutions that have enjoyed the highest acclaim. Courts are tasked with overseeing the legislature and the executive for the constitutionality of their acts and with protecting unpopular individuals and minorities against the vagaries of the popular will. Yet despite the high legitimacy enjoyed by human rights protection instruments, and despite the universal acclaim for human rights – the 'the last utopia'[75] – criticisms against the human rights movement, even against constitutionalism, are growing.[76] That courts contribute to the growing depoliticisation of democratic politics is behind some of these criticisms.

C. De-democratisation and the Rise of Democratic Illiberalism

The globally observed de-democratisation goes under different names: 'democratic recession',[77] 'regression',[78] 'democratic backsliding',[79] 'democratic erosion',[80] even 'democratic decay'.[81] These labels, however, only partly describe the specific nature of the current wave of de-democratisation – that what is currently being eroded is the *liberal* component in the liberal-democracy nexus in particular. This omission is somewhat perplexing given that in 2007 analysts had already identified the sources of the current problems of the regime as problems of liberalism specifically. Ivan Krastev, for example, sought it in the 'death of the liberal consensus' and the 'rise of democratic illiberalism'.[82] The liberal component of the liberal-democracy nexus can thus be seen both as the main culprit for the

[75] S Moyn, *The Last Utopia: Human Rights in History* (Cambridge, MA, Harvard University Press, 2012).

[76] ibid; S Moyn, *Not Enough* (Cambridge, MA, Harvard University Press, 2018); S Hopgood, *The Endtimes of Human Rights* (Ithaca, NY, Cornell University Press, 2013); E Posner, *The Twilight of Human Rights Law* (New York, Oxford University Press, 2014); C Mouffe, *For a Left Populism* (London, Verso Books, 2018); M Loughlin, *Against Constitutionalism* (Cambridge, MA, Harvard University Press, 2022).

[77] L Diamond, 'Facing up to the Democratic Recession' (2015) 26(1) *Journal of Democracy* 141.

[78] J Rupnik and J Zielonka, 'Introduction: The State of Democracy 20 Years On: Domestic and External Factors' (2012) 27(1) *East European Politics and Societies and Cultures* 3.

[79] N Bermeo, 'On Democratic Backsliding' (2016) 27(1) *Journal of Democracy* 5.

[80] T Ginsburg and A Huq, *How to Save a Constitutional Democracy* (Chicago, University of Chicago Press, 2018).

[81] T Daly, 'Democratic Decay: Conceptualising an Emerging Research Field' (2019) 11(1) *Hague Journal on the Rule of Law* 9.

[82] I Krastev, 'Is East-Central Europe Backsliding? The Strange Death of the Liberal Consensus' (2007) 18(4) *Journal of Democracy* 56.

observed problems with democracy, but also as the main casualty. Indeed, illiberal democracy – the political regime Viktor Orbán and his associates promote as an alternative to liberal democracy, is an attempt to develop an attractive model of democracy without liberal components. Underlying the illiberal democracy experiment is an ideological construct – 'democratic illiberalism'. Even if not fully coherent, it has a distinct ideational core, sufficiently strong to serve as a model of political order, alternative to liberal democracy.[83]

The explanation for the liberal malaise is well known: liberalism has become the globally hegemonic ideology once its twentieth-century totalitarian rivals – fascism and communism – faded away. As no alternative regime pressed a plausible challenge to liberalism for over 20 years, this contributed to liberalism's image of the regime-without-alternative to be imitated by all.[84] The ideological triumph of liberalism, however, made liberal elites complacent,[85] unable or unwilling to address some of the pressing problems of societies in the liberal age. This failure left many both dissatisfied with liberalism's performance as well as resentful towards 'meritocratic' elites, perceived to be too distant, even disloyal, to society at large.[86]

D. 'Democracy without Choice' and Depoliticisation

A related yet distinct way to conceptualise the problem was already alluded to above: the delicate balance between the two constitutive elements of liberal democracy, which are always in a tense relationship, has been broken. The trend in recent years was of the liberal component overtaking the democratic one. As Mounk puts it, liberal democracy has gradually turned into a rule of 'rights without democracy', where unelected, unaccountable, 'technocratic' experts uphold liberal rights at the expense of the popular will.

This state of affairs was reached through the combined forces of various mechanisms of outsourcing decision-making to non-elected bodies – a process often summarised under the rubric 'technocracy'.[87] Depoliticisation is a more apt term to describe these phenomena, in my view. It clearly spells out the mechanisms through which democracy is eroded when decision-making is outsourced to experts. When politics – democratic discussion and decision-making – is removed, democracy is emptied of its democratic content and remains democracy in name

[83] R Smilova, 'The Ideational Core of Democratic Illiberalism' in A Sajó et al (eds), *Routledge Handbook of Illiberalism* (Abingdon, Routledge, 2021) 177.

[84] I Krastev and S Holmes, *The Light That Failed: A Reckoning* (London, Allen Lane, 2019).

[85] W Galston, *Anti-Pluralism: The Populist Threat to Liberal Democracy* (New Haven, CT, Yale University Press, 2018) 17.

[86] Krastev (n 82) 90.

[87] F Fischer, *Technocracy and the Politics of Expertise* (Newbury Park, CA, Sage, 1990).

only. Depoliticisation works through multiple mechanisms: 'agencification'[88] – outsourcing decision-making on complex issues requiring technical expertise to non-democratically accountable autonomous agencies, appointed by the executive; 'judicialisation'[89] – 'the reliance on courts and judicial means for addressing core moral predicaments, public policy questions, and political controversies';[90] 'constitutionalisation' of democratic politics[91] (where 'issues concerning the design of democratic institutions and the central processes of democracy have increasingly become questions of constitutional law';[92] 'NGO-isation' – the often ideologically motivated outsourcing of democratic decision-making and provision of public services to national and international NGOs as allegedly providing better expertise/services than the state,[93] etc. Globalisation of decision-making[94] – the outsourcing of national democratic decision-making to supranational bodies and fora – is considered such an ominous threat to democracy that its rapid progression prompted prominent democratic theorists to ask whether and how democracy may survive globalisation.[95]

In the list above we see different manifestations of a trend that has long been noted – turning liberal democracies into 'democracy without choice'.[96] In such a regime democratic say becomes irrelevant: people may be able to change the government but not its policies, as these have been outsourced to non-elected and non-democratically accountable bodies. It is this process of emptying democracy of its democratic content that is referred to here as 'depoliticisation'.

In a seminal article Richard Katz and Peter Mair have identified as the primary source of depoliticisation the cartelisation of party systems in developed democracies.[97] Cartelisation is a complex web of agreements between major parties, which minimise the gains of the winners and the losses of the losers, but at the same time make policy changes very difficult. The result is often 'democracy

[88] T Christensen and P Lægreid, 'Agencification and Regulatory Reforms' in T Christensen and P Lægreid (eds), *Autonomy and Regulation: Coping with Agencies in the Modern State* (Cheltenham, Edward Elgar, 2006) 8.

[89] M Shapiro and A Stone Sweet, *On Law, Politics, and Judicialization* (Oxford, Oxford University Press, 2002).

[90] R Hirschl, 'The Judicialization of Politics' in RE Goodin (ed), *The Oxford Handbook of Political Science* (Oxford, Oxford University Press, 2009) 253.

[91] M Loughlin, 'What Is Constitutionalisation?' in M Loughlin and P Dobner (eds), *The Twilight of Constitutionalism?* (New York, Oxford University Press, 2010) 47.

[92] R Pildes, 'The Constitutionalization of Democratic Politics' (2004) 118 *Harvard Law Review* 29.

[93] A Choudry and D Kapoor, *NGOization: Complicity, Contradictions and Prospects* (London, Zed Books Ltd, 2013).

[94] D Held, 'Democracy and Globalization' (1997) 3(3) *Global Governance: A Review of Multilateralism and International Organizations* 251; D Rodrik, *The Globalization Paradox: Democracy and the Future of the World Economy* (New York, WW Norton & Company, 2011).

[95] B Barber, 'Can Democracy Survive Globalization?' (2000) 35(3) *Government and Opposition* 275; R Dahrendorf, 'Can European Democracy Survive Globalization?' (2001) 65 *The National Interest* 17.

[96] I Krastev, 'The Balkans: Democracy without Choices' (2002) 13(3) *Journal of Democracy* 39.

[97] R Katz and P Mair, 'Changing Models of Party Organization and Party Democracy: The Emergence of the Cartel Party' (1995) 1(1) *Party Politics* 5.

without choice' where unpopular policies persist even after a change of government. As a result of cartelisation, but also due to the growth of many other forms of outsourcing democratic decision-making to experts, perceptions of political inefficacy – that one can change the government but not its policies – become widespread. This alienates voters from mainstream parties, who offer the same policy menu despite nominal ideological differences in their platforms.

A further major source of voter alienation from mainstream parties is the growing perception that elected governments are not sufficiently responsive, as they often respond not to their electorates but to other (external or internal) constraints and pressures – be these from international markets or national businesses, or even from media empires acting as 'PR divisions of business groups'.[98] Parties in government often fail to ensure the desired balance of responsible (acting responsibly in performing its governmental functions vis-à-vis multiple constraints) and responsive (sensitive to the demands of the electorate) government, which is 'a principal source of the democratic malaise that confronts many Western democracies today'.[99]

The growing sense of frustration at the loss of democratic control spurs discontent with how democracy works. The trend towards emptying liberal democracy of its democratic content is reinforced by globalisation, where the processes of outsourcing decision-making are accelerated and deepened. The transfer of decision-making power is increasingly not only to non-responsive and non-directly accountable national bodies, but to transnational bodies without any democratic legitimacy. This adds intensity to the citizen's feelings of a loss of control, further enhanced by the processes of accelerating globalisation to become a major driver of populist support. Recent empirical study of the profile of populist citizens across countries in Europe and Latin America demonstrates that these are dissatisfied democrats: they value democracy highly yet find faults with its performance as they feel they are not well represented.[100] Populist voters also feel less 'ontological security' and tend to feel less in control of their own lives than the voters for mainstream parties.[101]

Depoliticisation – be it in the form of outsourcing decision-making to non-democratic bodies or in the often-related form of 'there is no alternative' (TINA) politics – is at odds with the democratic credo. According to the credo, it is the sovereign – the plural citizens – who should decide, directly or through their representatives, all important political issues affecting their polity. The de facto depoliticisation of vast areas of decision-making disempowers citizens, leading to increased feelings of loss of control over their lives. There are, of course,

[98] R Smilova, 'The Media in Bulgaria: Business Enterprises or PR Divisions of Business Groups?' in E Psychogiopoulou (ed), *Media Policies Revisited* (London, Palgrave Macmillan, 2014) 175.

[99] P Mair, 'Representative versus Responsible Government' (2009) MPIfG Working Paper 09/8.

[100] C Rovira Kaltwasser and S Van Hauwaert, 'The Populist Citizen: Empirical Evidence from Europe and Latin America' (2020) 12(1) *European Political Science Review* 1.

[101] B Steele and A Homolar, 'Ontological Insecurities and the Politics of Contemporary Populism' (2019) 32(3) *Cambridge Review of International Affairs* 214.

benign justifications for removing areas of decision-making from popular control. However, taken to extremes, this often leads to 'democracy without choice' and even to 'rule of rights without democracy', which are the main sources of the populist backlash. The growing asymmetries of power under the rule of experts (especially when the influence of unregulated markets is added) leads to further growing inequalities.

Deepening processes of depoliticisation bring growing inequality of power between citizens, on the one hand, and experts and governing elites more generally, on the other. This inequality opens an ever-growing gap between these two groups, which is aptly exploited by populists, who promise to restore 'democracy' by taking power from the elites and giving it back to people.[102] Yet instead of restoring the healthy balance at the heart of liberal democracy's success – that between rights and the rule of law on the one hand, and democracy, on the other – what populists deliver when in power is 'democracy without rights'.

E. Conclusion: Taming Elitist Hubris is not Enough

A major source of the appeal of populists' easy fixes to democracy's problems is the anti-elitist rhetoric they use. It falls on fertile ground. Governing elites have attracted much frustration – not only on account of their broken promises to deliver better-quality democracy, but also because of the condescending attitude the more successful tend to display towards those less fortunate – their 'meritocratic hubris'.[103] It is tempting to argue, therefore, that taming elite hubris – say, by an 'admissions lottery' to select colleges, may help close the gap between elites and the average citizen. The lottery for the competent few in order to kick-start their careers may help make the former less arrogant, and the latter less resentful. Yet even if the psychological effects on the lottery winners are as envisioned by Michael Sandel, the author of this proposal, and they become humble, maybe even caring for the plight of the less fortunate, this would not address the main structural problem meritocracy poses for liberal democracy. The meritocratic ideal for selecting ruling elites, and for attributing value and prestige in Western liberal democracies, would remain in tension with the democratic requirement for equality – for *equal* participation in the democratic process.

Ironically, the lottery solution, which is unlikely to solve the 'meritocratic hubris' problem, may offer a way forward with regard to democratic participation. Opening democratic decision-making to more tangible citizen involvement – by, for example, including in collective decision-making bodies citizen quotas, where citizens, selected by lot, take part – may enable the average citizen to have

[102] R Smilova 'Популизъм и отдалечаване на меритократичните елити в либералните демокрации' [Populism and Detachment of Meritocratic Elites in the Liberal Democracies] (2017) (1–2) *Политически изследвания* 26, www.ceeol.com/search/article-detail?id=759135.

[103] M Sandel, *The Tyranny of Merit: What's Become of the Common Good?* (London, Penguin, 2020).

her 'democratic say', without endangering democratic polities.[104] If the experiment proves successful – and citizens demonstrate they are up to the task for taking responsibilities of decision-making – citizen quotas can be extended, further narrowing the gap between average citizens and the credentialed elites.

V. Policy Processes and Democracy in Crisis

FRANK VIBERT

A. Introduction

There are many different reasons put forward to describe why democracy is said to be in crisis. This contribution addresses just one question that faces all democratic architectures in today's world. It is about institutions and policy processes. Failures in democratic policy processes provide one reason why democracy might be said to be in crisis. The failures mean that democracy does not deliver what people want and expect from their institutions or from their own participation. Policy failure demotivates.

The key question centres on how we try to ensure that the critical choices made in public policy in democracies are well informed and knowledge-based as well as responsive to the normative judgements that are inseparable from public policy decisions. The American Founding Fathers hoped that the electoral process would produce representatives with knowledge and understanding of what needed to be done. What we see, however, in today's world is politicians making public policy on the hoof, ruled by short-term electoral considerations, and decisions made by those who don't have much grasp of the substance of what they are doing.

In today's world, knowledge and information is largely held in independent expert agencies outside central government, such as in central banks, public health authorities, inspectorates and regulatory agencies. Thus, in order to ensure that public policies are well informed we need to bring the kind of thinking that is lodged in the world of independent expert bodies together with the kind of thinking and reasoning that we see in electoral politics and electorally based institutions such as parliaments.

We *don't* want public policy to be decided by technocrats, experts and those who claim to have superior wisdom. However, we *do* want democratic policy choices, including our normative choices, to reflect the best knowledge and information available and the practical experience of the professionals who engage in the policy area concerned.

[104] Note that the proposal for citizen quotas selected by lot is distinct from the radical dismantling of electoral democracy, substituting elections to parliament with lotteries, proposed by David Van Reybrouck. For details, see D Van Reybrouck, *Against Elections* (New York, Seven Stories Press, 2018).

B. Approaches

There are three main possible answers to this question of how we can obtain well informed policy-making. The first is to rely on democratic discourse and deliberation. The second possible answer is to entrench our most important social values in the political framework, mainly in the form of rights, positioned so as to ensure that all institutions, elected and unelected, respect them. The third possibility is to respect the different core functions of the institutions of government, the core functions of electorally based bodies, expert bodies and the judiciary but to rely on cross connections so that there is a modern system of checks and balances.

i. Democratic Discourse

From a normative perspective we would like to think that democratic discourse itself would lead to reasoned decisions. In the nineteenth century John Stuart Mill pointed to the importance of discussion with those with whom we do not agree. But reasoned discourse seems to involve either an underlying agreement on basic democratic norms or stringent requirements for discourse itself. In today's intercultural and polarised societies neither condition is likely to apply. Models of Town Hall democracy attempt to ensure that all sides of an argument are presented. But there is a lack of evidence that such forums achieve their goals in a political context.

The ideal of reasoned democratic discourse is also challenged by cognitive studies on how we actually reason. These studies show how our preferences are biased, inconsistent and rely on short-cut methods of reasoning. We associate with and anchor our beliefs with those with whom we agree and don't discuss our differences with those with whom we disagree. We browse social media channels that feed our own views. Party debate does little to change this situation. Political leaders are mainly concerned with registering positions with an eye on short-term electoral advantage and with whatever might appeal to their core supporters. Bias and party politics trump content. Despite our normative reasons to point to the centrality of democratic discourse, the overall evidence on the role of reason remains contested. Political scientists tend to point to evidence of the role of reason; social psychologists to bias.[105]

ii. Rights

Rights-based democracy is the main model of democracy we see in the world today and it supplements political decision-taking with judicial decision-taking.[106]

[105] See D Caluwaerts et al, 'Deliberation and Polarization: A Multi-disciplinary Review' (2023) 5 *Frontiers of Political Science*.

[106] See R Pildes, 'Supranational Courts and the Law of Democracy' (2018) 9(2) *Journal of International Disputes Settlement* 154.

Rights help steer our policy choices as measured by values and principles on which, in theory, we can all agree. Rights provide benchmarks against which we can decide on priorities, help identify what is important in a choice and are said to 'trump' other factors in a decision. There is no standard categorisation of rights, but they can be and are asserted to cover many of our most important choices involving the individual, family, identity, social welfare and the environment. They apply to all bodies with authority, elected and unelected, public, and private.

The worldwide turn to rights for steering policy choices is more problematic than it might seem. Statements of rights can just provide cover for autocratic regimes. Even where the intention to respect rights is present, their role remains problematic. The status of rights is unsettled and ranges from those who contend that they have peremptory status to those who contend that they have a useful but limited role as benchmarks. Their foundation is also a matter of dispute. They are often anchored in claims about the dignity of the person; but claims about what constitutes dignity do not mark clear boundaries. Rights can be divisive, and do not necessarily settle disputes. Even the most important values can be subject to many different interpretations, each of which has a claim to be respected or tolerated. Moreover, unless a hard division is asserted between statements of facts and values, claims about rights have to be weighed against the facts of a situation and the context in which they are being applied. This typically involves judgements about proportionality, whether the proposed policy action is proportional both to the value being asserted and to the situation.[107] Judgements about what is proportional can be very subjective and convey considerable discretionary authority.

A different class of concern about rights centres on the relationship between electoral politics and the law around what is sometimes referred to as judicialisation or legalisation.[108] All assertions of rights involve claims on the distribution of resources. They impose costs on others. This creates a tension between those who say that differences of interpretation and resource distribution questions should be decided by electorally-based institutions and those who say we can rely on the decision processes of the law and the judiciary. The more that the law extends its reach into distributional questions, the greater the concern about judicialisation. The extension of rights into environmental policy is particularly likely to be associated with significant social costs that have to be paid for somewhere by someone. There are attempts to define where the imposition of costs under the label of environmental rights can be justified – for example, where benefits are large and the costs small.[109] But such situations are often not clear at all.

In order for the relationship between democratic politics and decision-taking through the law to become less contentious, the role of the judiciary in the relationship has itself to be justified. One well-known attempt to define the relationship

[107] K Moller, 'Proportionality' (2012) 10(3) *International Journal of Constitutional Law* 709.

[108] P Fawcett, 'Introduction' in P Fawcett (ed), *Anti-Politics, Depoliticisation and Governance* (Oxford, Oxford University Press, 2017).

[109] H Shue, *Climate Justice: Vulnerability and Protection* (Oxford, Oxford University Press, 2014).

rests on the idea that judicial decisions should be democracy 'enhancing'.[110] However, what is enhancing or not is often a matter of opinion. In general, there is no agreement on how to establish the relationship. In the meantime, a rights-based 'ecosystem' grows, driven by the courts, lawyers and NGOs who have a self-interest in the development of rights. The ecosystem has the potential to edge out political decision-taking.[111]

Either to rely on reason prevailing through democratic discourse or to rely on assertions of rights to settle political disputes looks much more problematic than might seem at first sight. In consequence the third alternative identified above looks more compelling. It involves respecting the different branches of government and looking for cross-connections that provide an updated form of checks and balances in democratic government.

iii. Checks and Balances

The original concept of checks and balances applied to the legislative branch, the judiciary and the executive. In the modern world we need to group elected bodies together as representing one style of reasoning, the judiciary another style of reasoning and expert bodies their own branch answering to the epistemic standards of the knowledge world.[112]

Each branch represents a different form of authority. The law is subject to its own specialised reasoning, elected bodies reflect the associational claims of party politics, and expert bodies are expected to observe standards such as peer review by fellow practitioners and the knowledge of academia in their own field.

The traditional concept of checks and balances was twinned with the separation of powers so as to ensure the independence of each branch. Independence remains important in the new separation of powers. Judicial independence remains important and so too does the independence of those bodies in the knowledge branch.

The importance of independence seems challenged by the fact that the terms of reference of bodies with epistemic authority such as regulators and inspectorates are set by the political branch and their life can be terminated by legislatures or executives. However, political interference with the decisions they make is just as damaging to their role as it is to the law. In practice, their epistemic standing gives them considerable authority of their own. The law also has a role in keeping such bodies to account.[113] But the role is confined to ensuring that they operate within their terms of reference and respect rules of procedure such as providing notice

[110] J Ely, *Democracy and Distrust* (Cambridge, MA, Harvard University Press, 1980).

[111] For a discussion of linked ecologies see A Abbott, 'Linked Ecologies' (2005) 23(3) *Sociological Theory* 245.

[112] B Ackerman, 'The New Separation of Powers' in R Bellamy (ed), *The Rule of Law and the Separation of Powers* (London, Routledge, 2000). See also F Vibert, *The Rise of the Unelected* (Cambridge, Cambridge University Press, 2007).

[113] NB *Loper Bright Enterprises v Raimondo* overturning the *Chevron* judement (603 US 2024).

of what they intend to do and the opportunity for comment by those affected. The law is not generally equipped to second-guess the substance of the decisions of expert bodies.

The relationship between the elected bodies of government and expert bodies belonging the knowledge branch can be seen as involving different types of authority and a form of mutual accountability. Elected bodies have a role in holding the unelected to account but at the same time the unelected have an increasing role in holding those with elected authority to account. In this respect there is also an echo of the original separation of powers in the American Constitution. It was not a pure separation but one where cross-connections were set in place to help ensure that each branch kept in its designated place. These cross-connections included the power of Congress to impeach the President and the power of the President, subject to approval by the Senate, to appoint members of the Supreme Court.

The combination of independence coupled with cross-connections can be illustrated by the roles of the US Congressional Budget Office and the Office of Budget Responsibility in the UK. Both bodies are attached to elected assemblies but they provide independent expert advice on economic prospects, public expenditure and debt trajectories. They are able to provide their own expert and independent views on where US administration and UK government forecasts and assumptions involve wishful thinking. Such independent financial institutions are now to be found throughout the member countries of the Organisation for Economic Co-operation and Development. Finance ministers cannot ignore their views. This example of checks and balances suggests new life in an old model. Perhaps it could be extended to other areas of public policy where expert bodies have a potentially determining role. Certainly, during the Covid-19 pandemic the handling of relationships between elected politicians and expert bodies in the public health sector did little credit to either and left the public confused.

C. Conclusion

How to arrive at better informed decision-taking is one of the most important questions facing democracies today. We cannot rely on electoral mechanisms as America's Founding Fathers had hoped. Nor can we rely on reasoned discourse to prevail in electoral and party debate. Those politicians that emerge into positions of authority will only rarely have expert knowledge themselves in the many fields and tasks of modern government. Contemporary government relies on independent expert agencies outside central government structures for policy knowledge. This is not to denigrate the role of ordinary politics.[114] Popular opinion plays an essential role in flagging new areas of concern to governments and in providing feedback to governments. The ability to vote a government out of office remains

[114] H Landemore, *Democratic Reason* (Princeton, NJ, Princeton University Press, 2013).

essential for the health of democracies. Committees of inquiry in legislatures also have an important role in bringing expert knowledge to bear on matters that are politically salient.[115] Nevertheless, the main task in modern policy-making in order to achieve knowledgeable and informed policy-making is to bring together expert knowledge in independent agencies outside central government with the normative judgements of politics. Cross-connections under a separation of powers provides the most relevant model.[116]

[115] F Baumgartner and B Jones, *The Politics of Information* (Chicago, University of Chicago Press, 2015).
[116] F Vibert, *Rethinking the Separation of Powers* (Cheltenham, Edward Elgar, 2024).

8

Electoral Systems and Political Parties

I. Populism, Self-Restraint and the Political Parties[1]

DANIEL SMILOV

The 'rise of populism' has become a dominant interpretative theory used for the understanding of contemporary politics.[2] Populism is a basic democratic ideology, according to which politicians should follow the will of the people no matter what: they should not attempt to distort this will or educate the people but should just reflect their preferences and and incorporate them in authoritative decisions. From this point of view populism is essentially the elimination of self-restraint in politics: it is a minimalistic democratic ideology, which argues that the people are mature enough to make up their own mind and take their own decisions, and that their choices should not be constrained by the instruments of constitutionalism or the guardianship of political parties and leaders.

It has been convincingly argued that contemporary populism has a very strong anti-liberal element since it is a rebellion on formal and informal constraints on the will of the people. Jan-Werner Muller has pointed out the anti-pluralistic and autocratic tendencies in populism,[3] while Takis Pappas has defined the very phenomenon of populism as democratic illiberalism.[4] This paper further develops the wide-shared scholarly position that populism is an opponent to liberal democracy. The main contention of the paper is that populism targets and erodes not so much the formal institutions of liberal democracy, but the political attitude of self-restraint, which is essential for the formal institutions to work.

And indeed, the situation in the Western liberal democracies is rather paradoxical. On the one hand, the formal constitutional institutions are still in place and are more or less intact in virtually all of those countries. With a few exceptions, like Hungary and to a certain degree Poland, the formal constraints on power as well as the democratic infrastructure of the state are preserved and are in good

[1] This study is financed by the European Union-NextGenerationEU, through the National Recovery and Resilience Plan of the Republic of Bulgaria, project No BG-RRP-2.004-0008.

[2] The main author to advance an 'ideational' concept of 'populism' in the early 2000s was Cas Mudde. For a more recent summary of the debate see C Mudde and C Rovira Kaltwasser, *Populism: A Very Short Introduction* (Oxford. Oxford University Press, 2017).

[3] J-W Muller, *What Is Populism* (Philadelphia, University of Pennsylvania, 2017).

[4] T Pappas, *Populism and Liberal Democracy* (Oxford, Oxford University Press, 2019).

shape. Yet, there is an apparent sense of anxiety and anticipation of an impending crisis, which may lead to the dismantling of democracy. The paper argues that the reason for this anxiety is the fact that self-restraint has been significantly eroded at the level of political parties and leaders. This erosion creates uncertainty and is favourable for future scenarios in which even the formal institutions of liberal democracy – separated powers, the rule of law, human rights – are reshaped into autocratic direction.

The paper first explores the importance of self-restraint among politicians and the people for the proper functioning of liberal democracy. Second, it argues that populism leads to the erosion of self-restraint. Even more than that, contemporary populism actually *is* the erosion of self-restraint since this is its central defining feature. Finally, the paper addresses a number of related issues, such as why self-restraint has been eroded during the last two decades and not earlier, for instance, in the 1990s, 1980s. Also, the transformation of political parties due to the erosion of self-restraint is briefly discussed.

A. Liberal Democracy and the Importance of Constraints

As is well known, liberal democracy combines the principle of popular sovereignty with the liberal principles of constitutionalism: separation of powers, the rule of law and the protection of individual rights. It is an ideal which tries to reconcile majority rule with the protection of rights, separation of powers and the rule of law. There is a certain tension between these two groups of principles: the democratic (self-government) and the liberal (limited power). But on the other hand, it seems that the two foundational principles are necessary for each other, because without the protection of individual rights and the rule of law, democracy as majority rule could hardly function. As Ronald Dworkin, among many others, has forcefully argued, in order for democracy to be acceptable, it needs to respect numerous rights and liberties of the people.[5] Otherwise, as an egalitarian procedure it could be easily distorted and turned into a tyranny of the majority just like John Stuart Mill and many others have anticipated. In short, liberal democracy does rely on a system of formal constraints on the power of the people, which are designed to preclude its subversion into a tyranny.

As Hume has put forward, political power cannot but depend on cooperation in some form by the people. The minimal form of such a cooperation in a dictatorship is acquiescence, which must exist under the form of broadly accepted social conventions. Liberal democracy is arguably more demanding from that perspective. Since it is a system of self-rule by the people, the people themselves should exercise self-restraint and should be committed to observe a set of limits on their own power. If a convention of self-restraint does not exist, democracy

[5] R Dworkin, 'The Moral Reading of the Constitution' in R Dworkin, *Freedom's Law* (Harvard University Press, 1996).

could reasonably quickly turn into a tyranny of the majority. As the Hungarian example suggests, an aggressive majority could capture the key institutions of the state and could turn them into instruments against the opposition. Formally, the constitutional structure of the state could still be there in one form or another – constitutional courts, judicial councils, judiciaries, fiscal councils, etc. But these institutions would not function as separated powers, independent of one another, and which check each other, but rather as instruments of self-entrenchment of specific political players.

As Ziblatt and Levitsky have argued, democracies die when politicians stop exercising restraint and abandon toleration.[6] Interestingly, contemporary populism urges exactly this. As we shall see, it is a minimalistic ideology, which encourages the people to leave self-constraint behind and promises to represent them if they decide to do so.

B. Populism as the Erosion of Self-Restraint

The 'rise of populism' is most commonly understood as the rise of a minimalist ideology, which praises the people as they are, and accuses the existing elites of corruption, treason or some other moral or political defect. It is a Manichaean discourse, which juxtaposes the people, who are always right, with the elites, which for corrupt and self-regarding reasons distort the popular will.

Ideologically, populism is little more than a revolt against constraints on the will of the people. This will be the ultimate justification for action and is the fountain of legitimate authority. Constraints on the will of the people are thus by definition illegitimate and should be ignored or dismantled.

Thus, populists argue and persuade the people that their will and decisions are of ultimate importance and value, whatever they are. In this way, populism becomes the identity politics of the majority of the people. The fact that the people have some characteristic or preference acquires normative value, which is overriding. In essence, populists argue that the majority has a right to be authentic, to express itself as it is. Not equality, but the right to authenticity is the major ideological tool of the populist party. In multiculturalism difference is just a precondition and a mobilisational means for the achievement of the goal – equality. In populism *authenticity* is both the goal and the justification for action: the difference of the majority is what is to be cherished and preserved. Majorities are not only allowed to believe in the superiority of their culture but are required to do so. Eastern Europe is again the champion in this regard: Russians, Bulgarians, Romanians and Greeks all have this superiority complex.[7] While this may be the cultural legacy

[6] S Levotsky and D Ziblatt, *How Democracies Die* (New York, Crown, 2018).

[7] M Lipka, 'Greek Attitudes Toward Religion, Minorities Align More with Central and Eastern Europe than West', available at www.pewresearch.org/fact-tank/2018/10/31/greek-attitudes-toward-religion-minorities-align-more-with-central-and-eastern-europe-than-west/ accessed 31 May 2025.

of Orthodox countries, majorities in other regions are also adopting this pride in their ethnic, cultural and racial identity as a justification for prioritising themselves over others.

The striving for authenticity precludes constraints on the will of the people under the form of respect for education, expertise, the voice of minorities, individual rights and so on: when the people have spoken, such constraints should not be respected.Apart from striving for authenticity, contemporary populists are eroding self-restraint by encouraging self-centredness and indeed some form of (rational) egoism. Putting yourself first, whether as a state or a person, has been turned into a political slogan. One of the defining features of contemporary populism is its lack of willingness to cooperate with others, either nationally or internationally. In this regard, contemporary populists are very different from their predecessors on both the left and the right. Thus, most of the political parties that are today called 'populist' are:

1. *Against distribution through taxes:* Most populist parties argue for low taxes. Viktor Orban introduced a flat income tax of 17 per cent in Hungary, much lower than the previous system. Donald Trump lowered corporate taxes in the US to unprecedented levels and promised to go even further in a second mandate. The populist government of the Lega and 5Stars in Italy vowed to increase social spending without increasing the tax burden, leading to violations of EU financial discipline rules. Even the left-wing Syriza in Greece did not advocate for higher taxes during the crisis of 2015. Redistribution through taxes, the ultimate mark of solidarity with the worse-off in society, has not been embraced by contemporary populism. Instead, it encourages the majority to be self-centred, indulging in policies that benefit themselves rather than others.
2. *In favour of economic constitutionalism:* In general, most populist parties support fiscal and financial constraints, particularly those preventing an increase in the tax burden. The 2010 Fundamental Law of Hungary exemplifies this, with provisions like fiscal councils and public debt ceilings to constrain irresponsible fiscal policy. In the US, many Trump supporters view the US Constitution as a nineteenth-century financial compact prioritising economic freedom and limiting taxation or social security schemes. Even radical left populists, such as Syriza, ultimately accepted externally imposed financial constraints from the EU to remain in the Eurozone. This support for fiscal and economic constitutionalism reflects an aversion to redistribution or public expenditure favouring the worse-off.
3. *Against emancipatory measures:* Populists generally disregard the plight of vulnerable minorities, be they economic, ethnic, cultural, or sexual. Redistribution or affirmative action in favour of such minorities is often portrayed as undue and unfair privilege. Contemporary populists focus on the concerns of the majority.

4. *Against empathy with foreigners, refugees, and migrants:* Populists are broadly opposed to migrants and foreigners, arguing that societal benefits should be restricted to the 'people' (the political majority). Populist leaders strongly discourage self-restraint in advancing this self-centredness. Migration has become central to debates about populism, though it has been argued that fears of 'destruction of the nation', rather than migration per se, drive societal hysteria. Eastern Europe is particularly notable for its fear of migration and lack of empathy, even for clear-cut cases such as Syrian refugees.
5. *Against universal social solidarity (and for inter-group solidarity):* Post-war politics centred on universal social solidarity, with the welfare state prioritising the most vulnerable. John Rawls's Difference Principle, which prioritises the needs of the least advantaged, epitomised this approach. Today, this principle has reversed: solidarity now extends primarily to those closest to oneself. This shift from universal to inter-group solidarity reflects another erosion of self-restraint and rise of egoism.
6. *Against supranational solidarity:* The rejection of universal solidarity extends internationally, often described as 'economic nationalism'. Donald Trump's 'America first' slogan typifies this shift, which has influenced other nations, even those without the vast resources of the US. In the West, the realist idea of national self-interest has replaced post-war ideals of regional integration and cooperation.
7. *Against individual sacrifices for the collective good:* Political egoism entails a low tolerance for individual sacrifices in the name of public good. While temporary sacrifices might be rational from a utilitarian perspective, prioritising tangible, immediate benefits often outweighs considerations for future, egalitarian gains.

Thus, the brief overview of some of the central features of contemporary populism drives home the point that their common basis is the erosion of self-constraint among politicians and among the people at large. Actually, the populist politician both praises the authenticity of the people and lures and encourages them to trespass on formal constraints and, most importantly, informal constraints of self-centredness in its multiple forms of 'putting yourself first'.

C. Why the Erosion of Self-Restraint Happened Only Over the Last Two Decades?

The Second World War left Europe devastated but convinced that social polarisation and national rivalries inevitably lead to tragic destruction of human life and value. These were the circumstances of political self-restraint and social solidarity, which became the dominant model of politics in post-war Europe (and to a lesser degree in the US). Social democracy and Christian democracy became the mainstream political ideologies of the post-war reconstruction: both of these were solidaristic, paternalistic and encouraged political actors to exercise considerable self-restraint in advancing ideological claims.[8] The present-day German party system, or at least its 'mainstream parties', is still the epitome of the model (although it also suffers from the rise of the populist far-left and especially the far-right Alternative for Germany). Political parties were obliged to educate the people: the task of de-Nazification was one of their major goals, which meant than no one could argue that the people were perfect as they were. For this purpose, powerful political educational programmes were set up, which were gradually transformed into the famous system of German party foundations. From an ideological perspective, both the right and the left saw social compromise and the emancipation of vulnerable groups as their central tasks. Emancipation required sharing and redistribution: corporatist capitalism and high taxes were the major policies of the European post-war consensus.

This well-known story at the national level was matched by self-restraining and solidaristic policies at the supra-national level. The process of elite-driven European integration started, which ultimately resulted in the creation of the EU: a supranational polity comprising currently 27 European states. NATO, WTO, and some structures of the UN could be interpreted as less ambitious global attempts to follow these trends.

The very success of the post-war model, however, started to undermine its own social foundations – the circumstances of self-restraint and solidarity. Towards the 1980s, economic crisis put a serious dent into the welfare state and brought Thatcherism and Reaganomics to the political scene. These developments acted more as a salvation of the political model created after the Scond World War rather than as its rejection: albeit curtailed, the welfare state and its basic institutions survived in the West and the liberal democracies of Europe and the US achieved unprecedented levels of prosperity. The end of the twentieth century was marked by extreme confidence in the superiority and the effectiveness of the political model of liberal democracy combined with market economy. Many believed that what lie ahead was only further progress. Even more people were convinced that the system was robust and could not be replaced by *any* alternative.

These beliefs are actually the social basis for the construction of self-centred and egoistic political majorities. These beliefs are also spelling out the erosion of self-restraint. They were partially questioned by the 2008 financial crisis, but after the initial scare they largely survived it. The system regenerated itself after a period of social distress.

More specifically, the attitudes, which are the circumstances of erosion of self-restraint, are the following:

1. *The system is robust and could survive even serious shocks:* When people are convinced that the institutional setup of democracy and market economy

[8] T Judt, *Postwar: A History of Europe since 1945* (London, Penguin Books, 2005).

is insulated from shocks, they become more bold and experimental in their behaviour. Self-centred and egoistic behaviour becomes more acceptable since its social cost is presumably not high: catastrophe is impossible.

2. *Competition rather than cooperation and compromise is beneficial for society:* Political greed, just like economic greed, is beneficial. If everyone pursues his or her own interest to the limit of the acceptable, the overall result for society could still be beneficial.
3. *There is no alternative to the present system:* No major alternative to liberal democracy has been proposed thus far. Champions of *illiberal* democracy, as Viktor Orban, have not convinced anybody yet of the virtues of their proposal. It is either read as a liberal democracy in which conservatives are the ruling party (which is acceptable and harmless) or as some sort of autocracy of the Putin type (which is dangerous to liberal democracy but is generally unattractive in the West).[9] The lack of any in-between feasible option further convinces the public that liberal democracy is still without an attractive alternative. This belief is conducive to experimental, opportunistic and ultimately egoistic political behaviour. When the citizens are convinced that the situation is different from the 1930s (when powerful totalitarian alternatives of democracy existed) they could go very far in pursuing narrow partisan interests in political competition.

Eastern Europe is a very good example of the causes of eroding self-restraint among politicians. The rise of populism or the infamous 'backsliding' began not in the economically and politically testing 1990s, but only in the beginning of the 2000s, when the Central European countries had economically stabilised and become members of NATO and the EU. Paradoxically, Eastern Europe became a hotbed of political populism during a period of most extraordinary economic rise and catching up with the developed West. This means that populism is not driven only (or even primarily) by economic hardship, inequality or cultural complaints. It is driven also by the rising self-confidence of the people, which is praised by populist political entrepreneurs, who fan their self-esteem and self-centredness. In such circumstance, the desire of the people to be(come) great (again) easily becomes central in politics.

D. The Populist Political Party as an Instrument for the Erosion of Self-Restraint

The rise of the populist party is the response of the political class to the above described self-centred, self-confident attitudes and circumstances. The populist party thrives on and nurtures such attitudes by having two general purposes. The

[9] For a discussion of the concept of 'illiberal democracy' see R Smilova, 'The Ideational Core of Democratic Illiberalism' in A Sajo et al (eds), *Handbook of Illiberalism* (Routledge, 2021).

first one is therapeutic and psychological. It has to heal the majorities from residual feelings of shame, guilt and owing to others, which are associated with the abandoning of self-restraint. For this purpose it very often presents these others not as fellow citizens, but as the enemy or at least as somebody of inferior moral status. Commonly, populist politicians are railing against 'political correctness' and use language which denigrates and politically assassinates the opponent.

The therapeutic function of the populist party is served also by its attack against educational authorities of any type. Most commonly it is positioned against established *expert* institutions and individuals: from the mainstream media to academia. Populists portray these institutions as self-interested and corrupt with the aim of depriving them of authority. Thus, society is left without a neutral critical vantage point: everything becomes a clash of self-interested groups, and the majority could be relieved that its egoism and lack of restraint is not a deplorable aberration but is actually the norm.

The second function of the populist party is ideological. It gives arguments to the majority that its behaviour is not only normal (in the sense of widespread) but also morally justified. This ideological function of the populist party has been generally neglected in the literature: instead, it has been argued that its central message is the representation of the people as a homogeneous group against the corrupt elite. Things are more subtle than this, however. The main message is that the majority is *right* to pursue its self-interest as much as possible. In a situation in which we have only clashing self-interests, what is *right* is the will of the majority.

This ideological message goes against deeply entrenched political attitudes in Western (and not only) history. From as early as Aristotle it is known that genuine politics exists only in power relationships that are mutually beneficial: both for the ruling and the ruled. In this sense politics is non-definable without a notion of a common, public interest: without it, it degenerates into master-slave or familial relationships.

This Aristotelian difficulty of the ideological task of the populist party is dealt with in two ways. On the one hand, populists often take on board libertarianism as an extreme form of justification of the pursuit of self-interest in politics. Not all are convinced by the virtues of libertarianism as a positive political programme, however. Therefore, the populist party employs mostly a negative agenda: convincing the people that public authority is incapable of advancing the public good. And the terrain for that in terms of public perceptions seems well prepared. Contemporary publics are characterised by extremely high levels of distrust in politicians. In many countries participation in politics is low or at least general trends are negative. This makes it hard to convince people that the pursuit of the common good is at all possible: suspicions of partiality and self-interest are so deep that the populist politician needs only to fan the flames a little bit. Ultimately, his main line is not that he is better than the others in terms of articulating and defending the common good. He or she actually argues that the people are better than all politicians, and that the politicians should be just fair and direct transmitters of the preferences of the public.

This negative agenda is more essential than libertarianism for the ideological function of the populist anti-paternalist party and it explains an apparent paradox: contemporary populists do not seem to expand the powers of democratically elected bodies as parliaments, for instance. A typical example was Viktor Orban's 2011 Fundamental Law, which instead of expanding the powers of parliament introduced a complex system of bodies and organs, each of which was subsequently taken over by the ruling party. In the future, in case of losing parliamentary elections, these formally independent checks would entrench Orban in power, even if he ends up in the parliamentary opposition. In general, the end result of populist politics is that political authority stops being a defender of the interest of society as a whole, and starts to advance narrower, partisan interests. Because of this, populists do not strive to empower democratic bodies (parliaments) against independent constraints, such as constitutional courts or central banks: populists rather seek partisan control over such independent regulators. Such partisan takeovers of judicial bodies have happened in Eastern Europe, most conspicuously in Hungary, Poland and Bulgaria. Even in established democracies such as the US there are fears that politicisation of the US Supreme Court and the federal judiciary could be interpreted along these lines. Ultimately, populists discourage people from believing that public authorities could defend *common* societal interests in principle. Their message normally is that the people have been cheated by particular groups – minorities, corrupt politicians, urban elites – and that the time for revenge has come. In this sense the populist party rides the waves of distrust in politics that characterise the West. Populists, as a rule, do not even try to convince the people that politics is something good and morally justified: on the contrary, their argument is that politics is a 'dirty business', in which the more unscrupulous and sly individual outsmarts the rest.

E. The Populist Party and the Evolution of Party Systems

Populist parties are the latest phase of development of western party systems. While the post-war catch-all party was paternalistic and compromise-oriented, the populist party is a vehicle of self-interested groups – a vehicle which has dropped most claims of an educational role. On the contrary, it claims that people are good as they are, and that their authenticity should be expressed in the public arena.

The 'cartel' party of the 1980s and 1990s was the first to openly abandon political education.[10] The cartel party is parliament-based, thinly ideological, increasingly memberless and dependent on the state through public funding and other privileges. But the 'cartel' party was animated by the search for compromise and solidaristic visions of politics. It was part of a team (albeit a cartel) and pretended

[10] R Katz and P Mair, 'Changing Models of Party Organization and Party Democracy: The Emergence of the Cartel Party' (1995) 1(1) *Party Politics*.

to offer something to everyone in society. In this sense, the cartel party preserved the 'catch-all' element of its predecessors, while abandoning its educational and paternalistic role.

The populists reject the social compromises and the appeal to society as a whole of the catch-all party. They thrive on social polarisation and promise to protect the interests of specific groups without altruism regarding others.

The populist party resembles the cartel party in another aspect: it does not decrease public distrust in party politics but rather increases it. The goal of the populist party is not to prove that it has *authority* and deserves the trust of the public. As argued, it is predominantly negatively oriented and tries to convince the public that there are in principle no reliable authorities beyond the people themselves.

This is the manipulative part of populism. It is in fact a utopian view, according to which people do not need authority to guide their decisions, but only vehicles of transmission of their preferences and beliefs. For various conceptual and practical reasons this is untrue and impossible in any complex society. After all, the populist party is an *authority*, which claims not to be one. It gets power and the ability to guide peoples' behaviour by claiming that they do not need to be guided.

This type of manipulation is bound to be noticed by the electorate at some point. Therefore, the populists come with an expiry date, which rarely goes beyond a few electoral cycles. This may be one of the reasons for the increased voter volatility and instability of contemporary party systems.

As mentioned, theories of contemporary populism exaggerate the communal homogeneity that this political phenomenon presupposes. In fact, populist majorities have been far from homogeneous: on the contrary, they often appear as temporary and unlikely coalitions of disparate sections of society. The populist party reflects this heterogeneity.[11] Although it often speaks of the nation and reveres its history, this rarely translates into committed party membership or any type of intense and integrated political community. Nationalistic populist rallies in Poland and Hungary do appear as actions of a communitarian nature. The rallies of Donald Trump, Syriza and Podemos had a similar air. But in fact, contemporary populism could function and operate without communitarian mobilisation and without the creation of homogenous communities. Political interaction in the populist era is very often close to anonymous on the Internet and social networks, and the constructed communities are a collection of individuals sharing common interests almost accidentally. Therefore, mobilisation of the voters through psychological (rather than political and ideological) profiling has proven vital, as the incidents with Cambridge Analytica have demonstrated.[12]

[11] R Eatwell and M Goodwin, *National Populism: The Revolt against Liberal Democracy* (London, Pelican Books, 2018) 17–25.

[12] M Hu, 'Cambridge Analytica's Black Box' (2020) 7(2) *Big Data & Society*, available at journals.sagepub.com/doi/full/10.1177/2053951720938091, accessed 31 May 2025.

To sum up, the populist party is a paradoxical organisation: it is an authority claiming to have little authority, and it creates communities with very weak communal obligations, held together by temporary coincidence of individual self-interests. Because of that the populist party is very close in nature to the mass media: it attracts diverse publics by trying to keep their interest and attention without a serious attempt at educating them.

F. How Far Could Populists Go?

Politics has become a clash of self-centred and egoistic players in the age of the populist party: and this is not a public choice theoretical model this time, but empirical reality. The question is, however, how far they can go in self-centred advancement of their interests. Eastern Europe has proven most vulnerable in this regard, and in countries like Hungary self-entrenchment of populist governments has verged on the instalment of autocracy. Viktor Orban has been so successful in partisan take-overs of institutions that Hungary has been transformed from a government of the many into a government of the few, if not of only one person. Similar dangers are observed in other countries in the region as well.

In Western Europe and the US, partisan and self-interested political action has so far resulted in less pronounced damages to the institutional set-up. Separation of powers and the protection of rights are still well-entrenched. But here the main danger is to supra-national forms of solidarity, such as the EU, NATO and long-standing elaborate trade agreements. As Brexit has shown, even an established liberal democracy like the UK could construct a majority narrowly focused on its national interest (rightly or wrongly interpreted in the specific case).

In essence, there is a *conceptual ambiguity* as to how far populists could go. Maybe this is a context-dependent issue: in Eastern Europe they have been bolder and more experimental than in the West. But there is one thing which appears common: the tendency is towards escalation: bolder experimentation with the limits imposed by liberal democracy. In Italy the centrist populist, Silvio Berlusconi, was eventually eclipsed by a more radical successor – Matteo Salvini. In Hungary, Victor Orban has grown more assertive with every election and had effectively displaced the radical right party Yobbik. The Tea Party spirit in the US graduated into President Donald Trump.[13]

Boldness with experimentation with the limits of liberal democracy is a *guarantee of authenticity* in the eyes of the electorate. A self-interested majority needs to know that its representatives will faithfully follow its preferences and wishes, no matter what. Radicalisation, opportunism and experimentalism are 'proof' that

[13] For more on the tendency of populist parties to radicalise see D Smilov and R Smilova, 'Centrist and Radical Populism in Central and Eastern Europe' in R Heinisch et al (eds), *Perspectives on Populism* (Baden-Baden, Nomos, 2024) Ch 2.

the party is ready to follow any turn of the preferences of its electorate. Radicalism is, therefore, a pledge of faithfulness to the will of the people, even if it is self-centred and egoistic.

G. The Twin Dangers to Liberal Democracy

Thus far, liberals have been mostly worried that the 'rise of populism' could lead to subversion of liberal democracy into autocracy. The Hungarian example has been the major scare, where the rule of the many has gradually eroded into oligarchy with tyrannical elements. Aristotle's classical analysis offers another path for an even more fundamental corruption of democracy, however. In his view, a government by a self-centred majority transforms democracy into a rule of the mob, a tyranny of the majority. Rousseau and John Stuart Mill had similar worries: when self-centred and egoistic majorities take government control, democracy could easily be transformed into a political nightmare.

Not all liberals share this concern and this is the reason why 'the rise of populism' has effectively split the liberal community into warring factions. Adam Smith's view that unbridled competition of self-interested actors is beneficial to society as a whole is often transplanted from economics to politics. Many liberals, not necessarily fully-fledged libertarians, share such trust in the positive effect of competition among political players. Such liberals reject the Aristotelian wisdom that a well-governed *politea* needs a public good-minded majoritarian decision-making.[14]

Who is right, Aristotle or contemporary pluralists? This may seem an abstract question, but it has effectively split the liberal community in many countries. Some see the rise of populism as gross corruption of politics, while others are willing to view it as a mere extension of what they have always preached: the primacy of the markets, competition and self-interested political behaviour.[15]

There is reason to believe that the Aristotelian camp has the better argument, however. Thus far, liberal democracy has survived and thrived due to public-centred and public-minded majorities. Post-war Europe and Post-New Deal America were societies characterised by considerable levels of solidarity, sensitivity to the needs

[14] There has always been a tension between public choice accounts and the justification of democracy, starting from the puzzling consequences of Kenneth Arrow's Impossibility Theorem. More recently, concerns about the empirical validity of rationalistic accounts of politics have been powerfully raised in CH Achen and LM Bartels, *Democracy for Realist: Why Elections Do Not Produce Responsive Government* (Princeton, NJ, Princeton University Press, 2016).

[15] Committed liberals have been willing to admit that the 'rise of populism' is a political response to real failures of liberal democracy (such as the rising inequality) or its inadequate answer to novel developments, like the so-called 'migration revolution'. See I Krastev, *After Europe* (Philadelphia, PA, Pennsylvania University Press, 2017) and J Zielonka, *Counter-Revolution: Liberal Europe in Retreat* (Oxford, Oxford University Press, 2018).

of vulnerable groups and desire for compromise. More importantly, these were societies based on unwritten conventions about self-restraint by politicians. This ethos has been gradually eroded and the 'rise of populism' denotes the advent of its replacement – self-interest and political egoism.

Those who believe that institutions can function and shape behaviour even in the absence of corresponding ethos in the main political players have to take the Hungarian case seriously into account. Indeed, institutions could serve a constraining function, but for a limited amount of time. In Hungary, this was until Viktor Orban's party Fidesz gained a two-thirds constitutional majority: after that, the constitution itself became an instrument for self-entrenchment in power.

The constitutive ambiguity about the extent to which populists are willing and capable of changing the institutional setup of liberal democracy is only exacerbating the situation. What is the breaking point of liberal democracy? When the government forces a university out of the country? Or when it imposes 20 per cent tax on NGOs engaged in activities of which it does not approve? Or when it interferes with the judicial system by retiring overnight most of the senior judges? Or when it passes a 'foreign agents' law inspired by the legislation of Putin in Russia?

It is a pity that in today's Europe, public opinion is divided on such matters, and many think that such government actions are fair game. If anything, this shows that the public ethos in liberal democracies has changed dramatically. The *politea* is in danger of becoming a rule of the partisan mob.

H. Conclusion: Are Democracy and Liberalism Still Possible?

The predicament in which liberal democracy is at present is the following: it has constructed 'authentic', self-centred and self-interested majorities, which reject any form of political self-restraint and political education. Simultaneously, institutions that educate the people in the spirit of solidarity and the public good have been systematically eroded. The advent of the populist party is only one side of the phenomenon. Similar developments have taken place in the media and NGOs, and to a lesser extent in schools and academia. To put it crudely, we have societies which reject political self-restraint and education of the people, and political education institutions that have non-existent or vastly eroded authority.

The greatest danger to liberal democracy, therefore, may not be that it slides into autocracy or oligarchy, but that it gets a bad name as a corrupt and defective form of government. For long centuries people thought of democracy as the rule of the mob and the uneducated: therefore it was considered inferior to more enlightened options. Contemporary democracy risks portraying itself along exactly these lines. Here we could be reminded of Churchill's important caveat that democracy is the worst form of government but for all others. However, this optimism underestimates technological advancements, which could vastly improve the attractiveness of autocracy. In the brave new world of Big Data, AI, biometric information, and physical and moral enhancements of the human being, powerful governments or corporations will be able to:

1. Know better what the real preferences of individuals are. Machines could model human preferences better than the human being themselves.
2. Take decisions in the interest of society as a whole by avoiding the traps into which short-sighted egoistically minded *homo economicus* habitually falls (Prisoners' Dilemmas and other problems of collective action, for instance).
3. Take decisions by which individuals themselves will be better off if they follow them, compared to situations where they take these decisions themselves.

In such technological circumstances, which are not that far removed in the future, democracy as the rule of self-centred and egoistic political majorities will appear infinitely inferior to technologically advanced autocracies.

Philosophers dealing with the ethical concerns of post-humans have already raised similar questions while arguing in favour of a moral duty of the human being to accept moral enhancements, if they are technologically available.[16] It is an intriguing question whether this moral duty would entail the endorsement of technologically advanced enlightened autocracy over democracy functioning as the rule of egoistic majorities.

These questions have no easy answers. Thus far, liberal democracy has been repaired in one of two ways: either through more procedural democracy (including instruments of direct democracy as referendums and initiatives); or through more counter democracy in Rosanvallon's sense[17] – more supervisory bodies ensuring transparency and the following of uncontroversial standards. Both of these instruments work when there is a public-minded majority interested in the protection of the common good. If there is no such majority, democratic instruments could be used for tyranny of the majority, while the idea of uncontroversial common standards dissipates. All benchmarks, checklists and the accompanying NGOs or independent bodies become involved in a partisan game between self-interested players.

So, if the traditional paths of more procedural democracy or counter democracy are closed, is there a way forward for liberal democracy? One option will be an attempt to sanitise the idea of political perfectionism and political education with the goal of constructing public-minded majorities. This may be more difficult that it sounds, because it would require major reforms of the media, the political parties, the NGO sector and academia. These are the instruments that have to regain their authority in shaping the public imagination in a more solidaristic and empathic direction. Education does not necessarily mean paternalism, dogmatism

[16] I Persson and J Savulescu, 'The Duty to Be Morally Enhanced' (2019) 38 *Topoi* 17, available at link.springer.com/article/10.1007/s11245-017-9475-7, accessed 31 May 2025.

[17] P Rosanvallon, *Counter-Democracy: Politics in an Age of Distrust* (Cambridge, Cambridge University Press, 2008).

and forceful imposition of views. But it may involve nudging[18] the public towards valuable options, or at least providing the public with a set of valuable options to choose from.[19] Given that populism is going in exactly the opposite direction, it is a most serious danger to the future of democracy and liberalism.

II. The Politics of Internet Shutdowns

NICOLE STREMLAU

I'm going to take us in a different direction. I'm in Johannesburg now, so I will speak about some of my research in Africa. I'll be talking about Internet shutdowns as resistance and how we can use them as a way of rethinking oppositional practices, particularly during election times. As some of you might know, there's been a steady increase in Internet shutdowns as a response to online content that governments find concerning, and this is particularly the case around elections, especially in Africa.

This trend is also evident in India and other parts of Asia. It is a growing phenomenon, and by shutdowns, I mean the partial or complete closing of the Internet, also known as the Internet kill switch. It is a strategy used by governments as a way of attempting to address disinformation around elections or to mitigate the perceived impact hate speech may have on offline election-related violence in the aftermath of elections. It is usually done in the name of national security.

Shutdowns are almost uniformly broadly condemned by those who do not use them – they are usually discussed as a legal issue in terms of violating the rights to freedom of expression or access to information. Many international civil society groups that support freedom of expression are active in this area. They focus on language, such as digital rights and the freedom to connect.

Western governments have also been outspoken advocates of supporting media freedom. The US and EU recently came out with the declaration for the Future of the Internet, which is very ambitious, as the title might suggest, and in two and a half pages, the term human rights was mentioned no less than 20 or 25 times. Overarching this human rights approach or the Internet freedom agenda is this seemingly impenetrable binary, a struggle between democracies and autocracies, or as commonly being referred to now, this rise of digital authoritarianism, and so I want to be a bit provocative today and challenge this sort of dominant narrative that's coming up, because I think this human rights narrative of shutdowns is also blurring one of the real reasons why shutdowns are occurring. So, once again, it is framing African countries as these figures of lack, of falling short of international

[18] RH Thaler and CR Sunstein, *Nudge: Improving Decisions about Health, Wealth, and Happiness* (London, Penguin Books, 2009).

[19] J Raz, *The Morality of Freedom* (Oxford, Oxford University Press, 1988).

election standards, democracy, these norms that are expected, and it doesn't create the space to ask the right kinds of questions or uncover the alternative ways of identifying the rules, the regularities, and the logics around why shutdowns might be used.

I've been researching Internet shutdowns in Africa, specifically around government decision-making processes, asking why governments choose this relatively blunt tool of censorship as opposed to other forms of information control. What is the process of implementing shutdowns? What is the rule of law, if at all? And I think one reason we see this rise of shutdowns is because of the recent trends in social media companies like Meta to have end-to-end encryption, so surveillance is more challenging. Indeed, there are many cases of shutdowns being used by governments to assert power over opposition parties or deflect attention from protests around elections. Still, I think there's also another story going on. Our research is mainly focused on Ethiopia and Uganda but it has also involved dozens of interviews in other countries where there have been shutdowns, and I want to speak specifically about the case of Uganda today.

Recently, there were presidential elections in 2021. In the days immediately before the elections, Facebook took down a number of government accounts and pages that it argued engaged in coordinated inauthentic behaviour to target political debate ahead of an election. These accounts included President Museveni's press secretary and several accounts linked to the citizen centre at the Ministry of Information. And I think from the perspective of the national resistance movement, the ruling party, they were simply following the political tactics that they have seen elsewhere, other countries using, and they also said that they were following the same political tactics as the national unity platform, which the opposition leader Bobby Wine led, and he was aggressively using social media to campaign.

The government had previously complained that the opposition was misusing social media in a letter to social media companies. He requested the takedown of certain content, but no action was taken, and I will return to this point. So, for five days during the election, there was an Internet shutdown, and finally, when the Internet was restored, Facebook remained banned for more than six months after the election, and President Museveni argued (and here I will quote him) 'so if it's Facebook operating in Uganda, it should be used equitably by everyone who wants to use it. If you want to take sides against the [National Resistance Movement], then that group will not operate in Uganda [that group referring to Facebook]. Uganda is ours. It's not anybody's.' He continued, 'There's no way anybody can come here and play around with our country and decide who is good and who is bad. I'm therefore very sorry about the inconvenience to those who've been using this channel but we cannot tolerate the arrogance of anybody coming here to decide who's good and who's bad.' So, basically, Museveni expressed the belief that Facebook was making these kinds of decisions autonomously, and I think he raises two key issues.

First, who is writing the rules around what's allowed on social media, particularly around elections and especially about hate speech and misinformation?

Second, how these rules are being implemented, and then third, what shutdowns show us as a response. What do they tell us about freedom of expression, law, and governance in the post-colonial state, particularly around election time?

Right now, when it comes to large Western platforms like Meta, or X, the discussion around rules and content moderation is dominated by lawyers and technologists in the global north, and I think while there's some discussion of context around online speech or how the rules apply, it is usually from a cultural norms perspective about how to interpret certain speech. For decades, sociological scholars have been looking at issues of hate speech and argued how law is notoriously bad at accounting for context, and understanding the ambiguous factors of identity, motives, and history, but regulation has very much focused on the style and the superficial content of speech, and I think this has remained the case for social media.

So, what Internet shutdowns are actually exposing is this massive and crude response by the state, which is the broader theatre in which these speech rules are playing out. And I think what is missing from this is a discussion or accounting for the context of the post-colonial state and the various ways that governance or law works, as well as the history of media and communications before social media, particularly around elections that have been part of so many state and nation-building projects, and of course this idea of sovereignty that Museveni spoke about. At independence, African countries were asked to replicate the idea of the sovereign nation, a state with a monopoly on authority and justice. An ideal that took the Westphalian state 800 years to get rid of other sources of authority, and since independence, many of Africa's leaders, from Julius Nyerere to Kwame Nkrumah, had very definite ideas around what role the media should play in this project.

They tried to leverage print, radio, and television as tools for state and nation-building, forcing a type of authority that could not be achieved during long and bloody struggles that other countries had. But this control of the media combined with some authentic projects, some very genuine efforts of community building, was also coupled with self-serving tactics to benefit the few and retain or consolidate power. Now we see how social media platforms that are imbued with, on the one hand, a level of tremendous popularity channelled from their still powerful imageries of tools for activism and contestation, and on the other hand, their relative inaccessibility of control by national authorities, broke this system of communication for nation building.

Big Tech came in and changed everything, not least of all because they're operating from California or Beijing, and we need to see shutdowns within this context as well as within a broader understanding of the contemporary realities of the state in Africa rather than an idealised notion. Returning to the first point, when it comes to who writes the rules, digital technologies, digital cultures, and the rules that accompany platforms are not these free-floating global spheres or communities. They are rooted in national power centres in the US, China, and in Tencent, Meta, and Google.

The kinds of community standards or rules of service, as they are often termed, are primarily drafted in California. And these rules or standards are not translated and regularly updated into Africa's many diverse languages. At the moment, it's just a handful.

Algorithms are not trained in African languages, and the systems that feed fact-checkers mis- and disinformation that is trending have, again, little or no capacity in African languages. This comes at a time when the elevation, the integration of African languages is a firm priority of decolonisation for many institutions and governments, including, for example, where I am at the University of Johannesburg. And so, despite the discourse by social media companies to have a focus on 'communities', on bringing people together, we see an overwhelming emphasis on the state and how they relate to the state. Again, we see it in language. When it comes to content moderation, they focus on the language of the state. In Ethiopia, it is Amharic, which is actually spoken by a minority of people, but it is the language of the government, while there is little moderation in other languages that are not the language of the government, including historically marginalised groups.

On this issue of who writes the rules, the challenge is how to account for ideology's role in terms of how communication has been seen and regulated and what role it plays in post-liberation nation-building projects.

Like many countries, Uganda has a long history of debating and defining what kind of speech should be allowed. The NRM had a very ambitious media apparatus that was integral to its struggle. After coming to power, the media was liberalised, and the government even started independent newspapers, including the *New Vision*. This was seen as part of this unique experiment, whereby a government newspaper was supposed to be critical of the NRM as part of what it termed a single-party democracy.

But the rules that the government tried to devise were not ahistorical, and they were also negotiated with courts, opposition actors, and other public authorities. But these kinds of discussions or negotiation processes have not taken place with the rules and the rulers that govern social media. So for a poorer country like Uganda, which is not Germany or the EU, and has little power to negotiate and influence these rules, the rules and relationships are just thrust on them, and they are simply expected to adapt to them. There is no particular context realisation for their particular political projects.

We also see how unevenly and unequally these rules are being implemented globally. This was one of the major findings from the Francis Haugen Facebook leaks, in which Meta made it clear that they have priority countries and priority markets for content moderation. However, the overwhelming evidence suggested that they do very little in Africa.

Companies are slow to take down content around elections and marginal markets, and they have also been accused of ignoring genocide in places like Ethiopia and Myanmar. There has been far less research at a national level regarding the consistency and the even-handedness with which these rules might be implemented, particularly when it comes to political parties, opposition parties, and government parties. Uganda points to some of these challenges.

So for example, with the Facebook shutdown case, there was a question of whether the opposition was treated the same as the government when it came to the takedown of inauthentic behaviour. And here I think the evidence suggests no, that Facebook took down the government inauthentic behaviour, but did little to address the opposition, of which there was also evidence of inauthentic behaviour. And particularly for the government, this appeared uneven. It raised questions about the process, and they argued that Facebook had favoured the opposition by allowing them to create numerous accounts and post online, but it had blocked the government's efforts to do the same.

One challenge is that the only way the government saw or believed it could effectively fight back was to shut down the Internet. This raises the question of whose rules to follow when taking down content.

Before the elections, for example, the Ugandan Communications Commission wrote a letter to YouTube requesting the takedown of certain videos, arguing that they were inciting violence and compromising national security. Google declined the government's request, and they said there was not a court order. Nicholas Opiya, a human rights lawyer, argued that one problem was how the government approached Google. It reflected a gap in understanding or ignorance of how large social media companies operate and how content is assessed according to a company's community standards. And so basically he was arguing that Google would just throw the letter from the Ugandan government in the trash. It had no relevance. They couldn't take it seriously. But it also shows, in a way, the government was left humiliated. These companies do not have offices in Uganda. There's nowhere that you can go knock on the door and have a conversation about it. Decisions are often made hastily. They are often made with little evidence. They are often made with very, very, very little staffing as well.

So, in conclusion, I would like to be clear that I'm not trying to justify Internet shutdowns. I'm not saying they are a good or useful tool. But rather, I think we need to change how we think about them and also recognise shutdowns as forms of contestation, as forms of resistance, particularly in the Global South.

Rather than just dismissing them and just categorising them as abuses by despotic leaders around elections, we need to understand more why they are happening. And I think social media is creating the sense of moral panic for some governments. The platforms and companies seem out of reach. They can come in to countries and completely mess up with the politics of a place without knowing the rules or ideologies or even having effective processes in place for moderating content in local languages. So I think if we start to see shutdowns as a form of contestation, it might open up new ways of engaging with them, new avenues of how to effectively respond or even pre-empt their use, rather than just dismissing them.

9

Democracy Threatened from Within

THE HONOURABLE MALCOLM TURNBULL

Liberal democracy is threatened both from without and within.

We are seeing this in a very kinetic way in Ukraine at the moment, with Putin's brutal and illegal invasion of that country. And we've also seen real economic coercion of countries in our region from the People's Republic of China. But external threats are in many respects easier to grapple with, at least conceptually, than internal ones. And it is those threats from within to which I will turn.

Enoch Powell said a politician who complains about the newspapers is like a mariner complaining about the sea. And it's a good point because the media is the environment in which politics operates. There is a tendency to think that because in a parliament, the press sit in the press gallery and the politicians are in the chamber, that there's some distinction between the two; there isn't. It is a political ecosystem. And so the way in which that ecosystem operates and the way in which people communicate with each other is absolutely fundamental to the way politics operates.

Now, when I was first a journalist, in fact, a political journalist, about 50 years ago, in the mid-70s, the news media platforms had to seek a broad audience. Some of them leaned a bit to the left or a bit to the right, but they wanted to maximise the readers that they had in order to maximise their advertising revenues. Indeed, when the *Sydney Morning Herald* was founded by the Fairfax family in the 1840s, they had on the front page of their first edition some lines from Alexander Pope saying, 'In moderation, placing all my glory, while Tories call me Whig and Whigs a Tory.' Now those of you familiar with Australian media and politics would know that the old Fairfaxes were not especially broad-minded politically, but they knew on what side their advertising bread was buttered.

Now, all of that has dramatically changed in the last couple of decades. A whole range of technological changes have meant that it is now profitable to narrowcast as a broadcaster or publisher. That's to say, you can monetise an audience of a scale or percentage of the population that you would not hitherto have been able to monetise. And so narrowcasting is increasingly the norm.

And then when you turn to social media, there are few limits on the craziness or extremism that can be promoted. Most disturbingly, people are increasingly living in media and hence political silos or put another way, tribal echo chambers.

Recently in one of my podcasts I spoke with Alan Rusbridger, formerly editor of *The Guardian* for many years. And we were talking about what I regard as essentially an elitist view of media diversity. It's both elitist and anachronistic, and it's what I call the senior common room view of media diversity. You'd walk into the senior common room at a university or college, and you have all the newspapers laid out on a table. You've got a range of magazines, a range of publications, and you can dip into all of them or some of them, but they're all available for you. And so, you can say that the media of the right balance those of the left.

And because these newspapers on the SCR table have got enough overlapping casual readers, there is a limit to how much they can travel beyond the bounds of reality. But we are now in an environment where the media has become increasingly more partisan. And I'm speaking particularly of the US, the most consequential democracy on which pretty much all others rely. I'm speaking particularly of Fox News here, Mr Murdoch's channel. It has become angertainment.

In other words, it is seeking to enrage people to keep them engaged. And of course, the algorithms that the social media platforms use to keep people engaged are much the same. You keep people on YouTube or Facebook by continuing to feed them content that reinforces their prejudices, riles them up. And as a result, you get a more polarised environment. Now you can say, of course, well, there are media channels that are saying different things, alternatives. But we are not in that senior common room. *The New York Times* and MSNBC do not balance Fox News because the people who watch Fox News do not watch MSNBC and vice versa.

In fact, there you've got people living in silos. So, you have the extraordinary situation in this country where I'm speaking to you from New York at the moment. Today a majority of Republican voters still believe, despite all of the evidence and all of the court decisions, that Donald Trump won the 2020 election, and that Joe Biden is illegitimate. You have the extraordinary situation that this was not only peddled on social media, but Mr Murdoch's Fox News, by far the most influential news channel in the US, promoted and amplified this lie in circumstances where Mr Murdoch and his senior executives and commentators knew it was untrue.

Part of that Trump lie about the election was the claim that two voting machine companies had rigged their machines to favour Biden. Both sued and already Fox has had to pay a heavy price – $870 million – for settling the case brought by Dominion.

So that was a very big price paid to keep the Murdochs *père et fils* out of the witness box. Fox News did not send the mob to storm the Capitol but by promoting the stolen election lie it created a context which of course enabled the January 6 attempted coup d'état.

Now the challenge is what is to be done? You know, we've all assumed that freedom of speech will ensure that in the marketplace of ideas, the truth will prevail. But yet we are drowning in lies. And therein lies the challenge. In Australia, Murdoch's control of 70 per cent of metropolitan daily newspaper circulation has been an issue of concern for decades.

Now, obviously, there was a change of government in 2022 in Australia. The Liberal Party lost; the Labor Party won. That's important, it happens regularly, and many would say that parliamentary democracy depends on changes of government – not that anyone enjoys being tipped out of the office at the time!

But something remarkable happened in 2022 in Australia. When the votes were counted there were nine of what had been the Liberal Party's safest seats in the hands of small 'l' liberal independents. All women, all progressive on climate and other social issues. All, I might add, very capable and smart.

There are only 150 seats in Australia's House of Representatives and to form a government you need to have the confidence of a majority of them. How do you do that if 9 of your safest seats are now on the cross bench, and doesn't that send a powerful message to the Liberals (Australia's centre right party) that they have swung too far to the right, especially on climate?

After I ceased to be Prime Minister, and leader of the Liberal Party, in 2018, the party moved to the right and kept going and it did so because it was largely living in that right-wing media bubble. And this was the reality where so many of the party members were and so many of the MPs and senators were as well. And naturally, a lot of longstanding traditional Liberal voters, centre-right voters, felt this had gone too far.

Now in the US, where you've got a rusted-on two-party system, it is very hard for independents to break through. A Republican who is in that situation and can't stand Donald Trump and the whole MAGA thing, has a few choices. One, he or she can stay at home, they don't have to vote. Two, they can hold their nose and still vote Republican. Three, they can hold their nose even tighter perhaps, and vote for the Democrats.

Or they can, as Adam Kinsinger observed to me in another one of my podcast guests, self-radicalise. In other words, despite being a traditional Republican who was attracted to Reagan and the Bushes, persuade themselves that Trump is not a mountebank after all. Clearly many traditional Republicans have done that, and the increasing number of Republican Party leaders who oppose Trump are very, very much in the minority and have not seemed to dent Mr Trump's standing in the polls.

Australia has a very different electoral system to the US. It is not just that we have a traditional parliamentary system modelled in the UK, but that we have three features to our electoral system which are very different.

First, we have compulsory voting. We believe that 97 per cent of all Australians over the age of 18 are on the electoral roll and typically 93 per cent of all those on the roll vote at elections. If they do not vote without a valid excuse, they have to pay a small fine. This means parties and candidates do not have to run off to extremes to get the vote out – everyone votes.

While the fine for not voting is very small, it has developed a culture of high compliance and participation in voting. And to illustrate that, I held, when I was PM at the end of 2017, an absolutely voluntary postal ballot on the subject of whether we should legalise same-sex marriage or not, something I was very strongly in favour of, but it was hugely divisive politically. And so, we held this postal ballot. 80 per cent of Australians participated in it voluntarily and I might say 62 per cent voted yes. So that settled that issue very satisfactorily.

If you make voting compulsory, you have to make it easy to vote. So you don't get this problem you have in so many democracies, particularly the US, of voter suppression. So we have polling days on a weekend. Naturally, there are plenty of opportunities for postal voting, pre-poll voting and so forth. We make it easy to vote.

Second, we have preferential voting, what Americans called ranked choice voting. So, a candidate must get over 50 per cent of the vote either on first preferences or on the distribution of preferences. If there are four candidates, voters must number them 1 through 4. If no candidate has a majority on first preference votes, then the lower-ranked candidates preferences are distributed until one candidate has a majority. This is what Australians refer to as the 'two party preferred vote'.

These independent liberals (nicknamed Teals because of their campaign livery) typically received about 35 per cent of the first preference vote and the incumbent Liberal candidate about 40 per cent. In a first past-the-post system like the UK or the Americans have, the Liberal incumbent would have won because a plurality wins.

This was the situation in my old district of Wentworth. The independent Teal, Allegra Spender, ended up winning handsomely on the two-party preferred vote because she got most of the second preferences from the Labor candidate and the Greens candidate, who finished further behind. And that pattern, more or less, is what happened in all of these electorates.

This sends a very clear message, which is to say, if you move too far to the right, in this case you're not seen as doing enough on gender equity. You're seen as not doing enough on climate. You're perceived as being too socially conservative. Then centrist voters have got an option that is better than holding their nose and voting for the Liberal Party or holding it even tighter and voting for their political opponents. They've got that independent option.

We have had compulsory voting and preferential voting for a century. A third feature in our system, which is not quite as long-standing, is that the boundaries of parliamentary districts are drawn by an independent Australian Electoral Commission.[1] This ensures there is no gerrymandering in our system. By contrast, in the US, the combination of voluntary voting, first-past-the-post counting, and gerrymandering of districts by State congresses means that for the vast majority of the seats in the House of Representatives, the only contest that matters is the party primary, in which maybe 10 per cent of the electorate vote. Naturally, these are the most energised and zealous voters, and so candidates who wish to win the primary will steer to the right for Republicans and to the left for Democrats.

So, while the Australian system encourages politics to be mediated at the centre, the American system encourages polarisation. And the media, as I have described, amplifies and exacerbates that polarisation.

[1] Australian Electoral Commission, see www.aec.gov.au.

So the bottom line I want to make is that electoral systems really matter. It's not just a question of totting the votes up and having a transparent, democratic process. I mean, no one would suggest the UK is not democratic. But simply having that combination of compulsory voting so everyone's on the roll and preferential voting, those two things bring politics back to the centre.

Now I'll just conclude on this point because I think listening to the earlier speakers, I could anticipate this question. Why is it important that politics is focused on the centre? Well, the answer is that our systems, parliamentary democratic systems, have to be focused on the centre because people have to compromise. And they have to be reasonably resigned to changes of government and leadership.

I can illustrate this with a conversation I had over 30 years ago with someone who was not at all instinctively democratic, a gentleman called Vladimir Volfovich Zhirinovsky, who some of you may remember was a very right-wing Russian politician. I was doing some business in Russia at the time and we were trying to get some legislation passed. And the Liberals, Mr Gaidar's party, said they wouldn't talk to Zhirinovsky's party, because they were fascist, too right-wing, whatever the complaint was. And I said, well, you know, in a parliamentary system, you've got to talk to everyone.

So, I ended up talking to Zhirinovsky, and I remember Zhirinovsky said to me 'when I am president, I will have Yeltsin shot'. I said, okay. I said, that's your platform, is it? And he said, yes, 'I'm going to have him shot'.

And I said, 'Well, two points. One, given he is the president, if he takes you seriously, he's quite likely to shoot you first. Second point is what you should be saying is 'when I am president, Mister Yeltsin will have a very generous pension, palatial house on the Black Sea and every possible comfort known to man'.

And I said, 'If you say that, then he maybe won't feel so bad about losing an election to you'. And Zhirinovsky sat back and said, 'yes, that's a different way of looking at it – the Western model'.

This is the critical thing in democratic, parliamentary democracies. You've got to be prepared to live with the alternative and you've got to be able to compromise. It's very rare for an Australian government to have a majority in the Senate because of the way it's selected with proportional representation in the States.

When I was PM, the press and my critics would say, 'Turnbull's horse trading in the Senate and cutting deals with all sorts of people'. And I used to say, 'Look, you could put a big sign up in the Senate 'HORSE TRADING CENTRE'.

I said, 'That's what it's for. Parliaments are for doing deals. If you want to call them horse trading, fair enough. That's what it's all about. But you've got to get people together to compromise and that means bring them to the centre.'

Now, the difficulty is that we have a media environment, which is pushing people to the extremes and making it harder and harder to compromise. And that is the challenge that, frankly, that we have to address. And the answer is not simply diversity. It is actually responsibility.

Conclusion: Democracy in Crisis: A Review

DJ GALLIGAN

I. Representative Democracy: Nature, Appeal, Defects

The aim of The Putney Debates 2023 was to examine the state of democracy and to assess whether, as often claimed, it is in crisis. *Crisis* means a turning point; in social affairs, a situation of danger or suspense. The enquiry raises three issues: first, the meaning of democracy; second, the evidence as to how it is working and the defects; and, third, whether the evidence shows a state of crisis. It is plain from the earlier chapters that the enquiry is more complex than it seems at first sight and may be approached in different ways, while the answers are far from clear or certain. Nevertheless, the voyage is well-worthwhile, and much is learnt along the way. My purpose in this final chapter is to draw out the themes and remove some of the loose ends; to present a concept of democracy that is more complete than the conventional, then offer an opinion as to whether there is a crisis.

Representative democracy is at the centre of the enquiry. Richard Clary sets the scene by taking democracy to mean representative democracy. The 'government', or at least the leaders, are selected by 'fair and open election'. Citizens 'may participate equally' but must 'abide by the results' whatever they are. To the basic concept other features are added. Representatives work for the common good, which they settle by engaging in 'knowledgeable debate and deliberation', reflecting 'consensus through compromise'. Elected representatives exercise 'independent judgement' and are not bound by the views of electors or by citizens generally. Prudence and the force of an impending election might prompt the elected to consult and engage with their electors; but whether they do and the form it takes is up to them. The role of the people is limited to voting from time to time for one or other of the candidates.

The representative form conveys a thin concept of democracy. If democracy means the people, the *demos*, in some sense ruling themselves, representative democracy falls far short. The reasons are found in the origins. Representative democracy is in part a successor to princely rule, that is, rule by a monarch, czar, or emperor; and in part recognition that the people cannot be excluded from the constitutional order. In the UK, the House of Commons solved the problem by deeming itself, the elected chamber, to be or to embody the people, leaving no role for the actual people other than to vote. In the US, the elected few, the men of property, were deemed to know the common good. The master of French constitutional thought, the Abbé Sieyès, came to the same view by deeming the will of elected representatives to be the will of the people. The reality of power being in the hands of a few is then softened by being clothed in concepts of *sovereignty*, *representation*, and *consent*. What these concepts mean and their role in in the constitutional order is never explained.

Attempts by the people to establish more direct forms of democracy, even to engage vigorously in the processes of governing, historically, have been resisted and scorned. Contemporary ideas of democracy are caught in the shadow of history but not wholly captured. The people's gaining the right to vote, while a notable advance, rare historically and much valued, is not enough to constitute a worthwhile notion of democracy. It serves, however, as a base on and around which to build a justifiable and lasting relationship between the people on one side, and the elected leaders, officials, and institutions of government on the other side. As a prelude, let us be clear about the defects, the contradictions, and the conflicts inherent in representative democracy, which under scrutiny soon appear.

II. Representative Democracy under Scrutiny

Representative democracy under scrutiny gives rise to several issues: (i) the concept of democracy does not match the practice; (ii) confusion between form and substance; (iii) the uncertain place of the people and how it can be redefined to match the substantive purposes of government; (iv) how values, with origins outside, enter to regulate the relationship between the people and the officials; how they fit with representative democracy; (v) the place of agencies and institutions, including the courts, as sites of power within the system of government. Each is considered in turn.

A. Concept of Democracy

According to its Greek origins, democracy has two elements: *demos* (the people) and *cracy* (rule). The two elements are taken, rather loosely and summarily, to mean the people ruling themselves. Representative democracy makes no such pretence. The few elected by the people rule. Whether the people have a role between elections is left unstated. They might have some influence on the leaders but have no power to bind them. The next election's being never far away can be a source of influence; how much highly variable. The democratic element is the people's right to vote, nothing more. This is not to undervalue the right to vote, which has been hard-won and of critical importance in contemporary constitutional orders. The point is the right to vote on its own falls far short of the people ruling themselves. This gives rise to three issues. First: a system of government in which the people's engagement is restricted to voting for select leaders is democratic only in the narrowest sense. Second: the study of constitutional orders considered democratic shows that in practice the place and role of the people goes well beyond occasional voting. Third: in order to make sense of the empirical reality, the very concept of democracy has to be revised and restated.

B. Form Over Substance or Substance Over Form?

Representative democracy is presented as promoting form over substance. The people vote to elect leaders, *the form*, who then make decisions of policy as they think fit, *the substance*. If the people's role in rule by elected representatives is only to cast an occasional vote, it is hard to see the case for classing it as democracy. The people are not ruling themselves and between elections have no control over the leaders. The elected few may rule for the well-being of the people, but that depends on them, on their own sense of what that means and the strength of their commitment to rule accordingly. Why then has rule by the elected few not only become the standard of democracy but is defended as the best form? The answer in brief is that constitutional orders cast as representative democracies include much more than the people choosing the leaders. The mistake is to define such democracies as based on *form* not *substance*. The well-being of the people is the substantive part, the purpose of rule, while the means by which it is protected and advanced constitute the form. Form follows substance, rather than the other way around.

Let us return briefly to Lincoln's definition of democracy as 'government of the people, by the people, for the people'. That the three elements do not sit well together may be excused. It was after all a rhetorical flourish rather than a serious attempt to define democracy. Yet the very oddity hints at something deeper. If government be *of and by* the people, we may assume it is *for* the people, that is, serves the interests of the people. What then is the point of adding *for* the people? The classical definition presents the *demos* + *cracy*: the people rule themselves. *Cracy*, the form, prevails over *substance*, the well-being of the *demos*. As long as form is right, substance is served. Suppose the order be reversed: begin with the *demos*, the people, for whom the point of government is to protect and advance their well-being. Government has a *substantive* purpose; it is *for* the well-being of the people. Form then follows substance, is the means by which to achieve substance.

The confusion traces back to Madison's account of representative democracy as opposed to popular democracy. His account is based on the purpose or substantive goals of government, the common good, for which a suitable form has to be designed. The common good, the substantive purpose, is protection of property. The common good is best secured by men of property being in charge, the form. The democratic part consists in the people's choosing which men of property to entrust with governing. Form and substance are in harmony. In the real world, however, a glaring gap appears between the two. The common good, the well-being of the people, the substantive purpose of government, is more than protection of property.

Form and substance are out of step. There is no reason to expect a few men of property to know and understand, or wish to advance, the well-being of the people in a much wider sense; no guarantee rule is *for* the *demos*, the people in all the diversity of values and interests. The right to vote is important but not enough. Once Madison's account of democracy is understood as substantive, and that well-being has many dimensions, form is re-designed to cope. Ways and means have to be found to educate leaders about the well-being of the people; then values and processes need to be adopted to make sure well-being is served in practice. The consequences are twofold.

C. Place of the People Reconsidered

One concerns the place of the people. If their well-being is to be served, they need to be involved in the processes of government. First, in making known their interests, their sense of well-being, and how much they are valued. Second, the people need practical ways of ensuring well-being is protected and advanced, which in turn means engaging in the processes of rule, being vigilant, and having available modes of censure.

D. Ideas, Principles, Values: Allies of Democracy or Rivals?

The other consequence of tying democracy to well-being concerns ideas, principles, and values (referred to simply as *values*) that are brought into the constitutional field to guide the conduct of government. At the top, justice both substantive and procedural, rights and the rules of due process; at the next level, respect for law, allocation of functions among institutions, the role of the courts. Other levels could be added, other values, institutions and processes brought into the constitutional field, the unifying factor being that each in its own way contributes to the well-being of the people.

Several authors make reference to such principles and values, presenting them as having origins separate from democracy, conceptually and historically. In the leading chapter, Richard Clary, concedes the right to vote now-and-again is 'a fairly thin reed on which to base either participation or consent'; representative democracy needs them but their credentials to enter are unclear. Several 'secondary assumptions' are enlisted to add weight: the elected work for the common good; through debate and deliberation, the elected reach conclusions that 'reflect consensus through compromise'.

Other conditions are ready to be added. Fui Tsikata cites the work of Maurice Vile, who wrote about the need to reconcile 'values of liberty and equality' with representative democracy. How they are reconciled, and their exact status in the amended notion of democracy is not clear. The outcome seems to be a redefinition of democracy, now *liberal democracy*, not just representative. The concept of democracy broadens. Paul Craig writes eloquently of 'the constraints that flow from the rule of law'. Ruzha Smilova considers 'equality, the fundamental value and a necessary pre-supposition of democracy', that is, it has origins prior to and independent of democracy. Alessandra and Bogdan Iancu explain how 'liberal constitutionalism goes hand in hand with democratic ethos', the implication being that certain values enter into and moderate democracy.

Another dimension of a well-working democracy is the people's being well-informed. That depends on the availability of information and its accessibility. Nicole Stremlau presents a fresh approach to the issue. The subject of enquiry is the shutdown of the Internet, especially around the time of elections. The strategy is used and justified by governments as a counter to 'disinformation around elections' and in addition to 'mitigate the perceived impact' hate speech could have on 'election-related violence'. The strategy is opposed as 'violating the rights to freedom of expression or access to information'. Nicole's study, focused on experience in Africa with special attention to Uganda, offers guidance to a new and challenging situation that has lessons for all democracies. The power of the Internet and those who control it; the importance of the Internet in informing voters; the rules regulating provision and service; and not least the effect on the democratic constitutional order, are well-explained in Nicole's chapter and a solid foundation laid on which to build.

The citations could continue but the point is made: democracy as a form of government is both guided by and subject to such values. They enter the constitutional order to interact with the representative relationship, at times reinforcing, at times modifying. Values for which representative democracy in the thin sense has neither need nor room. In the absence of such values, representative democracy would be so limited in scope, restricted to one small portion of relations between the people and government, one would struggle to understand why democracy has such appeal, how it bears such weight in the ordering of societies. The case for redesign and redefinition is compelling, as we shall see shortly.

E. Agencies of Government, Sites of Power

Accounts of representative democracy are tied to the elected levels of government, barely noticing let along taking account of the machinery of government in all its forms – the many sites of power from the executive to administrative agencies, regulatory boards and bodies, and the apparatus of local government. At each site, aspects of well-being are in issue, covering matters from settling broad policy, to setting standards and rules, and then applying them in specific cases. One needs only to browse through a textbook on administrative law to see the extent to which persons, groups, and sectors with interests at stake may be involved, how they may engage, be vigilant, and impose censure. The bulk of governing occurs at such sites and the constitutional order displayed in all the diversity of values, purposes, and forms. At each site the relationship between the people and government is in issue, how it is handled a guide to the democratic process at work.

The role of the courts in a system of representative democracy is not clear. On one theory there is nothing to explain, no questions to answer because the courts simply protect the *form*, the procedures, of representative democracy. The more realistic view is that the courts are deep in matters of *substance* and at risk of being in conflict with the elected leaders, the executive, and the agencies. How that fits with representative democracy is left unsaid, a point to which I return later in this chapter.

III. Democracy Redesigned and Redefined

Democracy may now be redesigned and redefined to mean:

1. a system of government *for the people*, that is, to protect and advance their well-being;
2. the people have a place, a share in the processes of governing, shaped and guided by the dimension of well-being at issue and by the nature and function of each institution of government;
3. among the many forms of involvement, the election of leaders is first and foremost in laying the foundations of the constitutional order;
4. principles and values drawn from the wider society are admitted to the constitutional order to contribute to aspects of well-being.

Substantive constitutional democracy: let us name it. A clumsy name for an elegant conception but needed to avoid confusion with other conceptions: representative democracy, liberal democracy, parliamentary democracy, and any others the reader might wish to add. When in the remainder of the chapter the word *democracy* is used, it means *substantive constitutional democracy.*

According to this concept of democracy, government *for* the people takes the leading role, then quietly sets the scene for engagement *of* and *by* the people. The shift is subtle but critical. Well-being is served by a range of processes, some left to the people themselves, others stemming from other sources. The risks are reduced by the people's having the final say, for as David Hume pointed out 'the governors have nothing to sustain them but opinion', the opinion of the people. Government in all its forms is for the well-being of the people, who have the power to force change, to insist on other forms, other institutions and processes.

IV. Beyond Representative to Substantive Constitutional Democracy

Representative democracy is a normative principle defining the relationship between elected leaders and the people. It is a claim about how the relationship ought to be defined and structured. To treat the principle as if it were itself the constitutional order is a mistake commonly encountered. The distinction is critical. A constitutional order provides the full apparatus of government; distributes power among offices, agencies, and institutions; declares the values and principles of constitutional status; and defines the place of the people. The principle of representation is one part of the whole, a part much valued, even assigned by some the central part; but still only one part and not the whole. Once the conceptual distinction is made, the difference between a political principle and the constitutional order, the problems of practice, the merits and demerits of ideas and structures, are better understood.

The history, purpose, and value of constitutions are best approached in this way. The power of princes, the structure of institutions, the claims and expectations of the people, are all part of that history. Notions of justice, both as a *dynamic* force for change and as a *protective* principle, have long been embedded in social relations, including those between citizen and state. Ideas of juridical equality, respect for rights, and the need for courts and other institutions to declare and uphold rights, have deep foundations in western nations. Alexandra and Bogdan Iancu, in charting the history, show how such ideas evolved over time to secure a valued position in the constitutional framework. They also bring out the potential conflict between the ideas and the people's claims and efforts to have a place in the processes of governing. The need for agencies and the utility, in administering and implementing policies and programmes at various levels of society, has origins in the earliest forms of government.

Finally, another notion was born, grew, and took on weight: the idea that somehow, despite distractions and deviations, abuses and the wolfish appetites, the purpose of the constitutional order is to serve the needs and utilities, the well-being in all its modes, of the people. Concepts and principles come and go, adjust and change in tune with social and economic conditions. Some drop away, others become the base for constitutional invention and experiment; some as transient as the night, some passing with the seasons, others digging-in to stay.

Into this account the representative principle fits well. While traces are detected in earlier concepts and ideas, the relationship now at the core of representative democracy, that leaders be elected by the people, was late to reach the constitutional field. Despite modest origins, the principle has become entrenched, part of the foundation of relations between the people and government – part of the foundation, not the whole, being the critical point. Other principles flaunt equal rank. Respect for justice according to the standards set by law is one; protection of rights another. Hence the need for the courts and their being accessible to the people. Other principles of lesser rank, but still officer-class, guide the practice and process of governing. One is the separation of powers among the institutions of government. Another imposes on the agencies of government principles of due process and other standards to apply in exercising authority, including the use of discretion in all its forms and functions. A third set of principles defines the role of persons, groups, and sectors whose interests are affected by the actions of agencies, across the range from applying rules and standards to giving content to open discretion, a role based on forms of engagement, vigilance, and censure.

The list could go on but the point is plain: the constitutional order, depicted as a field to be cultivated, turns out to be busy and crowded, where values and principles at times work together but often are rivals competing for position and priority. This is neither a matter of regret nor reason for denouncing one as inferior to another. Overlap and conflict among ideas, values, and principles is normal, a standard feature of any field of social endeavour. Sometimes there is a right ranking, one value or principle's being obviously superior to another. At other times conflict occurs, with one asserting superiority rather than logic. Conflict among ideas, principles, and values is normal within fields of social endeavour, the constitutional order no exception. In a well-cultivated field, ways are found for the three to work together to make a coherent whole. The edges are bound to be frayed, the boundaries rough and uneven, rendering conflict unavoidable. Resolution is achieved partly by reaching back into the foundations to excavate the values, partly by reasoned argument, partly by moderation and restraint, sometimes by sheer power.

V. Tensions and Instabilities

Democracy redefined and redesigned contains tensions and instabilities some of which are discussed in the chapters, others left for the future. My purpose now is to single out for comment those that are said to weaken democracy and pose the most serious threats.

A. Electoral Process and Outcomes

The electoral process is open to abuse and distortion. The foundations of representative democracy are twofold: citizens vote for leaders and then accept the result. Having singled out the two main elements, Richard Clary goes on to consider the points of tension and instability. The main ones are: the selection of candidates; the undue influence of certain persons, groups, or sectors; the role of political parties; some voters feeling left out, their preferences not counting in the political process. The tensions heighten, leading in the US 'to refusal to accept elections'. The parliamentary system of the UK is said to be riddled with tensions: outcomes are not 'representative'; 'voters' intended results' are not reached; a majority produced that 'overstates the mandate of the winning party'. Other values are then enlisted to ground additional concerns: a lack of consensus and compromise, of deliberation and debate; and the absence of 'basic cultural norms' embraced by all. These are serious criticisms of the British system and, presumably, other systems centred on the sovereignty of parliament. Whether the criticisms are justified is debatable and enough to prompt the gathering of more evidence.

A refreshing alternative to the electoral systems of both the British and American kinds is the preferential approach practised in Australia. In the final substantive chapter, Malcolm Turnbull outlines the method and the benefits. The three elements are: voting is compulsory for anyone over the age of 18; a culture of 'high compliance and participation' has developed; the boundaries of electorates are drawn by an independent commission. The results are commendable. One, the system 'encourages politics to be mediated at the centre', a striking contrast with electoral systems in the US, which 'encourage polarisation'. The other advantage is to urge the people to compromise, and to be 'reasonably resigned to changes of government and leadership'.

B. Relations between Electors and Elected

The role of the people in representative democracy is to elect the leaders. Between elections, the people are free to express their opinions and to influence the elected, but the openings are few and the leaders free to take notice or not. The power of election is not yet spent. Although limited constitutionally to voting, the next election being far away allows, potentially, the people to have some influence on the course of government, on the decisions and actions of leaders. The channels of influence are variable, some open and accessible, others secret and accessible only to a few. Who has influence and how much is unevenly spread among sectors, groups, and persons. Some develop close relations with leaders, have influence on policies and practices; others feel left out, their interests ignored, their well-being of no weight.

The question in the background, indeed the basic issue for democracy, is how to make decisions of policy that bring together several aims. The critical conditions are: that decisions be based on knowledge, evidence, and sound reasoning; that they take account of the interests and expectations of the persons, sectors, and groups affected; and that they respect and apply the values of substantive constitutional democracy. In building on these basic conditions, Frank Vibert offers guidance on how to bring together the several guiding factors. He addresses, with insight and understanding, the problem of agencies having expert knowledge and the risk of their acquiring independence and autonomy from the political process and the people.

C. Disaffection to Defiance

The resulting risks are of two kinds, different in nature and leading down different paths. Groups and sectors feeling neglected are inclined to single out certain leaders, gain influence over them, and push them down routes designed to serve and advance their select interests. The results are several and varied, some mild, some drastic. One is growing discontent with the workings of government, moderate at first but at risk of being inflamed, from breeding mild scepticism about the system of rule, to outright rejection, with many stages in between. As the cause deepens, the restraints needed to sustain a constitutional order, well-described in Daniel Smilov's chapter, are thrown aside. The processes and institutions of government come to be viewed with contempt, the constitutional order at risk of being rendered ineffective. Many staging posts line the way. The virus, at first mild and treatable, the constitutional conventions restored, on occasion spreads, becomes more intense, and proves hard to curb.

As passions prevail, the restraints needed not only on the part of officials but persons, groups, and sectors as well, are cast aside. The removal, or even the easing, of constitutional constraints opens the gate to the social and economic order. The differences and divisions, the inequalities of class, status, and wealth, smoothed and soothed by the constitutional order, are now in the open. The inequalities bared and the conventions of constraint weakened, the contest over the power to rule becomes inseparable from the social and economic structure. The tug-and-scramble among interests, normally moderated and made orderly by the constitution, is now unlicensed and unrestrained, constraints trampled and consensus trounced.

D. Containing the Majority: Respecting Minorities

Democracy, however defined, creates majorities and minorities. In a well-working democracy the majority, through the elected leaders, respects the minorities, takes account of differences as to notions of well-being, sentiments, and aspirations. Yet, the tension inherent in relations between them easily gets out of control. Several chapters make reference to the tension, how it needs to be managed and, if not, the consequences, not only to the alienated groups and sectors, but to the stability and functioning of government. In analysing the nations of Africa, Zim Nwokora notes how the risk of domination by the majority is especially high in systems of direct democracy where the people vote on specific issues and policies.

In her study of democracy in India, Angana Chatterji gives a stark and sobering account of persistent and seemingly ruthless oppression of Muslim minorities by the government, whose main support is the Hindu majority. Angana describes the efforts of the government 'to configure a Hindu nationalist state in India'. The strong support of the majority enables the government to declare and enforce states of emergency, to take 'extra-legal and authoritarian-to dictatorial measures'. At the local level, supporters of the government are active in creating institutions and practices, using 'local and symbolic imaginaries to incite the Hindu majority to unparalleled dominance'.

The division is not usually so egregious, nor the potential for dominance so extreme. Diversity, whatever the kind, whether cultural or religious, ethnic or economic, is a common feature of nation-states and the tensions are always present. In settled and well-functioning constitutional orders, ways are found and measures taken to respect minorities and restrict majorities. Acknowledging diversity is the first stage; attributing value to it the second; taking practical measures the third. The measures are many, the scope open-ended, from conferring rights at one end, to granting within the constitutional order a degree of autonomy and independence at the other end. For present purposes two points warrant special notice. First, the relationship between majorities and minorities is an issue to be addressed in designing a constitutional order. Second, the need to take account of the relationship, and to provide measures capable of containing the tension, strengthens the case for a concept of democracy based on substance not form.

E. Executive Power: Presidents, Prime Ministers, and Populists

In his speech to the Greek generals as the war against Troy stalled, Ulysses spoke of the *universal wolf*, the insatiable appetite for power. The constitutional order is not exempt. The wolf of biggest appetite enters the field in the form of executive authority in the hands of presidents, prime ministers, and other holders of high office. Executive power is needed for effective government; executive power by nature poses risks.

Executive dominance, as depicted by Sionaidh Douglas-Scott, captures the sense of executive power and its tendency to dominate parliament. The power of the Prime Minister, alone or in league with a handful of ministers and advisers, has the potential 'to cripple democracy in the United Kingdom'. If that be an inescapable feature of a parliamentary system, the risk is bound to be more serious in systems where the executive, normally designated president, is elected by the people and empowered directly by the constitution. A casual observer of the behaviour of the current President of the US might well conclude that the powers of office are unbounded.

The risks of executive power and the consequences in the nations of South America are disclosed and discussed by Pedro Fortes. Despite each nation being distinct, a product of its own history, social structure and culture, Pedro finds patterns and practices of a general, even of a universal kind. Several themes stand out and are worth noting. One is to confirm the strength of the wolfish appetite for power. Another is the temptation to use the office of president to weaken, even to the point of getting rid of, the other institutions, parliament and courts in particular. A third theme concerns the institutions and agencies of government, which are kept weak and unable to deliver the services the people expect. A fourth theme is the passion of presidents to stay in power and the means they invent for doing so, which signals a fifth theme. The political parties, although normally weak, are nevertheless potentially a valued means of support for the presidential ambition to stay in office, a form presidents are keen to cultivate. A final and rather surprising pattern emerging from the South American experience is the vulnerability of presidents, the ease with which they are un-seated, no matter how powerful they become.

F. Beyond Leaders: Recourse to Other Institutions and Processes: Agencies of Government

The other main route open to the people is to have recourse to the other processes and institutions of government. They divide roughly into the many agencies that deliver aspects of well-being, and the courts, which have a more defined and limited place in the constitutional order. A few remarks about the agencies, then attention to the courts.

The first thing to notice is the absence of the agencies from accounts of democracy. This I try to remedy in my own chapter where I propose an approach in which the agencies take a leading role in the grand theatre of government and the staging of democracy. The orthodox idea seems to be that the agencies, from the highest regulatory bodies to the lowliest administrative ones, are within the domain of the higher organs, the legislative and executive. They create the agencies, define their powers, and hold them to account. On this approach the agencies are simply tools to give effect to the wishes of leaders, and so of little interest either to the people or to democracy. The account is partly true but seriously incomplete. Each agency has a sphere of autonomy and independence, a discretionary space in which to decide policies, and to draw up and apply rules and standards. And not least to encounter those persons, groups, and sectors whose interests are affected by the agency's actions. How the encounter is conducted, the relationship with interested parties constructed, the consequences for the well-being of the parties, taken together constitute a dimension of democracy of critical concern.

How well the agencies perform in serving well-being, in whatever form it appears at each site of government, is one barometer of democracy. Evidence is abundant in developed systems of administrative law and in empirical studies, although more is needed for a more complete understanding and assessment. The effects of poorly constructed and badly functioning institutions and agencies are shown in Pedro's chapter on South America. In his chapter on the nation-states of Africa, Zim considers the weakness of the state in general, and the agencies in particular, to be a common feature of government. Incomes are low and economic growth is slow, yet the state is unable to provide some of the basic forms of aid and welfare. The people have few ways of engaging in the processes of government and administration. There is, in short, a serious gap between the people and the organs of government. As the gap widens, the less the well-being of the people is served and the democratic character is weakened. The gap varies in size from one nation to another; just how much depends on empirical study and gathering evidence.

The agencies of government, critical to the well-being of the people and to the practice of democracy, are prone to traps and snares that put at risk relations with the people in general and the parties, whose interests are in issue, in particular. A 'fundamental tension' according to Ruzha Smilova is 'the meritocracy problem': the appointment of 'unelected, democratically unaccountable technocratic experts' who 'uphold individual and minority rights at the expense of the popular will'. The delegation of power to such 'experts' breeds 'inequality, distrust, and dissatisfaction'. The experts form part of the governing elite, remote from the people; democracy is eroded and the people are resentful. In short, the conferring of power on 'technocratic experts' drains power away from the elected leaders and 'at the expense of the popular will'. The risk is that sectors of the people, feeling their well-being neglected, turn to direct forms of political action and seek solutions in alliance with selected leaders willing to advance their cause. The further risk is that the processes and the constraints of the constitutional order, now deemed to be obstructions rather than supports, are abandoned.

The risk is real and the consequences so potentially serious that the turn to popular action, or populism as it is known, will be the subject of the next Putney Debates. For now, we have to be content with just two points. One is the need for more empirical evidence as to cause and extent of dissatisfaction, and the consequences for democracy. The other point concerns the design and function of the agencies of government. On the one hand, the independence and detachment of agencies, driven and made easy by advances in technology; one the other hand, the need to strengthen the involvement of persons, groups, and sectors in the processes of agencies. The task is daunting; but that, rather than unleashed populism, is the route to practical remedies and the preservation of substantive constitutional democracy.

G. Courts and the People

The Putney Debates 2019 examined the relationship between the people and the courts: *Courts and the People: Friend or Foe*? The place of the courts in the constitutional order generally, and how they relate to the people in particular, are the subjects of a collection of studies of interest and quality. However, in the study of democracy and whether there is a crisis, the courts have a central place, whether to support and strengthen or to threaten and weaken.

The positive side appears most forcefully in the account of democracy in the nations of South America. Across the 15 nations, the record is mixed, but in general the courts are taking on a fuller and more effective role in preserving democracy.

Colombia merits special mention for the capacity of courts to strengthen democracy. The President's attempt to amend the Constitution to allow him to stand for a second term, was held by the Supreme Court to 'violate the democratic principles of the Federal Constitution'. After reviewing the courts across the nations, Pedro concludes that, generally, over recent decades the role of the courts has increased in scope and importance. 'Political conflicts are often solved through judicial intervention and decision-making mediated by law.' The trend, described by one scholar as a 'supremocracy', naturally has its critics. Despite the objections, some well-founded, others without merit, an active and dynamic judicial approach seems to be entrenched and justified as an ally of democracy not an enemy.

In the older democracies, the place and function of the superior courts is established but often contentious. The need in a democratic order for courts to interpret the constitution and the law, to declare and respect rights, is not controversial. To over-simplify a little, the elected leaders make the law and decide the rights people have; the courts interpret the law and settle disputes about the meaning and scope of the rights declared. The tension enters at the higher levels, when the constitutional standards are in issue and the courts are asked to rule on matters relating to such matters as the scope of executive action, relations between the executive and parliament, even in some cases the legality of legislation enacted by parliament. Judicial independence, as Paul Craig stresses, is part of the foundations of the democratic constitutional order. Hungary is singled out, here and often elsewhere, as an example of the courts losing their independence by being taken under the control of the executive.

The foundational role of courts is explained and developed in Sionaidh Douglas-Scott's chapter. The Supreme Court was confronted with an attempt by the executive to use the prerogative, here to prorogue Parliament, to legislate and 'to assert its power' over Parliament, in effect to exclude it from being engaged in a matter of high national concern. The Supreme Court held the prorogation to be unlawful in preventing Parliament from doing its 'constitutional duty', which was a threat, an 'extreme threat', to 'the fundamentals of our democracy'. Sionaidh ends her clear and convincing account with a quote from Suzanne Baer, former justice of the German Constitutional Court: 'Courts, then, do not replace politics but are the safety belts – that do not hurt anyone'.

H. Social Structure

'The rise of populism' are the opening words of Daniel Smilov's chapter, the threat posed to democracy the opening sentiment. Daniel goes on to argue that populism, soaked in 'anti-pluralist and autocratic tendencies', is the enemy of democracy. The reasoning is of interest. Populism is the enemy not because it 'targets and erodes' the formal constitutions of democracy, the usual reason. Populism undermines and threatens to destroy 'the political attitude of self-restraint'. The risk of populism, widely acknowledged, is serious enough to justify its being the subject of the next series of Putney Debates. In the meantime, Daniel explains the sense of 'an impending crisis', why populism puts democracy at risk and threatens its dismantling.

The focus on restraint draws attention to the need for politicians and people to develop and be guided by an attitude of restraint. Restraint with regard to the constitutional order, the political structure, and the institutions of government. Restraint is the contemporary term for an idea imbedded in constitutional and political history, often in other guises, appearing under other names, the need to dampen the *passions* being one of the more common. Whatever the name, the idea is simple, the purpose plain. Constitutional orders and institutions are in a sense artificial, standing above and outside the sentiments and dispositions of daily life, pursuing purposes that compete with more basic instincts and more tangible ends. Only by looking beyond that first circle do the people engage with the second and grasp how it also serves their well-being. To transcend the lower circle, and ascend to gain the benefits of the higher, depends on both the people and their leaders restraining the passions and showing a willingness to support the ideas and institutions of the constitutional order. Restraint, negative in nature, is essential. To this, I would add support in the form of positive actions that aid the efficacy and strengthen the foundations of the system.

Mention of restraint and support, and the metaphor of circles, leads at a deeper level to a third circle, to the social order and the conditions that help or hinder the well-functioning and effectiveness of democracy in the substantive sense. In more homely terms, 'the social glue' as Pedro puts it. What is the glue needed to sustain the democratic order, and what are the ingredients? He goes on to display the glue's weak grip, at least in some of the nations of South America. Other signs of the social glue and its absence are brought out in Zim's account of the nations of Africa. The history, including the colonial legacy, the nature of traditional societies and the fragmentation across nations, all shape the social foundations, the sentiments and dispositions of the people, and in turn their attitudes to the constitutional order and the demands of democracy. Studies of the two continents, Africa and South America, enable invaluable insight into relations between the social structure and the democratic constitution. India even more dramatically raises the question of what social factors and formations would lead a majority, dominant and dominating, to tolerance and respect for a sector of society at the foundations so different.

Even within societies less vulnerable to deep social division, creating a constitutional order centred on democracy, and making it work properly, is a major undertaking, a formidable task. Here we enter another circle of enduring interest and importance, the subject of endless enquiry and imagination. Enough for now to end with two points, two words of wisdom from the eighteenth century, one from the twenty-first. The first, modest in ambition, aims to achieve a balance or *equilibrium* as described by Giambattista Vico. The second concerns the means, which in the wisdom of David Hume is *moderation*. The two together offer a worldly wisdom, easy to state, but hard to practise.

To the worldly wisdom of the eighteenth century should be added one from the twenty-first. After an account of the Australian system of preferential voting and its virtues, Malcolm Turnbull in ending his chapter and in effect the volume, praises the practice of 'horse-trading', not often encountered in constitutional discourse, described by the press as 'cutting deals with all sorts of people'. Parliaments are for doing deals. Call it horse-trading if you like; but, he writes, that is what it's all about: 'you've got to get people together to compromise and that means bring them to the centre'. Let us re-name parliaments, he suggests, and put a sign on the door of the chamber: *Horse Trading Centre.*

VI. Crisis or Not?

The point of The Putney Debates was to consider whether democracy is in crisis. The stages of the enquiry, stated at the start of this chapter, are brief and worth repeating: the meaning of democracy; the evidence as to how democracy is working in practice; the conclusions to be drawn from the evidence. To meet the three criteria across all nations considered democratic would be a huge task, well beyond the ambition of The Putney Debates and this volume of essays. The aim, more modest and more manageable, has been to study certain aspects of democracy in a few selected nation-states. The results, equally modest, are of interest and importance: of interest in showing the many points of tension and the instabilities, whether actual or potential, in a constitutional system of democracy; of importance in demonstrating just how complex such systems are and the range of variables, some common to all democracies, some unique to one or other.

INDEX

accountability and authority, 150
Adichie, Chimamanda, on Nigerian presidential elections, 98–9
administrative agencies, 42–3
advisory bodies, checks on government, 135–6
Africa:
colonialism, effects of in, 55
languages not used in algorithms, 170
RD factors for, 50–1
African countries:
corruption in, 52
internet shutdowns in, 169
profiles of, 63–4
societies, lack of trust in, 54–5
African states:
national income of, 53–4
state capacity of, 53
weakness in, reasons for, 52–3
African Union (AU), 60
Agreement of the People (document) "Putney", 99
algorithms, African languages not used in, 170
all-India register (2019), 70
Allende, Salvador, election and overthrow of, 103
Alvarado, General Juan Velasco (President 1968–75, Peru), 82
American Revolution, constitutions date from, 118–19
Añez, Jeanine (Interim President, Bolivia), 84–5
Argentina, military dictatorship and presidential elections in, 87
Assam:
Foreigners Tribunals, 71
Hindu supremacy and Muslims' inhabitancy claims in, 71
Australian Electoral Commission draws parliamentary districts' boundaries, 176
authenticity and populism, 156
authority:
accountability and, 150
constitutional, 33, 40
system, people's acceptance of, 10

Bagehot, Walter, on extension of franchise, 107
Banzer, Hugo (President, Bolivia), 84
Bermúdez, Francisco Morales (President, Peru), 82
Bolivia:
development of democracy, 84–5
presidents of, 84–5
Bolsonaro, Jair (President, Brazil), 90
Botswana:
Democratic Party, 58
entry into British Empire, 58
Boularte, Dina (Vice-President, Peru), 83
Brazil, 89–90
democratisation and military dictatorship of, 89
presidential buildings invaded, 90
'Broad Front' (Uruguay), 89
Burke, Edmund, on representative democracy (1774), 13
'by the people' (concept), 12

candidate selection, party control of (UK and US), 17–18
'cartel' party (1980s and 1990s), 161–2
cartelisation, 143–4
Castillo, Pedro (President 2022, Peru), 83
Chávez, Hugo, 81
checks and balances (separation of powers), 149–50
US, in, 24–5
Cherry, Joanna QC, 130–1
Chile, 87–8
Constitutional Convention, 88
elections 1988-, 88
citizenship:
exclusion of Muslims from, 70–1
requirements, changes to, 69–70

Citizenship (Amendment) Act (2019) (India), 70
civil service, role of (UK and US), 25–6
class and gender equalities and non-military political economy, 72
coalitions, failure of, 23–4
collective good, sacrifices for, populists' objection to, 157
Colombia, democratic development of, 85
colonialism in Africa, 55
Colorado Party (Paraguay), 83–4
common good (US), 35
elected representatives work for, 13
people and, 42
competition is beneficial for society, 159
compromise, consensus through, 13
Congressional districts, re-drawing of (US), 16
Constitution of Pennsylvannia 1776, 31–2
constitutional:
history, people's role in, 37–8
law (South America), 94–5
constitutional order, 40, 185
principles of, 185–6
purpose of, 42
restraints needed for, 188
constitutionalisation:
over- and under-, 122
transformative (South Africa), 61
***Constitutionalisation and the Separation of Powers* (Vile),** 99–100
constitutions:
balanced (US), 13–14
concept of, 185
courts' role in interpretating, 192
definition and concept of, 10
federal and state levels, division of power and, 120
French and American Revolutions, date from, 118–19
governmental institutions and, 119
history of, 118–19
horizontal dimension of, 119–20
people's roles in, 39–40
South America, in, 94–5
state obligations and, 119
structural dimension, 120
unwritten (UK), 123
vertical dimension, 120
written, democratic backsliding in (Poland and Hungary), 124–5
constraints and liberal democracy, 154–5
Contarini, Gasparo, on balance of forms, 33
Correa, Rafael (President, Ecuador), 86
Council of Censors, 32, 41–2
courts:
constitutions' and democracy's roles in, 191–2
representative democracy's role in, 184
crisis, definition of, 179

***Days and Nights of Love and War* (Galleano),** 103
de-democratisation, 141–2
decision-makers, House of Commons as, 24
decision-making:
globalisation of, 143
government and internet shutdowns, 168
judiciary and, 148–9
power, transfer of, 144
delegated legislation, 128
delegation of power, 41
democracy:
advance of, 103
concept of, 180–1
courts' role in preserving, 191–2
definition of, 184
deliberative (Africa), 61–2
denationalising, effects of, 112
erosion of, 2–3, 8, 104–5
'full democracies', 8
liberal constitutionalism and, 106
rights-based, concept of, 147–9
set-up of and self-restraint, 158–9
substantive constitutional, 184
unmediated, populism as, 112–13
'Democracy Index 2023, Age of Conflict' report, 7–8
democratic:
discourse, 147
politics and judiciary, 148–9
say, right to, 140–1
Democratic Unionist Party (DUP) (Northern Ireland), 9
refusal to vote, 17
democratisation:
Brazil, in, 89
time taken for, 62
demos, 44–5
depoliticisation, 142–4, 144–5
definition and concept of, 142–3
mechanisms of, 143
source of (Katz and Mair), 143–4

Dicey, AV, on extension of franchise, 107
discretion of administrative agencies, 43
disenfranchisement in United Kingdom (2022), 16–17
'divine principle', 34

economic constitutionalism, populist parties' support of, 156
Economist Intelligence Unit (EIU), 7–8
  indicators of, 50
Ecuador, electoral system of, 85–6
elected officials:
  change in role, 23
  representative democracies, role in, 22–3, 117
elected representatives, Madison variation of (UK and US), 26–7
elections:
  Ecuador, in (1979-), 85–6
  'fully free and fair', 7
  future, manipulation of, 15–16
  RD and, 47, 48
  refusal to accept results (US), 14–15
  systems' effect on representative government, 18
Electoral College (US), 11
electoral courts, establishment of (South America), 93
electoral process:
  operation of, 35
  overview of, 186–7
Elkins, Zachary, *'The Endurance of National Constitutions'*, 62
emancipatory measures, populists against, 156
***Endurance of National Constitutions, The* (Elkins),** 62
English Levellers, 21, 31, 99, 102
European States, historical development of, 52–3
European Union (EU):
  integration, modes of, 121–2
  treaties, Grimm on, 121–2
executive:
  leadership (UK), repeated rapid change in, 8–9
  power (South America), 91, 189–90
executive's dominance, 189
  UK Parliament, over, 127

Facebook:
  Francis Haugen leaks, 170
  people's use of, 174
  shutdown case, 171
  Uganda, in, 168
federal and state levels, division of power between, and constitutions, 120
federal constitution (James Madison), 33–4
first-past-the-post voting system replaces supplementary vote system, 20
***fixed point pact*,** 81
foreigners and migrants, populists' lack of empathy for, 157
form, 34–5
  substance over, 39
Fragile States Index, 51
franchise, extension of (Dicey), 106–7
French Revolution, constitutions date from, 118–19
Fujimori, Alberto, 82–3

Galeano, Eduardo, *Days and Nights of Love and War*, 103
Georgescue, Mr, 104
German party system, 158
Ghana, 59
  Constitution, 100
Goodwin, Doris Kearns, *No Ordinary Time*, 101–2
governance, representatives' role in, 22
government:
  bodies and independence (UK and US), 150
  independent regulators and advisory bodies check, 135–6
  mandate, 136–7
  organs of, and constitutions, 119–20
  parliamentary sovereignty, use of, 132
  people's support for, 40–1
  process, people's involvement in, 182
  regulators' checks on, 136
government agencies, 190–1
  people and, 191
governmental institutions and constitutions, 119
  definition and concept of, 10
Grimm, Dieter:
  constitutions, on, 118–19
  EU treaties, on, 121–2

Henry VIII powers and clauses, 128
Hindu:
  Right, consolidation of power, 75–6
  supremacy in Assam, 71

Hindu nationalism, 76
racialisation of nationalists, 76–7
House of Commons as decision-maker, 24
House of Lords Secondary Legislation Scrutiny Committee report, 128–9
human rights and internet shutdowns, 167–8
Hungary Constitution, 124

impeachment procedures (South America), 92
independence:
government bodies and (UK and US), 150
referendum, SNP's view on, 17
separation of powers and, 149–50
independent:
judgment, representatives' exercise of, 13
National Electoral Commission (INEC) (Nigeria), 100–1
regulator, checks on government by, 135–6
voters (Australian voting system), 176
India, internet and press freedom, 77
Indian citizenship, methods of acquisition, 69–70
Indian Constitution, Article 370 revoked, 72
indirect rule (Africa), 55–6
inequality in wealth and 'us versus them', 21–2
institute of 'crossed death' (Ecuador), 86
institutional fragility (South America), 94
institutions, mediating, 106, 108, 109–12, 112–13
inter-party advisory committee (IPAC) (Ghana), 59
internet shutdowns, 167
African countries, in, 169
government decision-making (Africa) and, 168
human rights and, 167–8

Jiménez, Marcos Perez, 81
judges, senior, vetting of, 134–5
judicial independence, threats to, (Baer), 135
Judicial Power Project (JPP) (UK), 133–4, 136
judicial review:
attempts to limit, 133
'hard', 134–5
prevention of, legislation for, 134
judicialisation, 148
judiciary:
democratic politics and decision-making and, 148–9
independence of, 100–1
representative democracy, in, 117

Kashmir:
government measures against, 72
impunity laws, 71–2
Muslims, treatment of in, 71–2
Kenya Constitution (2010), 59–60

Lasso, Guillermo (Ecuador), 86
leaders and people, relationship between, 36–7, 41
legal syncretism (Africa), 61
liberal constitutionalism and democracy, 106
liberal democracy, 183
no alternative to, 159
constraints and, 154–5
meritocracy and, 140
populism and, tension between, 164–5
technological developments, effect of on, 165–6
liberalism, failure of, 142
liberty and well-being, 38
Lincoln, Abraham, 12
definition of democracy, 12, 29, 181
Lugo, Fernando, 83–4

Madison, James:
federal constitution, on, 33–4
people's role in constitution, on, 39–40
representative democracy, on (1788), 13
Maduro, Nicolás, 82
majoritarianism (Africa), 61
majorities in democracy, 188–9
manipulation and populism, 162
media diversity (Australia), 174
meritocracy and liberal democracy, 140
Meta, hate speech on, 169
Miller, Gina, 129–30, 131
***Miller/Cherry v Prime Minister* (2019),** 130–1
minorities in democracy, 188–9
moderation, 169, 170, 173, 186, 193
Monti, Juan Carlos (Paraguay), 83
Morales, Evo, 84, 85
Moreno, Lenin (Vice-President and President, Ecuador), 86
multiculturism and 'us versus them', 21
Muslims excluded from citizenship, 70–1

Narendra Modi and Bharatiya Janata Party (BJP), 67–8
National Register of Citizens (NRC) (India), inclusion in, 68–9

NGO-isation, 143
Nigeria, 59
Presidential elections (Adichie), 98–9
***No Ordinary Time* (Goodwin),** 101–2
non-Kashmiris' residency in Kashmir, 72–3
non-military political economy and class and gender equalities, 72
Northern Ireland:
executive, leadership in, 9
power sharing, restoration of, 10

Orban, Victor, Fundamental Law (2011), 161
ouster clauses, 134

Paraguay, 83–4
Constitution (1992), 83
democracy in, 83–4
Parliament, prorogation of, and Supreme Court, 192
parliamentary democratic systems (Australia), centre-focus of, 177
parliamentary districts (Australia), Australian Electoral Commission draws boundaries, 176
parliamentary sovereignty, 123
government's use and legislative nature of, 131–2
partisanship, 23
party politics, democratic, demise of, 110
people:
authority system, acceptance of by, 10
common good and, 42
constitution, role of in, 39–40
constitutional history, role of in, 37–8
engagement with leaders, 41
government, support of by, 40–1
government agencies and, 191
government process, involvement in, 182
leaders and, relationship between, 36–7, 41
representative democracy, role of in, 187
ruling themselves, 31–2
well-being, 183
'peoples precede nations', 36
Pérez, Carlos Andrés, 81
Peru, heads of government since 2017, 82–3
Pinilla, Gustavo Rojas (Colombia), 85
Pinochet, General Augusto (1973–90) (Chile), 87–8
Poland Constitution, 124–5
political:
activity, juridical control of (South America), 92–3
actors, definition and concept of, 10
constitutionalism (UK), 137–8
minimalism, 101
stability (Africa), 63
violence (Africa), 63
political parties:
agents of governability, as, 109
candidate selection, control over, 17–18
internal organisation of (South America), 93
mediating roles of, 108–9
power of, 100
politics:
erosion of, 109–10
massification of, 108–9
professionalism of, 105
politics (Australia):
operation of, development of, 173
social media platforms' effect on, 174
popular:
government (rule by the people), 33
will, expression of, 99–100
populism, 153, 155–6, 192–3
authenticity and, 156
contemporary, 162
future development of, 163–4
liberal democracy and, tension between, 164–5
manipulation and, 162
unmediated democracy, as, 112–13
populist parties:
collective good, objection to, 157
distribution through taxes, opposition to, 156
economic constitutionalism, support for, 156
emancipatory measures, against, 156
foreigners and migrants, no empathy for, 157
functions of, 160
ideologist function and task of, 160–1
rise of, 159–61
sacrifices for collective good, against, 157
supranational solidarity, against, 157
universal social solidarity, against, 157
populists, leaders of, 105
power, personalisation of, 105
prerogative:
constitutional issues of, 129–30
exercise of, 129
'presidentialism of coalition' (South America), 91–2
primary assumption, summary of, 11
princely rule, 30–1
property rights, 33

proportional representation, introduction of (UK), 19
prorogation of Parliament (UK), 130–1
public policy, effect of rise of, 110–11
purpose, 43
Putney Debates:
1647, in, 1–2
2017, 2018, 2019 and 2021, in, 2
2023, in, 2–3

***R (Miller) v Secretary of State for Exiting the EU* (2017),** 129–30
Rashtriya Swayamsevak Sangh (RSS), 74, 76, 77
'replacement theory' (US), 21
representative:
government, electoral system's effect on, 18
principle, 185
representative democracy (RD), 12, 35, 47–9
Africa, factors for, 50–1
Burke on (1774), 13
Clary on, 179
courts' role in, 184
development and examples of, 179–80
elected officials and, 22–3, 117
elections and, 47, 48
form and substance of, 181–2
institutions (Africa), 56–7
judiciary in, 117
liberal, 139
Madison on (1788), 13
people's role in, 187
primary assumptions for, 11–12
principles and values, constitutional effect of on, 182–3
secondary assumptions for, 13–14
representatives:
governance, role in, 22
independence and judgment, exercise of, 13
restraint, 193
Roosevelt, Franklin and Eleanor, 101–2
rule by representatives, 32–4
constitutional relationship of, 36–7
defects of, 35–6
rule of law (South America), 92–3

Scotland, executive leadership in, 9
Scottish National Party (SNP), independence referendum, view on, 17
self-restraint, 137–8
erosion of, background to, 157–8
set-up of democracy, and, 158–9
self-rule, 32
separation of powers and independence, 149–50
social:
media platforms (Australia) effect on politics, 174
order, overview, 193
socioeconomic development (South America), 93–4
solidarity, universal social and supranational, populists are against, 157
South Africa, Constitution and constitutional project, 58–9
state:
obligations and constitutions, 119
political power and influence of (Africa), 51–2
statements of rights, 148
Stroessner, General Alfredo, 83
Sub-Saharan Africa (SSA) region, democracy in, 50
substance over form, 39
Sunak, Rishi, 5, 8, 17, 132
supplementary vote system:
first-past-the-post system replaces (UK), 20
reduction of power of (Brazil), 92–3
Supreme Court and prorogation of Parliament, 192

taxes, populist parties' opposition to distribution through, 156
'there is no alternative' (TINA), 144–5
trans-Atlantic slave trade, 54–5
Truss, Liz:
election of (2022), 16–17
Treasury civil servants, sacking of two, 25–6
'tyranny of form' (Warr), 34–5

Uganda:
Facebook, in, 168
techmedia, use of, 170–1
Ugandan Communications Commission request to YouTube, 171
United Kingdom (UK):
administrative state of, 115
Civil Service, role of, 25–6
courts, attempts to reduce influence of, 134
executive leadership, changes in, 8–9
general elections 2024, 12, 18–19

legislation, enactment of through Parliament, 127–8
Parliament, executive dominance over, 127
right to vote in, 12
under-constitutionalised country, is, 122
voter identification, 15
United States (US):
administrative state of, 115–16
checks and balances in, 24–5
Civil Service, role of, 25–6
electoral insurrection, 9–10
erosion of democracy in, 8
right to vote in, 11
2020 Presidential election, 12
2024 Presidential election, 17–18
universal suffrage in, 11
voter identification, 15
universal suffrage, 107–8
US, in, 11
Uribe Álvaro, President of Colombia, 85
Uruguay, 88–9
'Broad Front', 89
politics of, 88–9
'us versus them' concept, 21–2
inequality in wealth and, 21–2
multiculturalism and, 21
Uttar Pradesh, extrajudicial killings in, 73–5

Venezuela, absence of democracy, 81–2
Vile, Maurice, *Constitutionalism and the Separation of Powers*, 99–100
Vizacarra, Martin, 83
voter:
accreditation system (BVAS) (Nigeria), 59
alienation, 144
identification, methods for (US and UK), 15
voting:
compulsory (Australia), 175–6
first-past-the-post system, 20
in-person voting, effect of, 20
methods (US), 15–16
ranked choice (US), 19
right to vote (UK and US), 11, 12
two-party preferred (Australia), 176

Wales, executive leadership in, 9
Warr, John, 37
tyranny of form, on, 34–5
'we the people' concept (US), 20
well-being and liberty, 38
written constitutions, democratic backsliding in (Poland and Hungary), 124–5

X, hate speech on, 169

YouTube, Ugandan Communications Commission request to, 171

www.ingramcontent.com/pod-product-compliance
Ingram Content Group UK Ltd.
Pitfield, Milton Keynes, MK11 3LW, UK
UKHW020815290926
15470UKWH00003B/1169

9 781509 980895